EARTH REPUBLIC

Chatter from the Capital's Cauldron (and Beyond)

V. SHRUTI DEVI

INDIA • SINGAPORE • MALAYSIA

Notion Press

Old No. 38, New No. 6
McNichols Road, Chetpet
Chennai - 600 031

First Published by Notion Press 2018
Copyright © V. Shruti Devi 2018
All Rights Reserved.

ISBN 978-1-64249-072-5

CONTENTS

Author's Note on the Book

Earth Republic: Chatter from the Capital's Cauldron (and Beyond) is a collection of ten free-wheeling articles, where I've kept the style conversational, verging on the informally careless.

A potpourri of commentaries on theatre, sport, food and agriculture, world politics, Bruce Springsteen, Imran Khan, women's rights, world peace, people's belief systems, the right to privacy judgement…all with a flavour of New Delhi, right up to the present-day NCR, with tribal India and outer space forming a billowing back-drop for the grand production that is the Republic of Earth.

I've been careful not to be too prescriptive with ideas and definitions, and have, on occasion, refrained from churning out concrete examples to illustrate each statement made. This is, after all, not a text book from the twentieth century, but an instrument of sorts, intended to be a channel of peace.

The final chapter on world peace works as a dream-catcher, and weaves into its outlook, the emerging trends and essences from the nine chapters that precede it. This is not intended to be a monolithic treatise, and one has visions of a second volume, possibly an entire series, rising from the blue planet.

The writings occasionally incorporate select extracts from my childhood diaries of the 1980s, a few Facebook and blog posts, and also feature a written commentary from 2013.

Earth Republic attempts to bring to the reader, thoughts from time and space, and last night's rally at the mantle-piece, and is an invitation to forge reality and rattle the galaxy, all in one pranayam yoga clarion call.

– V. Shruti Devi
November, 2017

Acknowledgements

Considering that this is a book of non-fiction that draws on my areas of expertise, learning and training, I would like to acknowledge, with thanks, all my formal and informal teachers, lecturers, professors, instructors, trainers and tutors, dead and alive, from across the centuries. In the same vein, I'd also like to thank all my class-mates from everywhere, because you've added significantly to the learning curve in the classroom.

I'd like to thank and acknowledge the thought-influences of friends, ideologues, writers and colleagues-along-the way, comrades, collaborators from all political parties and non-governmental organizations and academic institutions, the children, women and men of rural India, especially from tribal and other forest-dwelling communities, who have taught me much over the years, and those from my party who have assisted me, taken my views and works forward, and have encouraged me to continue to work for the party, and the many causes that we stand for.

I'd also like to take this opportunity to thank the editors and publishers of my free-lance writings in the print and digital media, that commenced in the late 1980s.

A word of thanks to Elizabeth Zopari, my friend from school and college, for lending an ear to my writing plans and for having suggested, long years ago, that I capitalize on my past scribbles, and have them published.

Thanks, also, to my friend from college, Sonal Sena, for the Skype conversation (from Belgium to Kurupam), to brain-storm with me, on how to prioritize the clearing-house of written material that I've aggregated over the years, and to my friend from school, Anshu Shourie, for staying in touch, and listening to all my earthly and unearthly ideas during her trips to India from the U.S.

For their appreciation of the draft chapter on cuisine emailed or read out to them, thankyoooo to my aunts Pushpa Bose and Kusum Debi. Special acknowledgements to my aunt, Sucharu Singh Deo, for helping to translate to English, the meanings of several Oriya words from my interview of my grandma, on food histories.

One would like to record fond remembrances of my aunt, Sneha Premkumar, whom we lost to cancer, and my dear departed grandmother, Rajmata Sobhalata Debi of Kurupam. Their work-in-progress, at one time, on my grandmother's recipe book, inspired me to record, in writing, interviews that form a part of the chapter on cuisine in *Earth Republic*.

Thanks to my cousin, Jaideep Deo Bhanj, for his opinion, in the affirmative, regarding the inclusion of photographs in the publication. These will feature in a future edition.

For their general enthusiasm for this book-writing venture in particular, thanks to my cousins Dr. Piya Bose, Nameeta Premkumar, Sujeet Singh Deo, Anjali Dhal Samanta and Pranab Dhal Samanta, to my aunt, Uttara Mahipal Singh, and my mother, V. Preeti Deo.

I will make a mention of my father, V. Kishore Chandra Suryanarayana Deo, (and his friends, voters and colleagues, they all know who they are), for having influenced my ideologies and my personal sacrifices during my formative years and thereafter, which this book sometimes discusses, though they have not been connected with the writing or publishing of this book.

To all the other near-and-dear cousins and friends and relatives, if you've not been mentioned by name, it's because this isn't meant to be a lifetime-achievements award list, but is restricted to those directly connected to this book. Happy reading, and see you all soon, in any case!

A word of thanks to Abesh Choudhury, who is a Senior Lawyer in England and Wales, and a friend from my St. Stephen's days, for his prompt response to my request to read the chapter on the Right to Privacy judgement for a legal vetting of the text.

And to my class-mate from my days at Environmental Law, Shishir Gagan Singh, Advocate at the Steel Authority of India, Ltd., for hearing out my ideas and analyses regarding the tone and tenor of some of the essays.

And to my friends, colleagues and seniors at the bar (legally speaking), and especially colleagues at the Supreme Court Bar Association of India (SCBA), including V.R. Reddy, Senior Advocate, who was an Additional Solicitor General of India when I worked at his chamber, and similarly, Indu Malhotra, Senior Advocate, for ensuring that a modicum of gravitas has been retained in my conversations over the years.

For listening to strings of ideas and to readings over the phone, from the sections of *Earth Republic* that touch upon the 1980s, thanks to my friends, Shaila Faleiro and Nirmala Faleiro, respectively, who date back to that era of our lives. Thanks to my friend, Sonia Faleiro, for reminding me that I'd planned to be an author! And here, a word of credit to the Process Documentation aspect of the NBSAP Project in India, that now realises that it brought the genre of Narrative Non-fiction to the world stage.

Thankyou, thankyou, to my brother, Shishir Chandra Deo, for his enthusiastic response to my writing, and to the chapter with the childhood diaries.

Thanks to Dr. V.A. Rao, who was the Head of the Department of English Literature when I passed out of college (as we say in India, and will continue to do so), for his recent responses to my emails in connection with my writing, including his detailed observations on a reading of my nine-part blog series that analysed Bruce Springsteen's autobiography, of which an updated version features in this book.

Dhanyavaadalu to Stephen Golub, Attorney and Senior International Consultant, U.S.A., whose valuable dialectics one was introduced to at a series of discussions on International Development at Boalt Hall, UC Berkeley, almost twenty years ago, for reconnecting at Kurupam, for bringing Bruce Springsteen back onto my radar, and for reading and responding to my first blog-post on Bruce Springsteen.

Thrilled acknowledgements and compliments to my friend and litterateur, Dr. Madhavi Menon, for declaring, telephonically, that she will buy a copy of my book!

I appreciate the constructive listening atmosphere that was created by my friend, Dr. Philippe Cullet, International Environmental Lawyer and Expert on Water Rights a few years ago at Delhi, for lending an ear to my free-wheeling monologue on Empire, that ranged from my views on the creative implementation of the forest rights act, to grassroots democracy, to the return of the kohinoor diamond and other artefacts, to my round table, to Creatures of the Current, and world peace in general.

Special posthumous acknowledgements to Dr. Chhatrapati Singh, whom I had the privilege of interacting with as a student of Environmental Law at the Centre for Environmental Law, WWF (India), when he was the Director in 1995, for reminding us to dream, and for having introduced our batch to a host of often useful and interesting guest speakers.

My acknowledgements to Dr. Armin Rosencranz, lawyer, political scientist, member of the US Supreme Court Bar, and former trustee, Stanford University, for the watchful eye that he keeps on the globe: war, peace, the environment, human biology, and the Rule of Law in general. Some of our conversations have had an overall impact on parts of this book.

I'd like to put on record, my solidarity with India's Campaign for Survival and Dignity, and our commitment and resolve to work for the upliftment of the downtrodden. Much of the resonance in work continues, and I hope *Earth Republic* proves to be useful.

Flash-back greetings and acknowledgements to friends and one-time colleagues and collaborators from the United Nations Development Programme (UNDP), the Government of India, and the NBSAP Network, for all the gyan. The time has now come, I hope we finally opine, to talk of spirulina, of the electromagnetic spectrum, of Mars, of space debris, of political networking, and many things! Do read.

To those on my Facebook list who expressed interest in perusing the draft chapter on e-shopping, many thanks, and you will be kept posted on web events connected to the book, and the e-shopping chapter in particular.

Wry nods to the character who suggested that the non-fiction book of essays ought to overflow with naughty humour and erotica. Point taken, but this might not be that book!

To my friends from school and college and elsewhere, they all know who they are, and to my nieces, Alaiya Singh Deo and Aisha Singh Deo, and my sister-in-law, Sukanya Singh, thanks for all the excitement!

A special thanks, and a high-five to all the people from theatre, dramatics and the performing and folk arts, music and environment, that I've ever worked and jammed with, and all those whose plays I've watched, and gone to the theatre with…it's all real, and there's more to come!

At this juncture of history, one needs to acknowledge the role of technology that enables a person to locate a publisher through a net-surf, sign agreements via email with perfect strangers, and have flurries of paper flying through the internet in order to finalize a document. Cheers in advance to my publishing partners, Notion Press, India, may we sell spaceship-loads of *Earth Republic*, and prosper!

The impacts of rivals and opponents also serve to challenge one's aims, and to improve the quality of one's work. For this, and for the circumstances of undisturbed peace and quiet that I managed to procure for myself in order to write this book, I am grateful to myself.

A final word of acknowledgement to our erstwhile zamindari estate. To its spirit, I say: Democracy has been the perfect guerrilla tactic for expanding empire and human rights in the 20th and early 21st centuries… enjoy the read!

– Shruti
November, 2017

Chapter I

Cuisine: Food for All, Family Histories, and Culture

Food and cuisine is an overloaded trolley of thought and action these days. Political, cultural, medical, economic, scientific – you name it, there's something to be said and done about *bhojanaalu* on all these fronts. Perhaps it's always been so, in which case, lets grab some ongoing trends (we're talking circa 2017 here).

First of all, who doesn't want their taste buds to tingle, and spark off all sorts of brain-cell activity, and to be a connoisseur of all foods known, unknown, and yet to be marketed or created. It's a part of general knowledge, a mark of being considered well-travelled, and heeled, and cultured, and adventurous.

In some other similarly opulent environ, there might be no such appreciation or aspiration. The insular equivalent would lie in satisfied acknowledgements of the fact that the service clatters with a conveyor-belt full of X number of veg and X number of nonveg dishes, plus all sorts of other delectables that have, no doubt, taken aeons of preparation-time and effort back-stage. Or pride over a single dish well-made, with recipes that have been passed down over generations, with secrets, and innovations, and modern-day adaptations, accompanied with stories of when each dish was once served to whom, and praise and awe in general for the production team/s.

Cut to geography books. The movements of rivers, of water under-ground, of water in the atmosphere. Different lands and continents and regions and smaller locales, and varying climate, temperature and weather. Different crops.

Then comes the gradual influence of modern science, and the ability to grow almost anything almost anywhere, and to move these about across the globe. Then come lots and lots of people who need housing, and other building activities (some necessary, and some not so necessary), and the area for growing crops begins to shrink.

Farmers. Who are farmers?

A large corporation that creates and sells seeds and uses techniques of mechanized agriculture and cultivates thousands of acres of land and sells the produce at multi-brand retail outlets is an agriculturist, or a modern-day farmer.

So is a rural person or family who grows a few things on a patch or two of land. A bit is sold, a bit is consumed, and lots of money is still needed. Sometimes, they are a part of a co-operative, but very rarely these days.

So is an agricultural labourer who has no land, who might not care who the owner is, but who wants good working and living conditions.

Everyone needs to be able to pay the same kind of medical bills for health problems caused by environmental factors. Some can afford the best medical treatment, others cannot. This discrepancy, to me, is at the heart of the ethical challenge of the present century.

There is, of course, the important ongoing effort by the government to provide free and excellent medical care for all. (Nutrition, lack of nutrition, environmental factors, ill-health: you get the link).

For the human race to justify evolution further, it needs to display that it comprehends the concept of equity in the area of universal healthcare. That this is not charity, but the right of every individual human being on the planet.

The concept of the Right to Food has gained legal sanctity in India over the years. Nutrition, environment, health-care, wages, and tools of economic planning need to be viewed through this sieve. The bottom-line is that none of these is, or ought to be in the realm of charity.

Human beings have basic rights.

In my opinion, charity ought to exist and kick in only to tackle situations that are too far gone, or as a safety-net for unforeseen aberrations.

The pessimistic, or the eager-to-be-charitable-benefactors-and-not-equal-fighters-for-rights might argue that today, everything is in dysfunctional mode, and therefore, the bigger and more expansive the charitable work, the better.

I disagree.

Charity needs to be present in society in a calibrated fashion. Allowing it to over-take the system actually creates a false sense of security and achievement vis-à-vis the big picture.

That said, I need to reiterate that governmental subsidies, loan waivers, and schemes and laws for affirmative action must not be looked upon by tax-payers as charities. It needs to be dinned into tax-payers' minds, that these are tools of organized governance that ensure a just society and world. That's what our government's goods and services tax (GST) regime intended.

Nobody's doing anybody a favour by supporting schemes and laws that aim to uplift the disempowered. Follow some other path, and you and the economy, and the state of governance will end up in a bigger mess than you could ever dream could exist.

Furthermore, nobody wants infuriated marauding mobs, hacked-into technologies, and exploding devices around every street corner and URL, and certainly not nuclear explosions or biological warfare. These are all projected scenarios that the far-sighted have been anticipating and combating for more time than most people realize.

Course-correction in economic policies, controlling corruption, and efficiently implementing programmes is what ultimately keeps the roti in the hands of the impoverished, and the mid-day meal on the plate of the school-going child.

Charities and society's efforts, however, via their own innovative work, must show a beacon to mainstream governance, and participate in it in an integrated way. Successful experiments, pilot projects, best practices all go a long way to enrich the experience and the efforts of the government.

As do criticisms, challenges, opposing views, contradictions and protests. These rights to free speech ought to flourish and expand in a democracy.

Beyond a certain threshold of charitable activity, concerned citizens who wish to expand their sphere of work or influence must thus either plunge into political activity and mainstream governance themselves, or do what they can, to support and assist those who they think are in the best position to do so.

On a global scale, there exists the Food and Agriculture Organization (FAO), that leads the world's conversation on access to food. A report of 2017 was reviewed recently by a number of countries. Other than all the very real and obvious causes that economists and all of us are aware of, in connection with why hunger exists, a connect that many who live in peaceful lands might not make, is: the factor of Conflict. Many countries warned that the primary cause of Hunger and starvation today is actually Conflict.

The world-peace-economics-conflict-and-hunger-resolution path needs to be followed and tackled.

Scientists and some yogics might confirm to you, that it is possible for the human body to exist primarily on sunlight. Sun-gazing. With this, are likely to be theories regarding space travel, vegetarianism, and the blasting of the Darwinian theory of origin and evolution. It might even be claimed that this could account for some sort of superior functioning of the human body, race, and all of known creation. While one might not be able to disprove any of this (and it all brims with recreational potential, frankly), one is not ready to trade off anyone's mid-day meal for that kind of a spot in the sun.

The same goes for theories of earthlings amongst us being some sort of space-originated divine entities. Hold your horses, all ye chariots of me glorious stables! Not while I have land rights to claim, and earthly addresses to hang on to, or seek, depending on whether I'm speaking for a mere holder of an UNHCR card, or an Aadhaar or Voter's ID card, or a potential claimant under the forest rights act.

Not just sun-gazing, there are other talked-about wonder-foods: spirulina, and at a less capsulized level: millets. A word of caution, though, to not bull-in-a-china-shop one's pet product/s forward in an insular fashion. Being insular sometimes translates to not standing for the right to life of all human beings.

So back to some cultural aspects of food (in order to arrive at world peace via the honouring of fusion foods, ancient recipes, laboratory-envisaged nutritives and more). This, in the days of emerging trends of manslaughter in the name of preventing cow-slaughter.

Food, when seen as a vehicle of culture, essentially binds itself to ideas of identity: social, political, historical…of an individual, and of communities.

Associations of memory and nostalgia, social status, historical paths or moorings, connections with society, the aspiration for a disease-free, healthy and exceptional body, and the pure satiation of the senses all feed into the food-debate.

A spiritually-inclined person might not ascribe as much importance to all the ego-related and other emotional aspects of individual association with food as those dependent on such factors do.

However, questions of health, nutrition and equitable access to food can be looked at through a scientific lens, with no cultural value-judgements.

Elements of history, and food habits and their origins are also not restricted solely to emotion and cultural pride, but to aspects of identity that are sometimes deemed to be essential to hark back to, in order to demonstrate and establish all dimensions of a person's legal identity.

Such legal requirements and practices sometimes only act as redundant shackles to peoples' pasts, being flogged into existence possibly only to enable some governmental scheme or the other to conveniently create exclusionary criteria, thus reducing the sheer numbers of intended beneficiaries. And in some countries, one might not be talking of only governmental schemes. The very nationality, social categorizing, and identification of a person might hinge around what the individual's eating habits are.

Other than seasonal and daily eating habits, it is during festivals and ceremonies that those of a community are primed to indulge in preparing and consuming thematic culinary delights. The selection of such ceremonial foods and dishes is also said to have a scientific basis, ranging from seasonal availability to medicinal value.

Thus, the apparently emotionally-driven cultural values related to food carry with them, scientific significance. The coping-mechanism of various societies on various parts of the globe are rooted in ever-evolving ancient knowledge.

These ancient coping systems that are more identifiable as behaviours of the animal kingdom, are not restricted to human-versus-nature, but, indeed, spill over to humans-versus-humans.

The game-changer in this process has been the nature of human evolution. (A recognition of the right to life of all humans, the growth of human-generated values of justice, equity, compassion and so on).

Or perhaps there has been no humane game-changer at all. It could be argued that all these so-called values, in fact, have their origins in a visionary and tactical bid for the survival, (not altruistically for future generations, but in optimistic anticipation of the fructifying of the possibility of some version of scientifically proven and tangible immortality around the bend of the century, if not earlier), of the species. This version of immortality, of course, might not require food as we know it. However, the decades (or centuries) of transition would call for the need for continued and equitable access to food for all of humanity.

In order to ensure equitable access to food for all on the planet, all that needs to be done is to balance out the availability across lands and peoples. This, of course, raises a number of issues of the production and movement of food (crops, livestock, fisheries), and associated issues of control over land, water, space and even near-by planets.

Each century brings with it, its own challenges. The need of the hour is to ensure global co-ordination on planning and implementation processes, while prioritizing and keeping in mind core values that represent the best avataars of the human race.

Detailed academic and activistic discussions on these topics, one shall save for another occasion.

I would like to share with you, a set of interviews that I carried out, of my grandmother, Late Rajmata Sobhalata Debi of Kurupam (my dad's mother), a few years before she passed away in 2013. It was Jejmama's ambition and desire to write, and to have published, a recipe book. (Jejmama is the Oriya word for father's mother).

Jejmama had dictated to my aunts, the recipes of much of the food that she had grown up eating and cooking. Oriya food, other Indian food, Anglo-Indan dishes from the days of the Raaj, and other delicacies from various sources.

Photographs were collected for the publication, and for a while, it was planned for the book to have a running narration interspersed with recipes, as per my suggestion. This was the purpose of the interviews.

However, Jejmama eventually decided that she did not want to include a narration, and was keen to publish just the recipes, which had then been put into a final compilation by one of her daughters, and spiral-bound, awaited publication.

Alas, before this could happen, she passed away in October 2013, and ironically, it was just around that time that Amazon came out with its Create Space publishing platform.

The interviews that I took of Jejmama have thus been a part of my clearing-house of writings, which I now choose to share with a larger audience:

VSD: First, a line or two on where you were born, and on your parents, and where they were from.

VSLD: I was born in Talcher in 1929. Talcher is now a part of the state of Orissa in eastern India, and is a part of the Eastern Ghaat hill range. When I was born, it was a part of Princely India, and was a Ruling State. My father was the younger son of Raja Bahadur Kishore Chandra Biroboro Harichandan of Talcher, and my mother was from the Ruling State of Bamra, which is also a part of Orissa today. I was born in Talcher Palace.

VSD: Now, let's talk about all the different ceremonies that would have been held for you after your birth, and what food must have been cooked for each of these.

VSLD: On the twenty-first day (Ekuisiya) from the day I was born, there was a Namkaran (naming ceremony). I was named Sobhalata Debi. It was treated like a very big festival. There was a bhujji (feast).

Some of the dishes at the bhujji would have been spotted deer, khirri, khechidi, borra (vadas), bhoja botta puan cutlets — meat ground and shaped into round cutlets, puri, aloo and chenna torkari (cottage cheese curry).

My Annaprasna (rice-eating ceremony) was held when I was six months old. This was when I was fed rice for the first time. The rice was made into a sweet Khiri out of Sagada Dhuli rice (rice winnowed by bullock carts - unpolished) from my Jejmama's rice fields in Balunga.

For the guests at the Annaprasna function, there would have been pulao, a vegetarian dish, a non-vegetarian dish, and sweets such as Kakra (rice-flour and jaggery stuffed with mildly spiced grated coconuts, and deep fried), and Birhi Nadi Boda (urad-daal-lentil, coil-shaped deep fried dumplings).

On my first birthday, (first Sonikhetro), the guests would have been served Polao, a mutton dish, some vegetarian preparations, and sweets like Jalebi and Khirri.

Food-wise, my Kano Nouli and Mundan (ear-piercing ceremony and tonsuring ceremony), were celebrated quite a bit like the first birthday was. This is also the day on which relatives gift ear-rings to the child.

My studies began at the age of five. I was home-tutored. To mark the beginning of my studies, there was a celebration and a function called Vidya Arombh. A large variety of sweets was made on this occasion specially for children from outside, and also for the pundits and masters.

In the course of the Vidya Arombh celebrations, there was horse riding, shooting, shikar, elephant rides, target shooting, playing with kites, tops, marbles, 'pua,' kabaddi etc. in the playground. All the royal children — all my cousins and brothers, participated in this. Over the years, we also learnt a little bit of driving.

Varieties of Orissa sweets made for the Vidya Arombh were loddu, rosgulla, gulabjamun, khirro malpua (deep fried condensed milk pancake with sugar syrup), omrut rosaboli (mini gulab jamuns floating in rabri), monda (same as Kakra, but spherical), kakara, paluo monda (arrowroot monda), paluo kotta (arrowroot halwa), puree-khua.

VSD: Please describe the food that you had everyday as a child at home. Were there different kinds of dishes for different meals and seasons?

VSLD: *During our childhood, we used to have a big breakfast: fried eggs, omelette, scrambled eggs, nimki, bread, cheese that used to be covered in red wax, etc. Nimki is a dish that used to be prepared with wild meats like venison, wild boar and sambar. You need a big chunk of meat from the hind leg for Nimki.*

The food used to be different during different seasons, and there were also some dishes that were made all year round.

During the hot summer months, pokhalo bhato (fermented cold rice), was a must at lunch-time. This was eaten with sago khorada (sautéed indian saag), ambila (tomatoes cooked in yogurt and other flavours) and bodi sijha (mashed, sundried lentil balls boiled in gravy), pyajo, morcho (raw onions, raw chillies) and non-vegetarian dishes that went with it were macho jhura bhoja (flaked crispy-fried fish), chingudi thotha (prawns cooked with yogurt and mustard), chingudi mosala bhoja (prawns fried with chilli powder and turmeric). Usually, no dishes with gravy are served with Pokhalo.

On summer nights, the typical dinner used to include rice with potla jhulo (thin gravy), chapatti with korido acharo (bamboo shoot pickle), and baigono bhorta (smoked and mashed brinjals), aloo sijha with surso telo (boiled potato with mustard oil).

Aloo maunso (potato and meat) was a favourite for winter lunches. This was eaten with rice and daal. Other dishes we enjoyed in the winter months were maunso munda bhoja (fried minced-meat balls), fried fish and fried prawns, and prawn curry with gravy.

Birhi chokkuli chincho potro (a lentil-based savoury pancake sprinkled onto the pan with a leaf), sukha aloo dum, baingono dum (in this context, mashed potatoes and brinjals) were the winter dinner dishes. For dessert, there was a dessert bowl full of khua (thickened condensed milk), or mitha chenna (sweet cottage-cheese), or cream with sugar.

There were dishes that were made all year round for lunch and dinner. These were not always typical Oriya dishes. For example, we used to have mutton vindaloo, chicken with coconut milk, prawn malai curry, prawn masala curry, prawn cutlets with tails, mutton cutlets, murg musallam.

Some of the Oriya dishes that were made all year round were kosa maunso (mutton fried with spices), bhondaro handi (literally meaning store-room cauldron), macho petti bhoja (fish belly fry), macho masala bhoja (spicy fried fish), macho tomato suriso tota (fish with mustard and tomato), macho kalia (fish gravy), macho mundo dalna (fish head cooked with lentils and vegetables), konkada puro diya (stuffed crabs), konkada cutlet (crab cutlet), konkada jhura bhoja (deep fried crispy spicy crab flakes).

There were some dishes that we used to have all year round at dinner-time. When it was English food, it was served in courses. There were soups like jug soup, mutton soup, chicken soup, mullagtanny soup, followed by fish dishes like grilled fish and fish pie. There was also roast mutton or mutton cutlet with vegetable, minced mutton cottage pie and whole chicken roast. Some of the puddings were caramel custard, baked custard, pudding diplomat.

Teatime: dugdho soro (milk with cream), lia mua (sweet popped rice balls), singada (oriya-style samosas). In-between, whenever the garden is full with fruit, go and eat fruit – guava, suppota, banana, talo sojjo (ice apple), borkuli! Pluck green peas from the garden and big tomatoes and eat. Straight from the tree! Arisa pittha, gojjas, balushai etc. made from jaggery. Murhi tomato chokta (puffed rice with tomato paste) -famous-, baigono puda chokta (mashed smoked brinjals), aloo mudhi chokta (mashed potato with puffed rice), chuda palao (pulao made of flattened rice/poha), tomato mudhi chokta. Cakes baked at home. Biscuits (golden puffs, cream crackers, cream biscuits, Lily sweetish biscuits, Nice biscuits all shipped from England). Patties, mutton puffs, vegetable puffs all from Calcutta- Grand Hotel. Rasgullas from KC Das, Calcutta. Sandesh from Sen Mahashai.

Monsoon: Butto, Simbo (local flat or broad beans), Chinna badam (peanuts), mottor (green peas), corn all roasted in sand and eaten hot-hot with murhi. (There's a Meghua pago song).

VSD: What about festive foods?

VSLD: *Coming of age function (Ghoro jogyo). Girl wears a sari, restrictions of movements like jumping, running etc. Behave like a girl. On the 7ᵗʰ day, there's a big function with a nonveg feast. During the seven days, the girl eats vegetarian food. Guests bring big gifts like wedding gifts.*
Poojas: Ratha jatra (special food at home).
Dasara Feast at home for family, guests and staff and others. Talcher Dasara recipes.
Holi (normal feast food at home). Normal feast recipes.
Hingula Jatara. The Talcher royal family's Ishta Devi, Hingula Debi. The Goddess is fire. Everyone throws meat (live goats, hens etc.) into the fire. Lia, jaggery also (and red and black sarees). The burnt meat is eaten later.
Wedding was in Scotlandpur, Talcher. Feast-food. (Ask Bini babu).
Mithais were distributed during the wedding to villagers (very large laddus to take home).

There is a wedding laddoo recipe.

The wedding reception was in Kurupam:

Didn't know what was being cooked or who was eating what- wasn't supposed to know.

Mrs. Sundari Mani's father was the ward (of your Jejbaba and Sanjejbaba) in the court of wards. Mrs. Sundari Mani came for the wedding. There were parties, receptions for such people.

(Ask Kurupam people for details about the food).

At night, there was tennis on the tennis court, Annapurna theatre group from Orissa, and Andhra actors Banda, Prayaga, Lalita and Padmini of Trivandrum had all come to do dramas.

VSD: What about food after your marriage, in Kurupam?

VSLD: *Due to the family connections, food felt the same for me. Nothing new in the home cuisine. Silver utensils were used for daily meals. A number of help. Different kitchens for different purposes. Food for the horses (kultho- horse-gram, was cooked), also, uncooked, for elephants. For the cows, wheat, birhi (urad daal lentil), moong, mahua fruit, husk of til (rasi pidua), and cooked broken grains. (Boiled in Hondas, mixed with grass, rice husk, wheat husk, pejjo, ie., starch water from rice- of the staff's rice).*

When I got married and came to Kurupam, I was not very good at cooking. My mother-in-law (who was also my Ata), and my father and my mother and my husband: Because of these four people. They were so eager to have my cooking. So I took interest and learnt all my cooking. My mother-in-law used to wait for my cooking. There was a special kitchen for me with charcoal and wood-fire. A maid and my younger sister-in-law used to sit and blow the fire with a phoonknola.

Started cooking when Dr. Marikar and the nurses came.

VSD: What about after (my) Jejbaba (your husband) passed away?

VSLD: *Husband passed away July 29ᵗʰ 1952. Left Kurupam Aug., 29ᵗʰ 1952 – went first to Scotlandpur, Talcher, accompanied by Mrs. Boyen and Mrs. Strong (both tutors and nannies of the children). Spent one year in Orissa, made decisions on where to educate children. Finally, the original plan of my husband was kept to (of educating the children in Madras).*

Introduction to jatiya concept and cooking. Pattern of food and life changed.

VSD: You went to Madras, and kept to the jatiya concept of cooking for yourself. Please describe that first.

VSLD: *Reached Madras on Jan 14th, 1955 with children, accompanied by my younger brother. Also, Soito (Satyavati) old maid from Talcher and Tarini Nani from Palasa.*

Upaso food: Ekadasi: two Ekadasis a month, 24 a year, as per the panchang tithis.

My Ekadasi fasting food: No vegetables except potato, sweet potato, kuji saroo, cucumber. Only mugo allowed (can make daal). Out of fruit: Ponso, kodli, mango, guava, orange, lime allowed. (Only Indian fruit allowed). But apples, grapes also allowed though there were no apples and grapes at that time. Oil, onion, garlic not allowed. Only black pepper, jeera seed, ginger and pure ghee (bholo ghiyo) and rock salt allowed. Milk allowed. Wheat allowed, but not rice.

Ekadasi dishes: puri, chapaties, paratha, gohomo bhato, fries.

Sodo Jayanti (Jayantis of the main six Gods and Goddesses: Krishna Jayanti, Sri Ram Navami, Bamana Janama, Maha Ashtamai, Siva Ratri, Radha Ashtami or Chaitanya Janma). On all these days, it's the same food as the Ekadasi fasting food, except on Siva Ratri.

On Siva ratri: Whole day, only milk and fruit, usually bananas and coconut, sprouted moong (no cooked food).

Dhavaleshwar (Siva puja in the month of Kartik): Same as Siva Ratri fasting.

Kartik month Hobiso food: Different dishes on different days. (One day is an Ekadasi and one day is Dhavaleshwar. For the rest of the days of Kartika month): Cooked mugo, saroo, sweet potato, dahi, green tamarind, kodoli manja (core of the banana stem), koncha kodoli (raw banana) allowed. Cooked food only to be had once a day. Ghee allowed. During the day, one can eat bananas, coconut and curd. No sugar or jaggery.

Margasira Maso fasting: Lakshmi puja (not full fasting except that no onion or garlic on Thursdays and on Prathamashtami day), but special dishes such as manda, malpua, paluo manda. Birhi and mugo chokuli, and rice and Indian vegetables like brinjal, pumpkin, potato and borgudi (string beans) is allowed. No other English vegetable is allowed.

Magho Maso (Magho month) – Saraswati Pooja: khoja, pitha, monda.

Chaitra Maso: (Chaitra month) – Basantiko Puja ie., Navaratri (same as Dasara).

Chaitra Maso (Chaitra month) – Dasara recipes for Jatiya cooking.

Bhadro Maso: (Bhadro month) – Khudrukuni is the name of the fast to worship goddess Mangala Devi. Every Sunday of the month, followed by Budhei Usha (to worship Shashti Devi, especially for children, every Wednesday). On both these days, diet is same as Ekadasi plus Suji Khiri, liya mua, or just plain liya. Also, for these two only, no water the whole day, except after pooja in the evening.

In Bhadro maso falls Krushno Jayanti. On this day, there is a big celebration. About four or five girls who used to play with me in the village when I was young in Talcher used to be trained by me to do Leela Nato (Krishna Leela, ie., the story of Krishna, including Mano Bhanjan, Maya Simantani and Maya Savari etc). I used to play the harmonium and mridangam, and they used to sing (songs with raag raagini). They used to be in full costumes. My jejbaba, jejmama, ata and other relations used to witness this and give presents to the children, and things to eat (laddu, goja, badusha), and they used to sit and eat this at the mandap. On one such occasion, my Jejbaba presented me with a harmonium which is still in Bhuvaneshwar with Mojhia, she uses it during her Tulsi Ramayan path and Akhand Ramayan path. The Talcher performances were just like the Kurupam Kirtonos (by the oriya-speaking Goudo community). That's called the Leela Nato.

Ashwini Maso (Ashwini month) – (Dasara Maha Ashtami recipes).

Every month, fasting on Purnami day (full moon). Same diet as Ekadasi.

Soito was in charge of the jatiya kitchen.

Tarani Nani of Palasa was in charge of vegetarian cooking of the whole house.

Tarini nani made rice, daal, vegetables. Soito used to make all the jolikhya (tiffin) and used to train new cooks like Obhi and all who used to learn a little and go. Eventually, there was Joga (Jogannatho goudo).

VSD: When you moved to Madras after being widowed, and followed the jatiya cooking system for yourself, what was the kind of food that you cooked for the children?

VSLD: *In the morning, the children used to have their usual English breakfast and go to school.*

School-time, the four sisters used to come home for lunch around twelve thirty. Pucca Oriya lunch: daal, rice, vegetables. Very light. Curd.

When they used to come home at 5 pm all very hungry, some days, there would be mutton cutlet, some days pishpash with cauliflower pickle, some days chops with bread, masala chops, and on the whole very heavy things. Aloo chops (with minced meat inside), roast and grilled partridges. This was tea-time. Such things were made by me. And some sweets. Not everyday, but often.

Till today, all my children's friends, whenever they see me, they say aunty, your prawn pickle! Your cauliflower pickle! When the children's friends used to come home, they used to have snack-like things: fried bread, small poories, fried corn, nimkies (deep fried and mildly spiced flour sticks) with many kinds of pickles. Fish rolls, finger chips, mutton bota puan (fried mutton balls). The children used to roam around the garden, upstairs, on the terrace, have these snacks and go home after half an hour or so.

At night, the children's music session and homework session would get over. At nine or nine thirty they would have stew: vegetable stew, brown stew, baked custard, caramel custard, diplomat pudding (diplomat wasn't there in Talcher), Three Coloured Jelly (made up by me), home-made Indian sweets. The meals used to be served at a dining table in silver divided trays, and a plate for Kishore because he used to not like the divided tray. He used to eat on the Kurupam monogram plate. His name was on the monogram plate, the others' names were on the divided trays.

All five used to have birthday parties. Those days, things were cheaper, we used to have at least fifty to sixty people for each birthday. We used to buy samosas from Buharis. Those days, the Buhari samosas were great. Egg sandwiches, fresh fish sandwiches and vegetable sandwiches, besan pakodas (we call those pyaaji), fish rolls, shammi kebabs made at home, ice-creams from quality's in paper cups. Those days, there was no habit of buying birthday cakes. That happened only when they reached college. And home-made squashes. Cheese pakodas…these sandwiches and cheese pakodas and all, I used to make up my own recipes. Fried bread with pickle, looking like shahi tukda. Everyone used to ask for that. All the pickles, whoever wanted whichever: prawn, mutton, game meat, cauliflower, brinjal (brinjal was the main), mixed vegetable, tomato. I used to make a One-Egg cake (like cupcakes), learnt from Mrs. Bramstone, the Australian nurse who was attending to me when I had a four-month relapse of typhoid (those days there was no medicine for typhoid, and I had three relapses. At that time, Kishore was one or two months old).

I used to cut the skin of grapefruit like petals, and decorate short-eats on toothpicks on these petals, to look like a blooming flower. These were meant for cocktails, but we used to serve it for children's birthday parties. For parties, Kusum used to decorate flowers and leaves from the garden in silver vases.

When the children were young, we used to have a big lunch at home in Madras on New Year's Day. When we came from Kurupam to Madras after my husband's death, then we brought about sixteen of the staff along. I had to bring them all along. They were not part-time. They used to live in the house. They used to eat good food that was cooked for them. And there was a special lunch for them on new year's day. On Diwali day, there were special sweets and crackers for everyone.

Those days, there was no health problem. No restrictions on food for children. Food had to be fresh and home-made.

I used to make kathi puda kebabs with knitting needles. Those days, there were no ovens, so this was made on charcoal. The knitting needles were held from one end with a Chimta, and pieces of meat, fish and vegetables were skewered onto it and held over a charcoal sigri. To make it more convenient, a makeshift stand could also be made for the knitting needles to rest on, if holding it with the chimta was too uncomfortable.

When my children were young, every day, Kishore, Sucharu and Pushpa used to play tennis before going to school…at the Gymkhana Club. Every evening, I used to take Sneha and Sucharu to play tennis, badminton and table tennis for two or three hours. The children used to learn the new-new names of all other foods other than our home food. We used to come home and try making all those. Kishore and Sucharu were very interested in making these. We did so much of cooking that the children became experienced. Anything they ate, they came to know how it was made. After that, they didn't have to learn from anyone. They could make their own recipes without learning from anyone.

VSD: Now, about us, all the grandchildren! And what you used to make for us!

VSLD: *I used to take the grandchildren during their summer holidays or Christmas holidays in Madras to the Gymkhana Club; the Lady's Recreation Club; the MCC (Madras Cricket Club). I used to take them there and play badminton and table tennis with them. I used to take them where children were allowed.*

When I go to Pushpa's house in the US, they invite all their friends, saying their mother has come. I cook all the good-good dishes I know. Once, I made bird's nest, mutton cutlet, fish pie, prawn cutlets with tails (to have with drinks in the evening), kheer sagar pudding. The other dishes like pulao etc., which Sano (Pushpa) made, (she) learnt from me. There, it is very easy. Anything you ask for, it comes. Not much cleaning to be done at home. The ingredients, of course, we get from the public stores. The big huge stores. The first time, everything looked so huge. I went with Salil, with Pushpa. Whatever list you take, you get immediately. Within half an hour, you are back with everything. The grandchildren, Piya and Sushil, used to like all the Indian cooking. They were too small that time to learn. Now, they are waiting for the recipe book, but they remember what I cooked. I've been six times to America. Each time, it was to different places. So different friends came and tried this food on each trip. The Indian community at Delaware (from Andhra, UP, the Parsi community, and many others) liked the chottu choka bhoja (fried mushroom pancakes). After they tasted it, every house wanted Pushpa's chokka bhoja and our type of vegetable curries. In Miami, there were many Bengali friends, so I cooked Oriya-Bengali food for them. It's almost the same. All the fruit, vegetables, whatever one wished for, was available in America those days.

Pushpa is also a cooking expert. She knows to cook everything I know, plus excellent Bengali dishes that she's learnt from her mother-in-law. She's cooking alone there without help, so she's very good at planning and organizing food, freezing it, so there's always good food. Her husband, Salil, does all the cutting and chopping like American husbands do.

When I went to Kolhapur to my daughter Sneha's place, all the Maharashtran friends used to visit with their families. There, we saw all the places connected to Chhatrapati Shivaji. The places where he used to ride his horse, where he fought his wars, where he used to hide. There, I saw many fig gardens on the Kolhapur-Puna road. Sneha's friends all came home for a gathering. Kusum had gone with me. The three of us made four or five special dishes. I saw the college where Sneha studied her MPhil in English Literature. Sneha's daughters, Smita and Nameeta, enjoy khua malpua and rabdi malpua that I make. I heard there was khua malpua at Smita's wedding reception party recently. Smita and Nameeta love any Oriya dish that is made. Sneha used to train her Maharashtran cooks to cook food without too many spices and without too much of ghee. Simple food, she used to love. Mostly plain, vegetarian dishes and sea food.

My daughter Sucharu once did a short course at the Cultural Academy in Madras which included cooking classes. I learnt one or two dishes from her after that. One such dish was patrel, which was fish wrapped in banana leaf with a greenish gravy, and also brinjal pattya and lemon delight. Her son, Sujeet, loves lemon delight. Sujeet likes everything. Sameer is the mutton wallah.

My daughter Kusum. Whom does she not cook for! All the old ladies, my friends, for other friends, she cooks things for what each person likes. For me, ruchoko, stuffed brinjal, vegetarian chinese and pasta. She is very fond of cooking. For any occasion, she likes to give good food to the servants and poor people. The staff all get food made by her. There isn't anyone here who hasn't had her cooking! She can single-handedly, without help, cook for fifty people. She does this every time there is an occasion.

When Kishore and Preeti had gone to the US for the UN General assembly, I was in Delhi for three months in North Avenue to be with the grandchildren. I used to go with Muriel to INA market and buy prawns and pomphret. At tea-time, I used to make chincho potro pithas and other pithas. Shruti and Shishir used to like those. There were two young cooks from Orissa at that time, who used to help me. Shruti and Shishir liked the prawn cutlets with tails. Then I bought pork and made Nimki. I used to make various sauces there, including mayonnaise and salad cream I had learnt from Mrs. Bramstone.

Kishore cooks all kinds of food. There is no type of food that Kishore doesn't know. He knows what goes with what, what will be good to combine with what. He is an expert in all kinds of cooking. He knows what menu to suggest where. For my grandson Shishir's thread ceremony, he made stuffed bamboo for the relatives. They still cannot forget that. He organized and planned the menus for all the functions, and the cooks prepared all the meals with his guidance. My daughter-in-law Preeti is also very good at cooking and knows all dishes, including food of many countries including Nepal, China and many other places. She also makes cakes and bakes.

This brief personal food-history of my paternal grandmother depicts, to me, how each individual's cultural journey is, indeed, unique, even if there are shared filters with one's nearest and dearest. My mother's mother, Ammama, for instance, has, figuratively speaking, never entered a kitchen in her life.

One has staunchly never been much of a foodie. As a child, one was a preferred vegetarian, something that was probably not discovered or comprehended for long enough for one to have been at the receiving end of innovative punitive measures that were thought to be just right for toddlers who refused to eat their food, like being incarcerated for possibly more than just a few minutes at a time, in a cubicle-sized rooftop bird-cage (it's been dismantled in decades past), under the expansive sky on the deck of the ancestral home.

There are, to balance out the account, idyllic accounts of a Jersey Cow having been reared just for me, and other fresh farm-produce being available in my toddler-days at Kurupam, before I was sent forth to attend the kindergarten and a few months of class one at St. Joseph's Convent, Vizag.

My baby brother was born, (during which time I attended a few months of nursery school at Luz House, Madras), I was then sent off to my mother's parents' home at Vizag, my father got elected to parliament for the first time, my parents and brother left for Delhi. I received post-cards, such as one with a picture of Parliament House, in 1977 from my dad saying something to the effect of this is where daddy goes everyday. The food at my mother's parents' house was famed for being fabulous, but somehow, the routine of rushing home for lunch and returning to school for a post-lunch session didn't quite gel with my system, and almost every lunch was followed by a retching session, followed by a reluctant return to school!

A year later, I moved to Delhi. With a tin of biscuits, or chocolates, or both, that my grandma's sister gave me at the airport as a send-off gift. I was on the flight with my dad and uncle, and had the cookie-tin under my seat, and helped myself to something from it every few minutes.

Stepping out of the flight for the first time in the Delhi summer, the hot desert wind greeted me, and when we reached Meena Bagh, I was chewing gum. The government quarters for first-term members of parliament were set around a common lawn, with apartments on the ground and first floors. In our quadrangle, we had people from Kerala, Goa, Ladakh (the Queen), Uttar Pradesh, Orissa and Kashmir (the Kashmiris were officials of the government). An evening walk past peoples' houses and windows would get you wafts of goan sausages, mustard oil, coconut, north indian curries, and criss-crossing aromas and flavours that evoked the environs of far-flung kitchens of India.

After we moved to 15 AB Pandara Road, the walks into the colony held similar scents. After-dinner walks to the ice-cream cart near the post-box would afford us glimpses of warmly-lit interiors and wall-spaces adorned with the arts and craft of India and of neighbours' creativity. The famous Pandara Market with its restaurants that serve Mughlai and other north-Indian dishes, and some Chinese, was down the road. Walks towards the market-side would have you walking through occasional air-corridoors of butter-chicken masala or daal makhani. It was close enough to send the help on a bicycle with an ice-bucket for orange bars, a fun and economical dessert for kids like us. The lawns of India Gate had carts with chuski, crushed ice-bars dipped into many-hued sweet-and-sour syrups. The chuski expeditions were with a gang from school, usually after having watched a rollicking comedy by Stagedoor at Kamani auditorium, all crammed into a brand new Maruti 800 of the badminton champion from school who'd learnt to drive before most others.

The first thing one learnt to cook was custard with chopped bananas, something that I was pleasantly surprised to find on the menu, years later, at our St. Stephen's college mess lunch. In fact, I recall trading my chicken curry for a friend's dessert at the inaugural lunch!

At school, one's interest in cooking was kindled by my friend, Gunjan, who was an amazing teenage chef, and taught me how to make butter chicken, malai paneer, and had creative and impromptu ideas for icing cakes as a tween. Gunjan passed away soon after college in a car accident, after having been in a coma for almost fifteen months, first at the All India Institute of Medical Sciences, and later, at her home at Jangpura.

In the Pandara Road neighbourhood, cooking expeditions with other kids were with: Swati, who had a recipe for kebabs, Tanu, for mango ice cream, and Nitu, for quite a few gourmet dishes which we used to experiment with.

In our final years of school, the school acquired a range of kitchen equipment, and there used to be a class called S.U.P.W (Socially Useful Productive Work), where, among other things, we learnt how to make an Indianized macaroni dish, and something called Whacky Cake, that you were supposed to be able to make in a jiffy. I'm not sure if the intent was to also churn out marriageable young ladies, I choose to believe the aim was to equip us for survival in the modern world. Maggi Noodles was allowed to go from class-to-class and advertise its brand-new noodles-in-two-minutes product that made waves, we even stuck a sticker outside our classroom door! The rather uncharitable joke amongst us used to be that S.U.P.W stood for Some Useful Period Wasted!

To do full justice to reveries of dining out in the 80s and beyond, including at friends' places, and comparatively recent jaunts to Delhi's restaurants with the CC (self-christened cuisine club that began by sampling Blinis in the 2000s at an NDMC restaurant after reading about it in the papers), one might set a book or two a-simmer on the backburner for now.

But dining out for south Indian food in the 1980s, apart from Dasaprakash (where the Ambassador now stands), was the residence of our family friends, the Gopals. Radha Gopal aunty's south-Indian lunches with the most steaming and delicious doasas, stews, sambar, gun-powder and appams and uttapams on this (or that) side of the Vindhyas. Honest politician and ever-helpful, Gopal uncle…RIP.

All the noise that has been made over the years, and continues to be made, about how politicians receive too many perks, and are criticised for voting in their own pay-raises can be not only infuriating, but can create great resentment, helplessness and rage amongst children of honest politicians (yes, there are, and have been such creatures).

The public often confuses the issues of corruption in politics, and the fact that the system mandates that the politicians legislate on their own pay-scales. Add to this, the lack of understanding of official protocol that is required to maintain an appropriate balance of powers between wings of state and the bureaucracy, and you get disproportionate criticisms each time there's a miniscule hike in salaries to a comparatively miniscule existing paycheque.

And to add to the confusion, MPs are given unnecessary duties that are sometimes viewed as perks. The local area development scheme, for example. This shifts all the focus of an MPs work to a small whirlpool of sarpanch-like and NGO-like activities in the MP's own constituency. These functions need to be pruned. Back in the 1980s and 1990s, its equivalent was the MPs' quota of doling out limited, much-coveted cooking gas connections and telephone connections to people, using discretion.

The Pandara restaurants used to home-deliver to the neighbourhood, and were an option for when guests suddenly dropped in. Khan market, with its aromas of kebabs and the beginnings of fast-food was a longer walk away. A walk that one did quite frequently, to help mom carry back bags of vegetables from the road-side vegetable seller. The mouth-watering papri chaat, sold near the Shah Jahan Road bus-stops was another few-minutes' walk away. A route on which Shadow, the family Labrador, was sometimes taken on a walk. This chaat was a rare treat, and was sometimes brought in when there were guests for teatime who knew and appreciated what it was all about. Nathu's Sweets of Bengali market used to home-deliver to Pandara as well. It was possible to dial in a few modest orders of jalebis and rasmalai once in a while from there. If we did really, really well for the half-yearlies, like got above twenty-on-twenty-five for quite a few subjects, then off we were whisked, in the fiat driven by dad, to Nirula's for a hot chocolate fudge ice-cream. Movies were considered to be too decadent, and could not be afforded in any case.

Well-budgeted, very rare visits to five-star hotels were treated almost as a part of our overall education. Around the time of the Asian Games in Delhi in 1982, a number of new hotels had mushroomed in the city.

Our occasional visits were to the House of Ming and the Machaan coffee-shop at the Taj, and to the Frontier at the government's Ashoka hotel.

There used to be a musician at the Frontier, who used to play an ukulele-like instrument with the most enchanting, rippley music from the mountains.

The family used to go to The Ashoka for haircuts, followed by a grilled sandwich and ice-cream at the Samovar coffee shop there, and rum-ball pastries from the pastry shop to take home. Hair-dressers thereafter have been at The Claridges and the Taj, with, coincidentally, names of US First Ladies like Barbara and Nancy, and also Debbie.

When I started going for haircuts on my own, or with friends, I switched to Sunflower at Khan Market, and, thereafter, for many, many years, to Aina (meaning mirror), a tiny place run by an ex-Stephanian in an armed forces locality near India Gate.

Luckily, there was the Gymkhana Club, where the bills could be paid at the end of the month, and where club sodas as quaint as ice-cream soda, vimto and lemonade were sold at what could only have been a loss to the soda factory that's now shut down.

In keeping with the great tradition of connoisseurship of food that my Jejmama had built, however, the approach was to ensure that it was possible to partake of every imaginable delicacy. Not by going to five-star hotels, but by embracing food-appreciation and cooking as a hobby. And making at home, better and more generous helpings of what the five-stars served.

In the 1980s, I noticed that the political culture was that it was possible to frequently host important meetings for important people in Lutyens' Delhi only if you had the budget to serve the best of scotch whiskeys and air-conditioned drawing rooms at a time when ACs in more than one room were quite a luxury for anyone, and certainly for an honest MP.

Having resolved, by then, to be a lawyer like Perry Mason, and to be a politician like myself ☺, I believe I did manage to do my bit, over the next three decades, to gradually change the ways and platforms through which high-level political and other political and social meets took place in Delhi.

The advent of a retro punch-bowl that Jejmama spotted at an exhibition in Chennai and sent to us to Delhi crystallized the regular flow of no-frills, sometimes potluck parties with home-made mass-prepared patès and bakes. My parents both love cooking, and personally spend time and energy preparing specialities for their parties, beginning with a trip to the fish-market.

My brother and his wife, Sukanya, keep up some of these traditions, and are also adept at sourcing appropriate caterers for appropriate occasions at Gurgaon. Barbecues, Lebanese food, and the current zeitgeist of the millennium city with the foods of the world reachable to your doorstep. The home-made food is delicious, and made with health in mind. Sukanya's mother, Gul, makes the most authentic north-Indian pickles, the kind my friend, Aparna, used to bring to school with mathari in her tiffin box!

My nieces sometimes regale me by participating in various baking-with-premixes-and-adding-other-stuff-to-make-it-even-better activities occasionally! Alaiya was introduced to the wonders of plucking and uprooting Aloe Vera, and herbs and carrots and fruit amongst monkeys and peacocks and flying foxes and eagles at 4 Janpath. Aisha rolls cinnamon sugar bread with the deftness of a veteran playdough diva. We have ascertained, at ages three and six, that yeast is not exactly an insect, but consists of tiny creatures that go into the making of bread to make it fluffy. Food-craft as science-lab for tots!

As it probably always has been, from the days of wandering about in the wildernesses, and not-so-wild greens for medicinal plants, hungry for knowledge, moulding cake with silicon, and ways of thinking with ethical experimentation. And books and papers are sometimes the crucibles that take on journeys of their own in the minds of readers, making fairies and angels, unicorns and frankensteins, or just rip-van-winkles of those who read.

This is also a city where working people can opt for daily meals to be delivered home via websites, and where many corporate offices have canteens and cafeterias for the staff.

Creative state governments are also catching on to this trend (or public requirement), of people's time and energy needing to be freed from compulsory cooking.

In Tamil Nadu, there are government-initiated Canteens, where basic, simple, and, I believe, inexpensive food can be bought by citizens. Political parties in other states seem to be en route to making similar poll promises.

I, for one, often find it most convenient to buy packets of heat-and-eat-readymade food, and team it up with a freshly-cut salad, and am reminded of Plato's Republic, where society was envisaged so that each could contribute to society, what they were best at doing (and, I might add, even if Plato didn't, where this interfaced with what they enjoyed doing), and where all other duty-related activities meant for society could be carried out at one's own time and convenience. This becomes possible when the said functions (of being duty-bound to, let's say, accompany a person to a hospital), are not dictated by chance, but by each one's convenience.

This is possible in a society where people assign a part of their time to attend to the sick, to fight a war, to fight for causes, to do public service. In an organized way, irrespective of who the individual recipients are. In turn, individuals ought not to expect any specific individuals to attend to them when they are sick, to take them to their funerals, or to fight their battles for them as acts of individual duty or largesse. However, they are to expect, as their right, the role of the state, to seamlessly and systematically ensure that these basic human requirements are met for each individual.

This is not a path of restriction or of the limiting of human aspirations. It is the very opposite of it. This is the only way through which to be able to give the entire human race it's best shot to aspire for the stars, and for earthly fulfilment. By not having to bother about the mechanics of daily food and nutrition, or any other enforced duties-towards-proximate-individuals.

Once the intake of food is seen as a scientific method through which to attain and maintain a fit human body. Once all cultural and value-based judgements are disassociated form people's eating habits, and once appropriate forms of food are available to all, then we will still be left with the physical human desire to consume cuisines of varying flavours, textures, aromas and visual appeals. And to be educated on the history of food through experiential methods (by partaking of these elements of the planet's heritage). It will be fair to make such opportunities available to all the children of the world first. To the extent that dietary stimuli are also connected to other brain-functions, such dietary inputs are also to be understood and appreciated from the perspective of the development or restriction of the growth of the intellect.

It is possible to have a world where there is ready-to-eat food for all, with additional options of do-it-yourself shopping and cooking, and to bring this about without stepping on anyone else's toes. What constitutes the definition of ready-to-eat, and what constitutes the definition of stepping on anyone's toes can be debated ad infinitum at seminars to which, no doubt, relevant people will ensure that they are invited, papers et al. Especially since one is not drafting legislation at this point of writing.

Food as fine art and entertainment in this century has been brought to the masses through cooking-based entertainment game shows such as the Masterchef series, putting the world of chefs and khansammas on the world stage, and adding to the phenomenon of bringing world street foods and exotica alike to the high table.

One does believe that one has watched and lived the entire cauldron bubble- from walking the walk, and talking the talk, to digging the non-dug-outs of real rural fields and fallows.

Of having put one's foot down at appropriate times, when the beast of the caste system has reared its ugly head at communal feasts and gatherings, of having learnt to eat like the hungry, and of having nudged the world of table manners forward to include the honouring of golgappas, and eating with one's fingers at hoitey-toitey and well laid out dinner environs, discussing matters that might range from the Indian Penal Code, to cultural ties with Asian nations, or the rights of employers, employees, and inmates of houses in countries where populations employ house help on an ad hoc basis.

Of having one's preferred vegetarian grandeur interspersed with foods such as raw, sliced sun-dried limbs of African beasts, to lotus seeds and whiffs of pig's blood, and silver-foil-lined sweetmeats.

Of having surfed the net to create New Delhi versions of the foods and beverages of many lands: Japan, New Zealand, Canada, South America, and on and on and on.

And of having surfed one's memory and imagination to conjure an outer-space-tribes-of-the-planet spread: Organically grown food; grains that consume less water, and are drought-resistant such as barley and numerous other millets; star trek-inspired blue-curacao-lemonade that could well be interpreted as the poison that Lord Shiva consumed after the churning of the ocean.

Of having brewed many a fruit, green and grain into mellowing woodland victuals, and having received the holy waters of rivers…Ganga Jal, and Zam Zam from the Haj.

One might be comparatively ahead of one's times in terms of accessing much of one's larder needs through the internet- e-shopping and home-delivery. The digital marketplace is still the wild west of hawkers and consumers, in many ways, and requires an entire forward-looking chapter unto itself.

Until then, you may either shop for a slice of cake, or of the moon, on the world wide web!

CHAPTER II

PRIVATE, NOT SECRET VERSUS SECRET, NOT TRANSPARENT

There's a whole bunch of people that think that the recent, much talked-about Right to Privacy judgement is all about the Aadhaar card only. Guess what, it's not. Because that would be like saying that the Dasara pooja is all about Raavan. Guess what: It's not. Not in Sri Lanka, not in many parts of India.

So, Happy Vijaya Dashami, everyone. (Yes, it's Dasara in India, and the divine feminine that's not restricted to only the reproductive role at all, but the transcendent, victorious, multi-faceted version, is venerated across the realms of Vasudaiva Kutumbakam today).

Technology has enabled one to speak to the global community on the topic of the right to privacy judgement even before scurrying into this word file in a bid to complete at least a rough cut of this manuscript and send it off to the publishers on this day on which millions are primed to believe (arguably, for valid reasons providable by High Science), that all beginnings and ventures will meet with success and victory.

The status update on my Facebook wall, updated several hours ago, was:

"my advice to the judiciary is to refrain from writing lengthy judgements and obiter"

And as an explanatory note, I wrote:

"Sometimes, lengthy judgements are required, such as in the recent right to privacy judgement, esp. because we don't want judgements without reasons or justifications. But they should, in general, stick to the point, and not get carried away by opportunities to exercise judicial over-reach, or judicial irrelevance. i say this mainly because the non-legal public (who are equally entitled to try and understand the law -including the media, sometimes-), jump to their own conclusions about what the declared law is. furthermore, it is the duty of all in the legal community to educate people on how to read and comment on judgements, if they must"

Voila! One had begun this chapter, pretty much unbeknownst to myself, at the very instant of the writing of the Facebook comment. Of course, all and sundry (whoever those are), must be encouraged to discuss the law, but when in positions of influence, a rash pouncing on fragments on air serves to entangle rather than unravel the law.

So the right to privacy judgement, as it's popularly being referred to, is an approx. 600-page judgement.

The three judges hearing the Aadhaar matter in court decided that the right to privacy aspect of the entire debate was a matter that needed serious legal scrutiny. Not only as far as the Aadhaar card was concerned, but also as far as figuring out (or putting a "quietus" to) what the law of the land is, (and, to some extent, what it should be), as far as the right to privacy on-the-whole goes. So a reference was made, to a bench of nine judges, to do just that.

Think of this process as the rules of a Diwali card game. Different sets of people sit at different card-tables. If it's a party for intense, apex card-players, it is likely that the tables with the higher stakes will have more people sitting at it.

There is a Supreme Court. It has many court-rooms. Each courtroom has a bench. Each of the benches have judges that sit at them. (Thanks to legal-eagle kind of movies and serials, nobody thinks garden bench or creaky clerk bench when you talk of the courts). At the Supreme Court, it is, indeed, a permanent Durga Pandal-like scenario in polished wood, with their Lordships perched at the various altars all year round, with a few breaks.

The number of judges at each bench depends on the kind of case that is being heard. There could be a one or two-judge bench, or there could be a many-judge bench. Once a bench makes a legally significant decision, then only a bench with more judges on it can revise (or change) what has already been said. This is how the court-made law grows.

The job of the courts is mainly to use certain approaches (no pun intended), and guidelines to interpret the written laws that are made by parliament, the legislative assemblies, and so on. If matters come to them, that are not their business, they are not expected to admit the matters to that court.

While writing judgements, there are sooo many legal topics that might arise. But if you're holding jokers in a game that doesn't allow jokers, then you might ask yourself why the cards were in the pack to begin with. Or realise that you do not, in fact, have any jokers or trumps.

But Deepavali is twenty days away. And to be sure, many won't want any to know how much money they made or lost. Because where does the money come from, silly?! Cash. Blackmoney? Untaxed? People were probably even beginning to think: Fake notes?

And then, of course, demonetisation happened. Good for the country, good for the government and people. Idea-wise. In a sense. But what actually happened? Did cancelling those old five-hundred rupee and thousand-rupee notes all of a sudden make any difference? We'll know only if there's a guarantee that they won't now fake the two-thousand rupee notes. And apparently, it's unclear whether any black money made it to banks. Everyone who had pulled money out of ATMs had to go and return it, and then stand, without money, in long queues, to be doled out limited amounts of one's own cash in denominations that nobody was willing to accept for quite some time.

That was about cash and money, and whose business it is to know what. People playing serious cards don't drink. So not much booze at Diwali parties, one might assume. No such luck. Arrey, half the junta might be there to play cards, but what about the other half? And party-hoppers. Punch bowls were a good invention, I tell you! Everyone keeps all kinds of timings. Not only these days, but since we were young. So the kids have quite a ball. It's a free world, as long as you're driving safe. Boys, girls, they all mix quite freely. Many don't know how it is in other parts of India or the world. Or they do, and feel lucky that here, at least, we all respect each other's privacy.

India's right to privacy judgement does quite a thorough job of looking at the laws connected to privacy in many other democracies. Wait, I must confess, here, that I've only read the first two-hundred pages or so in great detail as of now.

But you know what happens in judgements, sometimes, there are some judges on the bench, who do not agree with what the majority is saying. So there could be a majority opinion, and that would then be the main judgement.

At the same time, the other judges are free to write judgements. If they disagree, it is called a dissenting judgement. If they partially agree, they can write that down. If they agree, but for different reasons, then they can write that down as well. All this forms a part of the judgement. Then there is a Court Order.

A bit like ordering food at a restaurant. If the majority decides that you're going to a Chinese restaurant, and the understanding is that you will go where the majority decides to go, then all the food you're going to get there will be Chinese. However, this is a system where you can also dial in Tandoori food, or South Indian khaana to the table, and insist that everything is packed with the left-overs.

When the restaurant review gets written, you are free to mention the Idlis and Kebabs while headlining the Manchurian, the Cantonese and the Schezwan. For the next round of restaurant-going, if there's a bigger crowd, don't forget to book a larger table, maybe even a buffet. And while deciding what cuisine to go for, if the fresh blood votes for Frontier Food, then the whole flavour will be different this time round. Fangs a lot for zat.

So now we're at the buffet, trying to form opinions on how the recipes of all the dishes could be altered in order to suit everyone's taste-buds.

You get what one is saying, right? There were some already-existing judgements on the right to privacy here in India. But there was stuff lacking in those judgements. So it was felt by a particular bench of judges, that the whole matter should be looked at by a much more crowded (and potentially noisier) bench.

So the almost-600 pages is the whole buffet served up by the bench. What I've just finished reading is the majority judgement that's there right at the beginning, and I've also skipped to the Court Order that's there towards the end. I plan to read the entire thing, and write a more serious-sounding piece on it somewhere else.

If you're not a lawyer, and you're reading a judgement, then you're quite lucky. Because then you're more like a person who's reading a series of short stories, except that they're real-life, and you could even try to do something about anything you might not agree with.

I don't know if this is possible in the world of TV serials. Well, yes, to some extent, I believe the turn of the story of a soap travels along with where the TRPs go. I know a bit about things like this because I used to watch The Bold and the Beautiful. (The serial where there was a Hilary Clinton kind of lady named Stephanie, and an Imran Khan kind of person named Ridge Forrester, and a Bill Clinton kind of person named Eric. Sally Spectra was quite a memorable character, there's a Whitehouse correspondent who looks quite a bit like her these days!).

There have been movies made, in Bollywood, based on famous court-cases. But it would be quite cool if there was an entire series of plays or serials that dramatized, topic-by-topic (with legal expertise, -no, I'm not careening around ghaat-bends, chasing one-nought-eights-), the main judgements of all important court-cases.

The commentary in a judgement basically examines the already-existing law made by politicians and those they are supposed to delegate tasks to. Acts, rules, guidelines, government orders and so on.

Then, it examines the already-existing judgements on the topic, or on related topics. This is the fun part. Each of these past judgements is basically a true story, obviously. After looking at all these factors, the final decision is made.

It's a bit like trying to decide where to go for the winter vacation. First, you look at the existing framework of dates, budget, visa restrictions etc.

Then, you look at what your priorities are, for a holiday.

Then, you examine the short-listed destinations, ask people for their stories on each of their travel experiences, or read up on the places, and make your final decision about where you're going to spend Christmas and New Year's.

For this Right to Privacy judgement, the judges looked at what's written in the Constitution of India; then they read a number of past judgements. I've read many of these past judgements long ago (or recently, depending on when they were written), as have most lawyers.

But it makes sense to refresh one's memory before writing about these things, or making court appearances where your memory has to dredge up the relevant nuggets. If you've been in the profession for quite some time, and you have someone refreshing your memory, it's called being briefed. I believe there are all kinds of dictionaries these days.

Striking up conversations or discussions, or worse, arguments, with lawyers on legal matters in social interactions (and possibly passing judgement on their lack of awareness of some micro-clause in the very-important-in-the-conversant's-life-document) is like nonchalantly helping yourself to the magazines and books that are displayed for sale as you walk along the open arcades at airports without as much as a by-your-leave to the holder of the keys.

Also, if you've noticed, these days, with technology, it is no longer necessary to try and remember many things that we used to try and remember in a world before the dawn of internet search-engines. That frees up a lot of mind-space. In fact, those who can remember too many things too quickly, are those whose surface-memories are like a jam-packed desktop on the computer.

The Right to Privacy judges looked at the laws (statutory, as well as judge-made, of other parts of the world. And international case-studies).

More stories, more foreign locations for film shoots, more things to sound knowledgeable about on one's international travels! Speech-writers of world leaders may also take note.

Let me quickly remind you that you now know why people keep thinking that the right to privacy judgement is THE Aadhaar judgement. (You know, the Aadhaar card that the government's been asking people to have, and which many are protesting against. One of the reasons that people and lawyers are protesting against the Aadhaar Card is because it is thought that it will go against a person's right to privacy).

While hearing arguments related to the Aadhaar card in the Supreme Court, a three-judge bench of the Supreme Court felt that there were many larger legal matters that needed to be sorted out, as far as the right to privacy is concerned. Therefore, they referred the matter to a nine-judge bench led by the Chief Justice of India, to look into the matter. (We've already talked about this, but it doesn't harm to make doubly sure that folks are up to speed with what's being said).

So the Right to Privacy judgement that we're talking about right now is the one delivered by those nine judges. The majority view was delivered by Justice Dr. D.Y. Chandrachud.

It is a historic judgement that can influence many things, and therefore it is worth knowing more about it.

Once a person understands the structure of how most judgements are written, a meaningful and efficient reading becomes easier.

I might zoom in and out of bits and pieces of the judgement in a non-comprehensive manner, primarily to recommend ways in which to read judgements, unless a better idea seizes me along the sentences. Methods, rather than diligent recipes. La Rousse.

The reference that was made to the bench was for them to scrutinize two earlier judgements, where it was ruled (or, as the legal jargon goes, where it was held), that there was no such fundamental right to privacy in the Constitution of India.

No point mentioning the full case titles of all these litigations. One will only refer to each saga by its abbreviated nomenclature or buzz-word.

The two cases that had to be scrutinized to begin with were the cases of M.P. Sharma, and of Kharak Singh. (The day that I was reading the Kharak Singh part of this judgement, I actually dreamt of a loud rattling of doors- as we say in Hindi- a khat-khat-khat-khat sound!) Anyone else who might've had the same dream might wonder what the message from the surreal world was! Well, it was a reminder to analyse Kharak Singh.

In the case of M.P. Sharma, complaints had been filed, and with a warrant, there had been searches and seizures made, to recover a company's records. This was because the company was being investigated for malpractices, and for taking its share-holders for a ride. The court held that there was no right to privacy that was violated there.

Then, there was what happened in the Kharak Singh matter. A dacoit was challaned, and released due to a lack of evidence. But under rules pertaining to "history sheeters," the government of Uttar Pradesh kept tabs on the person. This included midnight knocks on the person's door, and a number of other surveillance measures.

The court held that the Constitutional Right to Freedom (in this case, to "move freely throughout the territory of India") was not violated by keeping a watch on the person's movements.

However, it also ruled that the Constitutional protection of life and personal liberty was violated as far as the domiciliary visits were concerned.

Overall, M.P. Sharma and Kharak Singh both relied on an earlier approach that the courts had taken in the matter of Gopalan.

This was an approach towards how fundamental rights are looked at in the Constitution of India. Is each of the enlisted rights a stand-alone, water-tight right without over-laps, or are there over-laps?

According to Gopalan, followed by M.P. Sharma and Kharak, the answer was yes, these rights are water-tight.

To understand how previous judgements, or precedents, as they are called, work, let us take an imaginary situation from a far-off, beautiful, green village.

If there was a girl, or group of girls who needed to go to the nearest town to attend a class, or report in to a job, and if they wanted to ride motorbikes that they could afford.

If, for example, a village elder of the yesteryear expressed a view that girls had the right to ride motorbikes, but did not automatically have the right to wear trousers. Then both these rights were being viewed in air-tight compartments, or silos by such a village elder of the yesteryear.

This is how the Gopalan judgement viewed individual fundamental rights. As separate, insular entities.

The Gopalan judgement chose to look at the legality of Preventive Detention only by testing it against one of the Fundamental Rights enlisted in the Constitution, Article 22, that deals with "Protection against arrest and detention in certain cases," and did not think that it was required to test Preventive Detention against the "touchstone" of Article 19(1)(d), which is the right to move freely throughout the territory of India.

Clearly, I'm not saying that village elders have the mandate or authority to make such decisions in independent India.

The imaginary scenario has been projected to illustrate the system of precedents in judgements, especially to semi-literate people who might read a regional-language translation of this piece of writing, or have it read out to them in the future.

In rural India, many people still gather around one person who reads out important articles from a daily newspaper. I need to find out if this holds true, not just for photographs, but for articles from the internet as well.

Even in the Gopalan (Preventive Detention) judgement, however, there was a dissenting opinion, where Justice Fazl Ali said that all fundamental rights "protect a common thread of liberty and freedom."

This would be like someone else in the far-away green village telling the village elder of the yesteryear that you cannot ignore the connection between girls' rights to ride a two-wheeler, and their rights to wear what they please, including trousers or jeans.

The judgements of M.P. Sharma and Kharak Singh adhered to the Gopalan judgement.

This is like if, after the passage of more time, or in any event, at a point in the future, people decided to assert that even if a girl had the right to wear a dhoti, she did not have the right to ride a motorbike, and to prove their point, they would remind you of what the village elder of the yesteryear had said.

In Kharak, there was a dissenting view of Justice Subba Rao, which opined that there are, in fact, over-laps when it comes to interpreting the scope of each of the fundamental rights mentioned in the Indian Constitution. This dissenting opinion was later (ie., in a future judgement that over-rode Kharak), held to be the decided law.

This would be like if a stray voice in the crowd disagreed with what the people in the far-away green village decided (which is not to say that there's a mobocracy that's supposed to decide peoples' wardrobes or means of transport). And if this stray voice was temporarily forgotten.

After the passage of time, if other similar questions were to arise, and if the opinion of the stray voice were to be declared to be the correct opinion, then this would describe the kind of role of the dissenting opinion of Subba Rao in the context of the caselaw on the right to privacy in India.

In fact, any dissenting opinion that is later taken up as the mainstream decision would follow a similar trajectory.

Whether or not the right to privacy is a specific right, located in one or two of the existing list of fundamental rights, or whether it is, in fact, a right that has a cross-cutting presence across the board of all fundamental rights, is another question that the courts have dealt with.

The Kharak, M.P. Sharma and Gopalan judgements (to do with the history-sheeter/dacoit, the person accused of financial malpracrices, and the attempts at Preventive Detention), were over-ruled by the cases of Maneka and Cooper.

A number of other Indian judgements (some of them quoting American law, some British law and writings), have been discussed. The origins of the concept of Privacy, while quoting from thinkers and philosophers that range from Aristotle to Austin have been brought onto the radar.

Evolution of the Privacy Doctrine in India, leading caselaw from the Supreme Court of India in the overall context of Fundamental Rights and the Basic Structure of the Constitution, elements from the Constitution Assembly Debates, and India's commitments under international law have been spelt out and discussed. An exercise in Comparative Law has also been carried out, with a focused review of the evolution of International positions on the Right to Privacy.

Eventually, there is a set of nine Principles that the majority judgement lays out, and these are at the core of my current discussion.

As a political person, it is of interest that we now have access to a wide-ranging set of principles, based on the interpretation of the existing law, and where none exists, an effort to fill a vacuum.

My principle-wise comments:

> A. *Life and personal liberty are inalienable rights. These are rights which are inseparable from a dignified human existence. The dignity of the individual, equality between human beings and the quest for liberty are the foundational pillars of the Indian Constitution;*

This first principle reaffirms the fact that life and personal liberty are inalienable rights. This pre-dates even the Constitution, with signals harking back almost to the cradle of civilization, and also happens to be a part of the bedrock of the Constitution of India, patch-work and all intact.

Caselaw has been discussed, international scenarios have been scrutinized, and the said articulation in the current judgement puts any doubts that might have existed to the contrary, to rest.

The use of the subjective term "dignity" and "dignified" makes room for various interpretations, not only in terms of bench-marks or standards for what would be universally accepted as a minimum standard of living from a health and environment point of view, but also for diverse interpretations of "dignity".

> B. *Life and personal liberty are not creations of the Constitution. These rights are recognised by the Constitution as inhering in each individual as an intrinsic and inseparable part of the human element which dwells within;*

This principle also gains greater significance if viewed from a futuristic perspective. In a world where rivers and deities gain legal identities, with the law willing to recognize them as persons, and with reports rolling in, of a genetically engineered combination of a pig and human having been successfully conducted in a laboratory, the right to life and personal liberty of humans, specifically, needs to be distinguished and to continue to be protected. (This is not to say that one should disregard the new-fangled ethical issues presented to us by the world of emerging scientific endeavour and technological advancement).

A court of law states, here, that the "human element" "dwells within". This is not to be read, in my opinion, as a religious or even a purely scientific construct, but a legal one that takes into account, language, science, and a general human consensus.

This is also a reiteration, by an Indian court, that our legal position is that of honouring the life and liberty of all human beings, irrespective of their citizenship or location.

It is worth examining the legalities of how the Indian government reacts to situations of refugees through this legal filter held up by the Supreme Court.

> C. *Privacy is a constitutionally protected right which emerges primarily from the guarantee of life and personal liberty in Article 21 of the Constitution. Elements of privacy also arise in varying contexts from the other facets of freedom and dignity recognised and guaranteed by the fundamental rights contained in Part III;*

This principle is at the heart of the answer to the question that has been put to this bench.

Essentially, the scope from which to derive legal backing for the Right to Privacy has been interpreted expansively. The Right has not been boxed into, or restricted to any one fundamental right, but the all-pervasive, cross-cutting nature of the Constitutional Right to Privacy has been confirmed by the Supreme Court of India.

> D. *Judicial recognition of the existence of a constitutional right of privacy is not an exercise in the nature of amending the Constitution nor is the Court embarking on a constitutional function of that nature which is entrusted to Parliament;*

There is no judicial over-reach in ruling that there does exist a Constitutional Right to Privacy.

Not only is the view that has been expressed not contrary to the Constitutional scheme of things, the recognition of the Right to Privacy is an intrinsic part of the Constitution.

This conclusion has been arrived at after taking into consideration, the views expressed in the Constitution Assembly debates (where, in fact, the right to privacy had not been thought fit to include in the articulated list of fundamental rights), and in the context of an ever-evolving civilization.

It must be noted that the court has used a slightly more generic phrase in saying Constitutional Right, and in not saying Fundamental Right, as far as the Right to Privacy is concerned, though there may not be much of a distinction.

> E. *Privacy is the constitutional core of human dignity. Privacy has both a normative and descriptive function. At a normative level privacy subserves those eternal values upon which the guarantees of life, liberty and freedom are founded. At a descriptive level, privacy postulates a bundle of entitlements and interests which lie at the foundation of ordered liberty;*

The court has expressed the view that privacy is the constitutional core of human dignity. Indeed, in order to be able to protect the fundamental rights that one is entitled to, privacy is a necessary prerequisite. Furthermore, this right is not restricted to spaces or areas, but is to do with the individual.

This view does, and must prevail, even in the face of belief-systems, worldviews, scientific realities and technologies that do not honour privacy.

It is appropriate for this articulation to have emerged from the courts of a country that is Secular, with no state religion, and where people of all faiths are meant to be on an equal footing.

There are, I believe, interpretations of Buddhist and of Hindu thought and belief, that would not, from an existential stand-point, attach much value to privacy. However, when demystified, these beliefs are likely to stem from the attempt to unify, homogenize and control not only society, but the very roots of consciousness and human awareness in favour of centralized diktats of religious leaders. Keeping this factor in mind, I think the law has taken quite a progressive step, in reiterating the rights of the individual.

However, it is important for the appropriate distinctions to be made on a case-to-case basis, so that privacy is not cited as an excuse to perpetrate opaqueness in governance and public spheres.

It is also equally important for the right to privacy and dignity to be equally available to all.

> F. *Privacy includes at its core the preservation of personal intimacies, the sanctity of family life, marriage, procreation, the home and sexual orientation. Privacy also connotes a right to be left alone.*

Privacy safeguards individual autonomy and recognises the ability of the individual to control vital aspects of his or her life. Personal choices governing a way of life are intrinsic to privacy. Privacy protects heterogeneity and recognises the plurality and diversity of our culture. While the legitimate expectation of privacy may vary from the intimate zone to the private zone and from the private to the public arenas, it is important to underscore that privacy is not lost or surrendered merely because the individual is in a public place. Privacy attaches to the person since it is an essential facet of the dignity of the human being;

Among other obvious things worth reading (and therefore reproduced here verbatim), by this definition of privacy, activity between or amongst consenting adults cannot be used as evidence against them in a court of law, since the very production of such evidence will impinge on a person's constitutional right to privacy. This is also potentially path-breaking for the LGBT community. However, I would still recommend that the political wing stick its neck out and lead and bolster that aspect of the held-up (word-scramble intended) law.

G. *This Court has not embarked upon an exhaustive enumeration or a catalogue of entitlements or interests comprised in the right to privacy. The Constitution must evolve with the felt necessities of time to meet the challenges thrown up in a democratic order governed by the rule of law. The meaning of the Constitution cannot be frozen on the perspectives present when it was adopted. Technological change has given rise to concerns which were not present seven decades ago and the rapid growth of technology may render obsolescent many notions of the present. Hence the interpretation of the Constitution must be resilient and flexible to allow future generations to adapt its content bearing in mind its basic or essential features;*

This is the beauty of our judicial system. Nothing is ever cast in stone. The law is, and is meant to be flexible, and evolve with, and respond to changing times – notions and all.

Core values, however, for which the Constitution and country exist, remain enshrined and protected.

Here, the court agrees with the view that any painstaking cataloguing or enlisting of what includes the right to privacy is not a good idea. That, instead, it makes more sense to have some basic guidelines, and then to look at each case as it comes up for challenge.

This is an appropriate position for the court to take, according to me.

It needs to be made easier for the citizenry to challenge violations of such privacy.

While we do not wish to over-burden the courts, the path of alternate dispute resolution must always be tread in a careful manner.

The way in which a court of law functions (and is equipped to function) is very different from the manner in which any other adjudicating body would function.

In India, over the past few decades, there have been concrete alternate dispute resolution (ADR) mechanisms that have been put in place, and do function where relevant. The fine balance that distinguishes an ADR platform from a kangaroo court has been maintained.

However, rather than referring more kinds of cases to the ADR route, it is high time that the elephant in the courtyard be taken cognizance of.

That, apart from reaching a proper resolution regarding the manner and method of making judicial appointments, the system itself needs to recognize, and act upon the need for exponentially increasing the number of benches that the regular courts should have, and the number of judges that there ought to be in the country. The proportion is laughable right now.

These guidelines serve as useful tools for politicians and bureaucrats who are meant to make and implement law and policy. The legal departments of various ministries would do well to run any planned surveillance measures through these filters, and desist from introducing methods and tactics of surveillance that would fall in the face of these guidelines. And to actively withdraw any that already do, within a specific deadline.

H. Like other rights which form part of the fundamental freedoms protected by Part III, including the right to life and personal liberty under Article 21, privacy is not an absolute right. A law which encroaches upon privacy will have to withstand the touchstone of permissible restrictions on fundamental rights. In the context of Article 21 an invasion of privacy must be justified on the basis of a law which stipulates a procedure which is fair, just and reasonable. The law must also be valid with reference to the encroachment on life and personal liberty under Article 21. An invasion of life or personal liberty must meet the three-fold requirement of (i) legality, which postulates the existence of law; (ii) need, defined in terms of a legitimate state aim; and (iii) proportionality which ensures a rational nexus between the objects and the means adopted to achieve them; and

As we all probably know, everyone in our country has the same fundamental rights. The Constitution does not envisage a different set of fundamental rights for me, and, if I don't like your face or your food or your language or clothes or behaviour, for you. That's not how it works.

We are all entitled to exercise our freedoms, but we need to sometimes accept what the courts refer to as reasonable restrictions, to the exercising of those freedoms.

So I might be entitled to move about freely anywhere in the country, but that does not mean that I am entitled to gate-crash your private party that's taking place in your house.

Such reasonable restrictions need to be fine-tuned, sometimes, and there are sooooo many grey areas.

The laws that the government makes, as well as the courts, keep interpreting these grey areas.

For example, for many years, people could smoke cigarettes anywhere they pleased. Then there came a time when a court ruled that smoking in public places should be banned. My right to breathe fresh air was in conflict with your right to smoke cigarettes. Therefore, smoking cigarettes in public places was banned in that state. The argument about passive smoking in private spaces continues. One arguably inadequate safeguard that's been made compulsory is that cigarette packets should print a line on the cover, saying cigarette smoking is injurious to health. There is, of course, an entire spectrum of livelihood-related rights of other people involved, that needs to be taken into consideration when such decisions are made. The points at which such livelihood needs cannot justify the rights-infringements, when identified, are the points that reflect the law in vogue at a given point of time.

Today, the air gets polluted enough for the manufacture, trade and use of firecrackers to be regulated more tightly than it already is. During Diwali, at least.

I.   Privacy has both positive and negative content. The negative content restrains the state from committing an intrusion upon the life and personal liberty of a citizen. Its positive content imposes an obligation on the state to take all necessary measures to protect the privacy of the individual.

Now that one's subjected the unsuspecting reader of hopefully lovely chatty book to impressionistic view of what the law is (articles with-held deliberately for staccato effect), and what the hoo haa is all about, in general, let's look at what is, and might be happening to peoples' privacy these days. (Kidding about the unsuspecting reader bit, no need to plot suing the author or any such thing).

Yes, yes, we're also all people, when it comes to surveillance. Nobody's above or below the interests of the potential perpetrator-of-surveillance.

The forces of the state, of the market, of the media, of one's immediate rivals and foes, the downright curious (and others), are the likely patrons of technologies, devices, and services that pertain to surveillance. These are available a dime-a-dozen (to nostalgically scurry into cliché-thorw-back-era for a bit), and there are also those that would demand an arm and a leg (pun intended). Nothing sleazy being suggested here – I wouldn't be surprized if some surveillance technologies involve the piercing of chips or other implants into the bodies of human beings.

And why just implants. There are all kinds of surveillance methods and technologies.

Some well-meaning expert on the topic would do well to write a piece like this one. Just not about law, but about the kinds of surveillance methods that exist, and are in use, and get it out to the general public. To the colleague, to the relative, the friend, the acquaintance and the various other service-providers of those who might be targeted for surveillance. Which is just about anybody, but who might happen to be the only target in his or her immediate circles.

This, in fact, could even be a tactic the surveillance-wallahs attempt to employ: isolate an individual who has many social circles, and put only that one individual under surveillance.

Do this in such a way that all the otherwise supportive and believing people suddenly think that the person targeted for surveillance is making preposterous claims of being pressurised in some manner, or spied upon.

Make no mistake, there is a very, very thin line, if any, that divides being under surveillance from being pressurised or harassed.

Covert surveillance, that's the problem. Covert surveillance that's revealed to a few targets, that might be the bigger problem. I'm still talking about what I just spoke about.

As I see it, many acts of surveillance involve not only acts of keeping tabs on people, their activities, their daily programmes, their every move, even when they think they're alone, their every bodily function, but also attempts to influence these, and to communicate or relay these back to the person and others in non-verifiable ways.

To an alert layperson, this is the mix in the cauldron so far: the internet, and it's much-discussed capacity to track, replicate, intuit and impact your actions; audio-visual recording and transmitting devices that might or might not involve in-situ installations (there are a whole a bunch of satellites up there, all working, no doubt, for the good of humanity); tracking devices on equipment that you carry, such as your phone, or that your body might contain; technologies and devices (chemical, psychological, socially engineered) that can communicate ideas to you via your conscious, semi-conscious, dream, and socially-disarmed states by transmitting to apparently abnormal frequencies or zones, to your senses of perception and cognizance.

So while humanity and the legal sphere maintain semblances of order and keep the concrete world order in check, those who dare to venture to state the bizarre, and to tackle it any which legal way that they can, will find it necessary to gently tuck into fluffy, irrelevant corners, those who might not comprehend all this.

Those whose egos drive them to refuse to believe that others might know better, perceive better, act better, lead better…the bones and relics of such saints are free to await their days of judgement. But in some faraway cookie-corner, please.

Immortality shall dawn gradually and silently on life on earth. Not via bodies preserved through present-day medicine, but through a scientific understanding of the nature of spirit and its movement through space and matter. Where, then, will these guidelines of privacy stand?

Or do we have these guidelines in place well in advance, in order to usher in the Futuristic New Age (of science), where privacy of the being will battle pure science, and where being human will still mean something to a handful of survivors from the distant past.

Perhaps it is in this same spirit that the very down-to-earth and exemplary-in-many-ways Supreme Court of India did indicate, to the world, through another judgement, that the electro-magnetic spectrum is, in fact, a natural resource, and needs to be regulated as such.

The electro-magnetic spectrum - yoga and spirituality - the human nerve-centres and chakras - the electro-magnetism associated with the human body - the interaction of these with the electro-magnetic spectrum of the planet. Not only humans, but all creatures.

Biodiversity, Interconnectedness - loop back to the search for freedom-realms of existence, also known as Dimensions in science- and back to the fact that the present realm, that we are aware of, and interacting with, is as real as any other.

That human rights, and the Constitution, and the right to privacy, therefore, do matter, and do need to be defended in the here and now.

For those who wish to continue attending this rally, one has, indeed, gleaned a few streaks of OTT ideas and responses from a detailed reading of the judgement. These, one plans to hold forth on in greater and a tad more excruciating and decadent detail in the near future, hopefully. Not like one is angling to get readers addicted or anything. But just so that you don't OD on this for now. Eventually, of course, the ideas ought to be pared down to more formal outputs. And certainly to be translated-in-one's-head-and-adapted-to-regional-language-public-speeches. Now who said that's a skill that requires any credit. Certainly not the fattened beneficiaries!

Toodle ca, then, off you go, feeling all important and superior for telling yourself that you are more legally knowledgeable (e-v-e-r-y excruciating detail of whatever your own personal or impersonal tryst with the law has been), than this fortune-telling specimen of a barefoot supreme court lawyer (winks conspiratorially at fellow-legal-eagles, many of who, frankly, look quite blank themselves). Alternate title for this work: Legal Empowerment, Sustainability, and the Last Laugh at Halloween (Take a Bow).

CHAPTER III

CHILDHOOD DIARIES, THE PLANET TODAY, AND INDIAN POLITICS YESTERDAY

India was the host, in 2012, to a meeting that takes place every two years, of all the countries that are a part of an international agreement to protect biodiversity.

The system of where the meeting takes place every two years is a bit like the system employed for the holding of semi-urban kitty parties in India, that were a rage in the 1980s, and today continue to be an emerging feature, maybe even backbone, of assorted social circles. Support groups of sorts.

One might even go so far as to say that the concept of village self-help groups (now registered as SHGs, and in some states, subject to all sorts of laws controlled by the government, before they can so much as accept a gift from an individual), took root from the concept of what began as ladies' kitty parties in urban and semi-urban India in the 1980s.

Those who intend to steal the thunder of the Buddha (Lord Gautam Buddha, who also spoke of Sanghas), might stake a claim to having heralded democracy onto the planet. Talking of stealing similar thunder, other victims (whose toofaani thanda would be in the danger of being low-voltaged) might be: some of the age-old systems and networks of grassroots democracies, and some of the value-addition by the likes of Mahatma Gandhi, and, more than just arguably, the Indian National Congress Party itself.

(If this kitty-party analogy -unlikely-, and the thunder-lightning analogy -vaguely familiar- have been transferred to text already by anyone, it's not because they've overheard and plagiarised my conversations and commended them to print, it's probably because this is a whole entire dialect that's been in vogue for some time).

What counts as a democracy, and the question of how a legitimate democracy (or democracies) interpret Human Rights, is the global lawn that needs to be kept trim on an ongoing basis. Too many split ends, and you'd need a drastic change of hairstyle. Unstructured body-building, and you'd need to plan a new routine.

Anyway, back to the international Convention on Biological Diversity. What I was saying was that a different country hosts it each time. I've not kept track of the politics (if any), behind the selection of each of the venues.

One might be thinking more on the lines of: Vah! What a place Egypt would be to visit. Africa jaana hai toh Egypt, pucca, is a must-do. (The COP 2018 is to be held in Egypt). So remember that this is going to be going on there in November. Useful to know, either way.

When we (proud Indians) hosted it in 2012, it was held in Hyderabad. The whole world was probably there (from the world of the United Nations Convention on Biological Diversity, which is a lot of countries).

I went.

For such things, participants usually plan well ahead of time, and are either experts, NGOs, community-stakeholders or formal representatives of governments. There are main events, side events, and then there are self-appointed observers such as one's self. I guess. Wearing many hats. Congress Party. Supreme Court. Activist. Expert. Cultural figure (sort of), to name a few from the coat-hanger. (Ref.: legal gown).

Before setting out for Hyderabad from my exclusive little development-sector-report-and-a-few-law-and-political-books-plus-my-own-professional-writings-lined study at 4, Janpath, New Delhi, with a magnificent view of greens and peacocks, peahens, raptors, a fish-tail palm, monkeys, medicinal plants and more, one did a quick analysis of the sate-of-the-art of the CBD, India, and main points of concern, seen through my (under-utilized) prismatic lens/es.

These thoughts and ideas were conveyed to a school-going audience and other eminent persons, when one was invited to speak on the subject at a South Delhi school on the eve of the then forthcoming trip to observe the 11th COP of the CBD at Hyderabad. (On a request from the Indian NGO, Kalpavriksh, one also wrote a post-event article for their news-letter, on most of the informal meetings and interactions that one initiated and learnt from, during the COP).

At the talk at the school in Delhi, as a part of the question-and-answer session, a student asked me whether it was possible to have dinosaurs roam the earth again! And my answer was: technically, yes! (Which, of course, does not imply that we wish for the various Rexes to make mincemeat of our skyscrapers and jungles, our own little skin, bones and earthly possessions and energy-fields included).

But all this talk of dinosaurs reminds me of some of my pet dinosaurs: my set of old diaries that I used to write as a school-student. And come to think of it, there's some stuff in those diaries that's quite connected to what I'm writing about here. Nature, environment, India, politics, and the world.

So, I'm now going to treat you all to some teeny little glimpses into my almost-secret childhood diaries (1980s). It wouldn't be surprising at all, though, if surveillance has been there way before Bill Clinton drafted himself to Vietnam to inaugurate their stock exchange. (One was invited, at around that time, to Vietnam, to attend a farmers' meeting, which I declined, as it was too last-minute, and I had other year-end plans). The diaries have been displayed, on a bookshelf in my room, as one would display published books, approximately since the beginning of the millennium.

The complete works in their original forms could be books-in-themselves in the future, since one's ambition, at one time, was to be a child-prodigy author. Can still be attempted, unedited and dated: How to be a detective; identity flick books with inter-changeable segments of whichever faces were available to cut from weekly magazines, such as a photograph of the actor Kamal Haasan who seems to be on Indian TV a lot these days, talking about a possible role in Tamil Nadu clean politics; statute-style commandments pertaining to life, loftily entitled Disciplinary Demands for a Superior Species; shrink-style categorized columns about the kinds of people that exist in the world; gazetteer-like daily repetitive accounts about having taken the dog for a walk, gone to school, come back, done homework and so on; analyses of governmental programmes that involved the participation of school students, or at least one such analysis; pre-exam study routines; things that the nuns said at the assembly that I found interesting; lists of things to do in anticipation of the summer holidays, including the much-ridiculed-by-snooping-rellies-those-days: 'breathe in and breathe out' bullet-point, and so on and so forth.

But for today, we are going to tip-toe into select extracts – about which I have things to say, looking back more than thirty years after these earnest writings.

An account of the days during and after the assassination of Indira Gandhi, who, as the Prime Minister of India, had represented India at a landmark United Nations Conference on the Human Environment at Stockholm, Sweden, in 1972.

This was a conference that had been boycotted by those from the USSR. The Stockholm Declaration, however, when it was finalised, had some pro-poor changes that countries like China and Brazil had introduced.

And of political importance was the fact that India had made a strong case for "poverty alleviation" at the Stockholm conference on Human Environment.

As a result, when the matter came up later at the UN General Assembly, even those from the USSR did not oppose any of the points of the historic Stockholm Declaration.

Today, the work and role of the BRICS nations: Brazil, Russia, China, India, South Africa, seems to be on a significant leg of a long-drawn plan for the world economy.

As I see it, this was one of the most globally significant doings of India via Indira Gandhi.

Today, as a lawyer concerned with sustainable development, one might wish to pay tribute to her memory by sharing with the world, these diary entries that one had made, as a thirteen-year-old, at the time of her assassination:

Extracts from the Brown DDA Diary (I noticed, only today, that it's a diary of the Delhi Development Authority, always only thought of it as just a brown diary):

"31ˢᵗ October '84

Dear Diary,

I'm writing myself after so long because something really unexpected and rather shocking happened.

Today, in the morning at 9:30 the Prime Minister of our country, Mrs. (late) Indira Gandhi passed away. She was assassinated by her own gunmen at point blank range as she was walking towards her car to go to her office.

Her body was riddled by sixteen bullets fired from the gun of a Sikh who was her gunman. Two of the three criminals were shot dead, and one was injured, and is now under arrest.

Mrs. Gandhi was rushed to the Indian Institute of Medical Science, and died at 11 O'Clock.

The public, however, were kept in the dark as to the condition of the Prime Minister.

Later on, the news was released on teleprinters and on A.I.R. and T.V. only after the arrival of the President Giani Zail Singh, at 5 pm. today. He was on a tour in Yemen, and has immediately flown back to the capital. Rajeev Gandhi who was on a tour in West Bengal, made for Delhi, too late to see her alive.

The cabinet of Cong. I was having a meeting to discuss the turn of events. The opposition, too, had a meeting which daddy has gone to attend. Most likely, they will be going to Safdarjung for condolence.

The big question now is what will happen. There is no deputy Prime Minister or any other person to take her place. Her intension was that Rajiv Gandhi would succeed her but that seems unlikely. The time for elections, too, is coming near and there are many political parties struggling. Then one more thing, the Tamil Nadu C.M. is very seriously ill, and it is doubted whether he'll live. As the sun sets and darkness grips this day of doom, leaders of nations and many others are sending their messages to the President and to Rajiv Gandhi.

Announcement at the end of the day: Rajiv Gandhi is now the Prime Minister of the country, and it seems quite incredible as he takes his oath from the President with mixed feelings that he is to be our Prime Minister. The sudden death of Mrs. Gandhi had stunned everyone, and we now await the message of our new P.M., Rajiv Gandhi."

"5th Nov.

It is now five days since Mrs. Gandhi was assassinated. Her body was in state in the Teen Murty Bhavan for three days, wrapped in the tricolour. According to people, there was not such a large crowd to see her, but the police couldn't even manage the thousand or so people who were there, and they were compelled to fire tear gas shells. Daddy and mummy had gone there with some of daddy's party members, but they came back because of the crowd. The funeral was day before yesterday, and we were just wondering about what would have happened if someone tried to kill President Zia!

After Mrs. Gandhi's assassination, there was terrible violence all over the north, especially in Delhi. Because a Sikh had assassinated her, the Hindus went about killing all the innocent Sikhs.

The condition became such that one life meant nothing to anyone. Later, it was not the anger of the Hindus, but it was the hoodlums who did all this, finding a good opportunity to loot and create a nuisance of themselves.

We, who live in a safe area did not realise how bad and gruesome things were, and could not believe how cold-blooded and inhuman people who called themselves human beings could be.

There was terror and death, people who surely had gone out of their senses were destroying and finishing the lives and property of any Sikh they came across. People were actually being burnt to death by hundreds, something that sounds impossible, and then do we think of the saying that man is the greatest enemy of man. Some people were hacked to death, and the police, they were silent onlookers of the whole thing.

Three or four truck-loads of dead bodies were found, and some desperate Sikhs had to hide under these corpses for safety, while…"

(Here, the ball-point pen with which I was writing in the diary seems to have run out of ink, and then something else must have cropped up while looking for another pen, so this diary note remains incomplete).

Today, when I delve back into this piece of writing, various responses come to mind:

First, of course, one is reminded of the trauma of that time in New Delhi, and of how events like these play a role in shaping one's world view, and the elements that go into making the resolves that one's made in terms of career, mission, call it what you will.

Second, one reads it from the perspective of a linguistic forensics expert (though one isn't one, any reader would, one assumes, take a lively interest in deciphering the layers of influences that might have impacted any set of writings. Lucky you if you have things you've written scores of years ago, that you can now pontificate over for a lark. Or a book).

Here, I find, that my reporting of it is (obviously, to those who were familiar with it), the jargon and tone of the government-run news channel, and other newspapers of the time. ("As the sun sets and darkness grips this day of doom" is decidedly 1980s Doordarshan!)

The violence and riots, one probably heard about from various cross-sections of society in the neighbourhood, the markets, and at school.

It was, indeed, a sad and ironic way for the life of a person who had connected with the citizens of India, and the word community, to have come to an end.

The Stockholm Convention (and Declaration) with which I associate her, was the beginning of a long journey towards environmental goals for the planet.

Twenty years after Stockholm, there was the Rio convention, by which time the world had started to fine-tune its international efforts for conservation.

From the Rio summit flowed the United Nations Convention on Biological Diversity, among other instruments.

Fourteen years after the assassination of Indira Gandhi, I found myself treading the lanes and by-lanes of one of her past constituencies – Medak, in Andhra Pradesh, in what is now the state of Telangana.

Circa 2000. A young Northern Andhra Pradesh Congress Party activist from New Delhi, drawn there by a set of events, in the avataar of a Supreme Court lawyer and legal expert on a United Nations-Government of India process, to help take forward India's commitments that dated back to the Stockholm and Rio conventions.

Walking and chatting with the women farmers of Zaheerabad, Medak District, we might have described ourselves as a Telugu-speaking 21st Century version of the spirit of Stockholm, Rio, and everything in-between, before and beyond.

There were many shackles to be broken, stories to be told, and wrongs to be corrected. An iota of this, we have managed to achieve, in the seventeen years that have played out since.

Today, the inevitability of globalization brings with it, the accelerated opportunity to manage the planet's resources in a co-ordinated and efficient fashion.

However, the need of the hour is to stave off the mis-utilization of this very socio-political and technological potential. The benchmarks and trade-offs in connection with standards set for democratic values such as Human Rights and Equity need to be watched and protected with utmost vigilance.

While the visible battles are in the arena of equitable access to Land, Water, and Air, the use of the other natural resource – Space and Outer Space, is now at our doorstep, in our cell-phones, and knocking loud and clear on the electro-magnetic and other waves of our very consciousness. The Supreme Court of India has taken the planetary lead in recognizing the electro-magnetic spectrum to be a natural resource.

Transparency in scientific knowledge and research, and the scientific empowerment of lay-persons is the need of the hour.

And by scientific empowerment, I do not mean merely access to user-friendly technologies, but the facility to comprehend the implications of various scientific uses and applications, and to make decisions, as individuals, citizens and leaders, on various aspects of life that will have more and more technological content and inter-face in the days to come.

The many factors that contribute to the establishment of the Rule of Law (and good governance), include the raising of any iron curtains that might still be Waiting for Godot.

This would include opaqueness in decision-making, and for this, the world today keeps a watchful eye on both, America's Trump, and on the nuclear activities of countries like North Korea.

New Delhi, which has been at the cross-roads of world history, has always observed and participated in the global conversation in a non-aligned way.

The heads of disparately-mandated governments visit us, we visit them, Modi has even made what appears to be a Prime Ministerial past-time of dropping in, swinging by, hangin' out, holding forth, and rambling on to (albeit homogeneous and possibly ego-driven) audiences worldwide. A bizarre taking-forward of much of the diplomatic outreach, effort and spade-work that the UPA and other preceding governments had diligently and unobtrusively laboured on for years.

Foremost on my mind, today, is Principle 26 of the Stockholm Declaration. The one about doing away with elements of mass destruction. The entire nuclear question, as we all realise, I'm sure, is an Environmental one.

In the mid-80s, Gorbachov coming to India was a big thing. A quick read from the brown diary again:

"27ᵗʰ Nov., 1986

Today, Mikhail Gorbachov addressed a joint session of parliament, for which daddy went. For the first time, T.V. cameras were allowed into parliament, and we saw daddy in the corner.

Gorbachov seems to be a very nice, capable person, calm and firm __that's the impression I gathered. Pity he's a communist __ but I guess they have their own reasons for their views. I'd surely HATE India to be a communist country. __It's okay, as long as it isn't applied to your own country! (I think.)

It's supposed to be really historic, and it is, as a matter of fact. But I still think that if Reagan comes, there'll be much more of 'public interest' or whatever. I think he's supposed to be coming next year."

Well, Reagan didn't make it the next year, though Springsteen did, two years after my diary noting. Indira Gandhi, however, had made visits to America, and I've just viewed a youtube video of her being received by Ronald Reagan and Nancy Reagan at the Reagan Library in 1982.

Strange histrionics with a white handbag, and an angry-sounding reference to the fact that she's been a Prime Minister since 1966. Either some sort of assertion of her own seniority on the world stage, or some irksome memory of Richard Nixon's 1969 visit to India…one but speculates… especially since it's come to light of late (four or five years ago), that Nixon and Kissinger, in telephonic conversations, had referred to her, using a word that rhymes with witch (and this was way before the days of Harry Potter and the snitch of the game of quidditch…people were still reading Nancy -Drew-, I reckon).

Though it was Dixon, not Nixon, who wrote the Hardy Boys series. People love to talk like this, I assure you! Once in a way, at least.

Nixon of the receding hair-line, and Kissinger who seemed to despise India those days. People could play those roles in the world of reality theatre if they haven't been doing so already!

I, for one, think, now, that the elderly gentleman who said he was a rancher, who sat next to me on a domestic airline in the USA in 1998, resembled Ronald Reagan, and his wife might have resembled Nancy Reagan, I don't quite recall how she looked. Asked me lots and lots of questions about my recently-concluded Environmental Law Fellowship in the USA.

This was on a flight from San Francisco to Detroit (to reach Michigan), with halts at Phoenix, Arizona; St. Louis, Missouri; Tulsa, Oklahoma, and maybe even somewhere in Texas. People literally wearing cowboy hats and straw hats boarded the craft. And here's the poetic thing: Did you know that the name of the person who was the first head of India's Research and Analysis Wing, (RAW), was Kao?!

Adds a whole new dimension to cow, Texas, poetry, and so on, to the literary kitty of those who did not know. I didn't, for example, till a few years ago.

The same goes for the witch-comment of Nixon's. After Michigan, I went to Boston via Chicago and Providence, from where my cousins drove me to their home in Boston. One of the weekend visits in the north-east during my stay at Boston was to Salem, the "witch city!"

Symbolically, this ties in with my views and political struggles connected to gender justice.

The election symbol of another new political party in India that I view today as preferred allies for my party, the Aam Aadmi Party (AAP), is a broomstick. I do not know what prompted them to opt for this symbol, but it calls to mind, the environmentalism of appropriate garbage disposal; gender justice; my trip to the witch city, and the 'yes we can' mentality – everything is possible.

The day we went to New York City was the day I got the news of my great-grand-mother having passed away. (My mum's dad's mother). Those who are familiar with the speech that's attributed to an indigenous Chief from Seattle, Washington (and has been quoted by the Supreme Court of India), will recognize the underlying cultural ethos of referring to, and thinking of places and elements in nature, and inanimate objects, as living entities. I might think of NYC as a great-grand-motherial figure.

My mum's dad had gone on a private vacation to the US years ago, as a young member of the Indian parliament, when Indira Gandhi's father, Jawaharlal Nehru, was the Prime Minister of India. My mother's father was the Congress MP from Bhuvaneshwar those days, and an ex-Rajah, and despised communists. His opponent for his seat back home was a commie.

He, however, greatly appreciated my political work and activities, and made it a point to say so, before he passed away in the year 2006.

My own politics has been more influenced by the positive aspects of democratic socialism. That's what I'd say the Congress Party still stands for today.

We've made this happen, over the past few decades, and even managed to resurrect the electoral career of my father, Kishore Deo, who, after 1984, won his next Lok Sabha election twenty years later in 2004 (he'd had a Rajya Sabha term starting in 1994, selected by the then Prime Minister, P.V. Narasimha Rao), and was brought into the UPA 2's central cabinet after its downhill journey gained momentum in 2011.

We had, through the ten years of Congress-led United Progressive Alliance (UPA) rule, struggled to keep our own government responsive, in check, and goaded it on to bring in a slew of progressive legislation.

Through most of the UPA 1 and UPA 2 years, we were allotted a government bungalow at 64, Lodhi Estate, located in Lutyen's Delhi, followed by the Cabinet-ministerial 4, Janpath.

Our presence in Delhi, as far as houses and addresses go, has been a nomadic one, and probably has the makings of yet another book: New Delhi Nomads! This, too, shall come to pass.

The teenage diary entries were mostly written out of 15 AB Pandara Road. This next one goes back even further into the past compared to the bits from 1986 that I quoted a little while ago.

This is from a 200-paged, 4-rupee notebook that I wrote in at Age 12 (the price has been mentioned here, so that we can all marvel, yet again, at the phenomenon of inflation and price rise).

Extracts from the Pink Bittoo Exercise Book:

"13ᵗʰ Sept., 1985

It's been a long time since I've written a diary. This is not exactly a diary. Whenever I feel like writing my views on something, or if something important happens, I'll just write it down. Actually, I was searching for my brown diary. I couldn't find it, but I'll look again, tomorrow. It had quite a few interesting events noted down, right from India winning the world cup, to Mrs. G.'s assassination.

Today is a Friday. Usually, there would have been a peaceful weekend to look forward to, but tomorrow, we have to perform our guitar item for the prize distribution day. Mrs. Banerjee the guitar teacher has also been training us for a song that our school's putting up for Bang Club. Hopefully, I'll be playing. It's on Monday.

Things have been going on as usual. Of course, Longowal, Maken etc. were killed, but there's the newspapers that keep a record of all THAT.

I'm not writing because I don't have a 'friend' to talk to or to record events, but it's just that I love writing. I also like the idea of one day having a diary that'll keep the memories of many times alive in my mind.

…Bruce Springsteen really is fantastic. Meeting him would be a dream come true. I don't think there's any chance that he'll come to India. At least, not now.

What's cricket coming to these days, man? Once, we go to Australia and win the world cup next, we lose against Sri Lanka, of all teams. I guess I'm being so pessimistic because we lost the match only day before yesterday. They aren't covering it on the T.V., and I haven't been listening to the commentary. I'm really looking forward to the cricket season this year. I hope the half-yearlies won't be in the way."

A slice of life of from the life of a New Delhi kid in the 1980s. Politics, cricket, 'extra-curricular' activities, friends in the neighbourhood, and occasional historic events. I learnt cycling on the lawns of India Gate; we'd create activities for ourselves, like drawing maps of the neighbourhood, and assigning names to all the lanes inside what later became a gated colony. I was reminded of this, years later, when community-based organizations in rural India invited me to exchange ideas with them, connected to their funded projects to map community resources.

We'd also learn, in Pandara Road and Pandara Park, to shrug off the whistles and lecherous behaviour of road-side romeos as we called them those days, as we expanded the circles and hours of where we could cycle and walk to, and what we could wear; we'd learn to catch auto-rickshaws, to close-by places, at first, and to haggle with auto-drivers for years to come. More from the pink book:

"14th Sept., Saturday

I had to stop quite abruptly while writing yesterday because it was getting late, and I had to sleep. I've just finished breakfast. There's nothing much to do this morning (Shaila has gone for a retreat and Pala is taking part in a play in her school) I hope our guitar performance goes off well this evening. What if it rains? There's nothing much to write now, because as I mentioned earlier, I've just got up. See ya tomorrow."

"15th Sept., 1985

I read the diary of Anne Frank yesterday, and to tell the truth, I didn't like it one bit! We played the guitar yesterday. It went off quite well. To our surprise, the T.V. people had landed up, and they recorded our item. It'll be coming on the 2nd channel tomorrow. How sad! Mamu won't be able to record it. Even I won't be able to see it because we have to go for bang club. Today, I've managed to gather up most of my costume except the black tie. I'll have to see to that after lunch.

...I've just remembered, there's Hot Tracks this week. Great! I hope they show Springsteen or at least WHAM. Last time for Live Aid, they showed Rick Springfield. He really tries to imitate Springsteen and I don't like him much. There's Live Aid today, but I don't think I'll see it because it's quite late (10:30 to 11:30) Today's a Sunday, so the morning programmes are going on as usual. (Shishir is watching them.) Star Trek was nice today. Thank goodness they've started it again."

A typical weekend, with some guitar-playing, television-entertainment, visiting relatives, and reading. Odd criticism of Rick Springfield. Whatever!

About the diary of Anne Frank, I think, what I remember impressionistically, is that I found the experience of even just reading about her situation unpleasant. In retrospect, it was probably unfair to say that the book was awful! On the contrary, the writing was probably powerful enough to evoke such a reaction.

I have to say, here, that studying about Hitler and the World War had a very deep impact on my world view. Other than the neighbourhood anti-Sikh riots, and stories of violence during the India-Pakistan partition (of which most Delhi families had many), the deeds of Hitler were etched in one's emerging understanding of what the human race was about.

Back home in our part of Andhra, Naxal violence was a thing of the distant past, and the only insights that I had into those times, were foggy parallels to be drawn from stories of Robin Hood and the like.

One had heard of a famous Telugu revolutionary book entitled Konda Gaali, which means Hill Breeze. Though I haven't yet read the book, the title, and the social equality that it's said to speak for, inspired the naming of a character in my work of short fiction, Creatures of the Current in 1999: the Halchal Hawa.

As far as Hitler was concerned, one has read, over the years, that the government of Germany, at some point of its post-world-war history, made efforts to go into a public-relations over-drive to restore its image of pre-Hitlerian glory.

To impress upon the world to not paint all the citizens and the youth with the same brush, and to engage with Germany, not as a villain, but as a responsible world power. This seems to have worked well for Germany, and it appears that gas-chamber associations don't overshadow their international persona today.

Indian democracy has benefited from that country in our learnings pertaining to Germany's Committee System, something that we applied to our own legislative processes, and thus enhanced the participatory aspect of the functioning of our chambers of democracy.

"Tuesday, 17ᵗʰ Sept., 1985

I didn't get a chance to write yesterday because straight from school, they took us for Bang Club, and I reached home around 9:30. It was almost eleven by the time I slept, so I couldn't possibly have written. Bang Club was real fun.

We dressed up in school, and left for Siri Fort at 1:30. After reaching there, we had to wait outside for sometime. Everyone was getting pretty restless, and there were quite a few Mater Dei-ites. Carmel came after sometime, with some of their girls wearing terribly short skirts__rather vague.

When it was time for us to go in, the participants had to enter through gate No. 5. We had to cross a lawn, and all of us followed Mrs. Banerjee, singing 'singin' in the kitchen' I felt quite proud of M.D.S. all the while. After drinking water, we went into the auditorium. First, there was dramatics. St. Columba's came on, and their play was something to do with wrong numbers and all. What cheek__they kept ringing up Mater Dei (in the play, of course!) The other skits were all rather boring 'cause we could hardly hear anything. I couldn't wait for our school to come on because I was sure we were much better at least, the 'Ghost Busters' dance made it more lively. When our chance did come, there was real appreciation from the crowd. HA! Gauri was acting as pope John Paul the second or something like that, and she did a bit of break dancing.

Then we had to go back stage to the green room to get our guitars tuned and all, so I missed the beginning of the western music, that included Carmel's Tom Dooley and others. From backstage, we saw M.S.M. singing we are the world. After that, we hung around in the green room for quite some time until Mrs. Banerjee asked us all to pray. At last, it was our chance. The song for which we guitarists were playing was first. Megna, the nursery girl was quite cute. Then we got off the stage, and Mary Anne, the instrumental by Benaz Dastoor and Nowhere Man followed. Mrs. B. was not at all happy with our performance. We went back to our places at gate No. 5 and there were some real noisy D.P. Sites behind us. I was sitting with Anuradha most of the time. It got a bit boring after some time because while waiting for the results, Amjad Ali Khan, the chief guest, played for us. It went on for quite long. Then, they started announcing the prize winners of the previous events. M.S.M., D.P.S and Columba's did quite well. Even Mater Dei was not bad. At last they announced the western music results. I'm still not sure whether it was M.S.M. or Columba's 1st but Mater Dei was second. We came second in quite a few other things but over-all we came 4th. At least it was a better show than last year.

Today in the assembly, all the results were announced, and they asked us, Bang Club participants to stay back. Sister Susan is not in town, so Mrs. Latif spoke to us about the effort we should make next year, and she congratulated us for this year. Gauri and the others also spoke to us, and the W. Music girls are being treated at Nirula's on Friday.

In school, the class has been busy preparing for the entertainment they're putting up tomorrow because we're going to the old age home.

…It's nearly dinner time now. I got Elizabeth's letter yesterday, and I've written today. I was wondering what I should send in the envelope. Maybe a handmade bookmark made by me! (with a fancy kind of Rakhi stuck on it for decoration!) I think I'll do that now if dinner isn't yet ready. There's Chinese and a cauliflower bake tonight!

One more thing, our guitar item that was supposed to come on the T.V. didn't come, instead they showed some Punjabi dance by our school that was terrible."

After much debate, I decided to include my note on the annual inter-school talent competition, Bang Club, as a part of this socio-political commentary. Not so much for the nostalgia that these memories evoke for a few, or to showcase the atmosphere of school life in Delhi at that time, but to revisit and comment on some of one's own attitudes.

We undoubtedly saw ourselves as, (and probably were), path-breakers when it came to the perceived boldness of teenage girls. In societal circles where talking loudly and wearing short skirts were seen as acts of defiance, and socializing with the opposite sex was the subject of scandal and alarm, where going on an Archies-comic-inspired double date to the good old Nirula's pizza shop was provenly unthinkable, where girls from co-ed schools who mildly flirted with boys were labelled tarts, it was a multi-pronged approach that had to be employed to eradicate this combination of Victorian and rustic attitudes.

Don't get me wrong on the rustic bit – I'm the champion of all things grassroots, have voluntarily put parts of my life on hold for more than a few short decades for honouring and empowering grassroots communities, and blah, blah, blah. Lost my elocution-winning and voice-over-rendering accent and deliberately allowed my grammar to be disempowered by the sweet spirit of global embracement, and no regrets. But this is being said now because public memory is short, and the voting age is young. For people who evolve, and reinvent themselves with the times, and with experiences gathered, it is important to document what they were and what they did, in order to put their present activities and stances into meaningful context for the uninitiated.

It was, apparently, possible to sometimes fall prey to prudish, moralistic tendencies. I'm surprised that I've referred to the short skirts of the Carmelites as "vague." (In my jargon those days, vague meant vague, not vulgar. But it was still not complimentary in this context. It was probably in vogue because even the use of the word vulgar was off-limits, forget actual vulgar utterances). Undoubtedly, it was the ruthless spirit of competition that made it alright to hit below the belt, and criticize short-skirted girls from another school, but this is so not on!

Particularly in the area of gender justice and women's rights, I believe that it is important for all those who stand for a just society to put aside all their petty and miscellaneous differences, and co-operate with each other in order to be effective.

Then there's the prim-and-propah comment about the guys from Columba's being cheeky because the script of their skit included making phone-calls to Mater Dei School…I'm like…WHAT WAS THAT AGAIN? Did we even talk like this? Straight out of Thomas Hardy or Pearl S. Buck, or the Bronte Sisters, or whichever-other-library books like Wee Wife came out of!

The Elizabeth that I've mentioned at the end of this note is not Elizabeth Zopari from school, and later, college, but Elizabeth, my American pen-pal from Colorado. They both have the same birthday, though, the 12th of January.

Regarding the Punjabi dance that was broadcast (instead of our guitar performance) being described as 'terrible', it must actually have been not too well rehearsed! And just for the record, a studio performance of the western music performance was broadcast on another day on national television, would be good to lay one's hands on a copy of it.

"18th Sept., 1985

Today our class went to the old age home: it's near civil lines in Old Delhi, and is called OZNAM or something, and it's also behind 'Rosary School', which I've never heard of before!

In school, we dressed up in the first period itself. (it was western music) then, we ate some of Gunjan's banana and walnut cake and mixture that I had taken. The girls doing the Punjabi 'Giddha' dance were looking typically Punjabi!

We waited near the school bus for around ten minutes, though it seemed ages, and then Mrs. Venugopal told us that a tyre of the bus was punctured. We went back to class, and on the way, passed many bewildered eleventh and twelfth standards who were wondering what we were up to, parading about in fancy clothes. Back in class, we ate again, and when we were called for, went down again.

The bus journey was about half an hour. The old people really made us feel wanted. There were some sweet old ladies who sang nursery rhymes for us. An old man sang some lovely songs like Elvis Presley's 'Are You Lonesome Tonight'. We sang for them too, and did the Punjabi dance. One old man played the mouth organ for us, while others told jokes and stories. An old lady on a wheelchair sang Punjabi songs, and I took a snap of her along with my friends. (I had taken my camera along). They appreciated the presents we had taken for them. We also served chips, bananas and biscuits.

I was just wondering, some girls were really moved by these old people. __the stories they had to tell about themselves. Sons and daughters who've abandoned them. They are also very affectionate to strangers such as us, because they know we care.

One may feel slightly drawn to these people and their sufferings, though some seem to be very happy, and keep themselves occupied, but it was not like as if my eyes were being opened for the first time, the way I sensed it in many other girls. I think it just shows how very limited some of their lives are, living in only one world, that of their own. Why? Because there just isn't any chance for them to do otherwise. I'm glad our school at least does this much. Now, I think of myself, for instance. How much more I know about the other half than my friends. I remain indebted to the circumstances through which I get to see a lot of rural India every year.

Now, it's become a common thing, a part of me, to sometimes be in the midst of such people. And imagine, for my friends, even one such opportunity would be the experience of a lifetime!

Another thing worth mentioning—Today at assembly, one girl was quoting certain people and here's what struck me the most—
'Never trouble trouble
Till trouble troubles you
You'll only double trouble
And trouble others too

—

Great minds talk about ideas
Ordinary minds talk about events
And small minds talk about people.'"

Funny how set phrases and "quotations" are sometimes treated like the word of the law, or the lord, or whoever. Full-grown adults fall for this kind of thing even today. In fact, I won't be surprised if acres and acres of Wassap messages and witty sms messages are made of wonders such as these.

About the visit to the old age home, I think I've said what I had to say in the note.

My contemporaries from school are, needless to say, much-travelled since, and are socially sensitive and proactive in their varied spheres of activity.

Perhaps it's time for our country to focus more on plans for the aged. This does not mean only appropriate retirement and insurance policies.

We've at least managed to ensure that the just demands of people retired from the armed forces were adequately addressed, to begin with.

Other systems of social security and contingency-planning for individuals in a welfare state need to be mulled over in greater detail, and legislated upon accordingly. We, the citizens, and the current opposition, will need to strategize and work towards extracting these objectives from the current dispensation.

CHAPTER IV

BORN TO INTERFACE: AN ANALYSIS OF BRUCE SPRINGSTEEN'S AUTOBIOGRAPHY, BORN TO RUN

I now bring to you, writings based on a series of blog-posts I made earlier this year. These were an analysis of Bruce Springsteen's autobiography.

On reading Born to Run, I found that it was juicily full of the kind of techniques and landmarks that would make someone who's studied English Literature long ago all nostalgic for wanting to write like a sophomore.

The articles were written with two kinds of people in mind, other than the fact that I simply wanted to write these notes.

One primarily had in mind, people who might never have heard of Springsteen, might know about him vaguely, but not enough, and those who are not likely to ever read Born to Run, but would be interested in its contents.

As I read the book, it became clear to me that the book seeks to, could, and does have a greater purpose than just an understanding or appreciation of a pop star, rock star, and cultural czar of the USA.

To those who have not yet read the book, but intend to, this, now, is a spoiler alert!

One made diligent, hand-written notes along the way, and has uncharacteristically and meticulously quoted these with almost scientific thoroughness. (I take the liberty to say so myself, being acutely aware of the fact that this kind of meticulousness is not particularly the kind of stuff the world of literature and the arts would prefer to distinguish themselves by).

I have chosen to review the book by specifically detailing in autobiographical elements of my own, that relate to Springsteen. This, the reader will find, is in the spirit of the writer's expectation from this book, as expressed by The Boss.

I've restricted my editing of the blog posts here to:

a merger of the nine-part blog series;

the insertion of sub-headings every time there's a distinguishable theme that the review explores;

tweaking and adding a few words and phrases, and maybe even sentences here and there;

introducing a new concluding section that strings together my own set of coincidences that I've either dredged or yoked together from out of the woodwork of the pages of Born to Run.

The reader may decide!

From the blog

Springsteen; India; the 1980s

In true Brechtian form, one shall begin with a transparent description of how and why one read Springsteen's book. Bring backstage to the front, as it were, while weaving ways forward for the nation and the party. Oh, and the planet.

I choose to write and upload Part 1 of this essay onto my political blog on the 15th of August, 2017, the seventieth anniversary of India's Independence. Independence Day. When Nation means India, and Party means the Indian National Congress Party, of which one is a member, a worker, dream-weaver, course-corrector and interpreter-of-things-in-retrospect. It's a democratic party.

So one emerged from a many-year hiatus from long-book-reading (while reading and analysing news almost twenty-four-seven), to dive into Bruce Springsteen's autobiography, Born to Run, that was released last year.

Back in the 1980s, 1988, to be precise, was the Amnesty International Human Rights Now concert tour that included Bruce Springsteen and the E Street Band (the main draw at the time), and they performed at the Jawahar Lal Nehru stadium of New Delhi on the 30th of September of that year.

Springsteen had caught the attention of school kids of my generation with his 1985 Grammy Awards win and performance, and the Born in the USA album.

In the days when the country was barely forty years into independence, and found the need for a stringent version of democratic socialism, there used to be only one, and later two, government-run television channels. Doordarshan 1 and DD 2 ran with fixed timings, and the government relayed cultural events and programmes in keeping with whatever the country's current foreign policy thrust required.

For one spell of Sundays, there were interviews and music of the Pakistani singer, Nazia Hasan and her brother; Russian ballets were a staple; the Japanese programme, Giant Robot for kids, as well as the American programme, Star Trek, and Carl Sagan's futuristic shows were all watched, discussed, and absorbed. There were also British programmes like Fawlty Towers, Jane Eyre movies, and The Jewel in the Crown. And the Old Fox detective serial about the German Herr.

These are only snippets that I mention here, of the entire mix that was broadcast, in the true tradition of the Non-aligned Movement (NAM), that India valued, especially against the back-drop of the waning days of the cold war.

Then came Hot Tracks. From what I recall, just four songs every Friday, divided by an ad-break. The entire school (or so we thought), waited to tune in, and hold forth the next day, starting at the bus-stop, and thereafter (in this case, possibly into the hereafter, given that one is still writing on the topic!).

And there was Bruce Springsteen. On stage on the screen, singing Dancing in the Dark, and Born in the USA. A leftist aunt passing by said look at you, you're a fan! And a gawking fan was described, and thus born.

One identified with the fact that The Boss (that's the moniker), wrote lyrics for and about the working class and the masses. As a teenager, one saw one's own role as a poet-politician in the making, much influenced by the fact that one's family was a political one, and that we were in New Delhi because my dad represented our hometown, a faraway constituency, at India's temple of democracy.

Some of my closest friends were kids of politicians, and politicians of all hues walked through our doors, giving one the opportunity to listen to debates and discussions that were to, in retrospect, have global impacts.

The then deputy-PM of the USSR and his delegation, for example, graced the government bungalow in New Delhi that we lived in those days, 15 AB Pandara Road, with their presence one evening for dinner.

Socialistic and other Indian political leaders who went on to become ministers and leaders of parties, and of the country, used to drop in and air their views on world politics and the state of what was described those days as the Third World.

Frankly, much of what they said sounded like another Bruce Springsteen song. This, along with the influence of Christian educational institutions, served to make one ponder, perhaps more than many of one's contemporaries, over the state of the world, famines in Ethiopia, the Constitution of India, the state of the Environment, and the work of the United Nations.

As a teenager, one had UNEP Save our Seas stickers alongside every Springsteen poster that was available in Khan Market for room décor those days.

One was in the school band, struggling to play the guitar, with our school, Mater Dei Convent, shining on at the inter-school Bang Club competitions, playing numbers like Come Young Citizens of the World, We Are One, at the Siri Fort auditorium where Obama, in the next century, made his New Delhi address.

So when the much-awaited Springsteen Human Rights concert came our way in '88, thanks to Amnesty, off went the gang, all excited and decked up, to listen to, and watch The Boss!

The Rule of Law; A Navajo Reservation; Springsteen's Known Hard Times Himself

More on the concert later, now back to the book at hand.

For those who believe in upholding the values of freedom, justice, equality (and diversity), it becomes evident (and that debate is held often and by many), that the best way forward is, indeed, the Rule of Law.

But for the rule of law to be truly actualized, you also need Truth (or Satya), a value that Mahatma Gandhi stood for. Honesty. Satya and Ahimsa. Truth and non-violence. And so we are a democracy that's proud of our Defence Forces. They're there to keep the peace. We owe our forces and our martyrs a country that practices good governance.

India has always played a pivotal role in world politics, and when we speak for the rule of law, we do so, not as lackeys of any greater power, but as the ever-evolving spirit of the roots of grassroots democracy that took a giant leap towards the parliamentary system when it drove the British away, and gave itself a Constitution, and the present parliamentary system. (Ironically, some elements of colonial media are, as I write, referring to these dates in history as the days of India and Pakistan's partition, rather than drawing attention to the freedom movement and the era of new democracy worldwide).

And the historic musical event of a generation (that Springsteen refers to in his book) also requires a mention. The one at Max Yasgur's farm. Better known as Woodstock. 15th August.

We learn from Born to Run (Springsteen's autobiography titled after a successful album by the same name, and an article on public transport that I wrote for a leading news daily in India in the 1990s), that before embarking on the Amnesty tour, the performers had to go back to school, in a manner of speaking, and study the human rights situations in all the countries of South America, Africa, Asia and Europe that they were on the brink of taking by storm with their performances.

Springsteen writes that Roy Bittan was the only one in the band with a college education, which is why he's known as The Professor.

Bruce himself had done a year at a community college, and was largely self-taught thereafter. For this, (or possibly despite this, and minus the self-consciousness of the demands of snobbery), Springsteen's lyrics that speak of the blue-collar working class ring true. They stem from a world of real experience.

In India, for decades, the best education has been available to people only via the English language. This colonial legacy has served to empower those who speak English. In the 1980s, it was automatically assumed that those who spoke English were from the higher echelons of society (whatever that might be).

Today, The Republic has progressed to valuing the roots of its linguistic culture, though there's a lot that remains to be done in the field of the rights of linguistic minorities. Especially tribal communities.

The inter-relatedness between a language, and a way of life…a culture: human interactions, as well as human interactions with the rest of creation, and how different languages play different roles in shaping these…the basic thread of connection is probably understood through the prism of science. Sound, light, matter, and the sounds and syllables uttered by humans. Even in these sounds, languages vary. From individual to individual, continent to continent.

One syllable that prevails is breath, to use the language of science. Or, as understood through yoga, the syllable Aum.

When Bruce met a Hopi boy at the fringe of a Navajo reservation, and in answer to the question "how much" (to play the role of a tourist guide), the Hopi boy answered, in translation from the languages probably closer to the surface of his awareness, than communities whose grooves are in a different state of evolution: "whatever it's worth to you." A bit like the code of honour Springsteen talks about, to describe the method that one of his bands employed, to share the money that they earned. There is, indeed, much to be said for incorporating the best practices from everywhere, while making decisions, especially those that impact entire civilizations. Case in point: The Constitution of India. And how each country places itself and its people in the emerging scenarios as far as the world economy goes. The country of Bhutan, for instance, has a Happiness Index, which is an officially recognized concept in the country's world of finance.

While one has been aware of much of the back-ground of Springsteen's work and influences, it still came as a surprise to me, in the year 2017, to learn, from Born to Run, that Bruce:

> lived in a house, during his childhood, where the living area was heated by a kerosene stove;

> lived in a house where cooking was done on wood coals;

> had no hot water at home in New Jersey;

> was once so broke, as a struggling musician, that he couldn't pay rent, and slept on the beach;

> lived in a neighbourhood where people only left their houses in suits if they were going to church;

> sometimes had girlfriends who used to tip him money for food;

> had never met anyone who'd been on an airplane…this was in the mid-70s;

> used to sometimes be slipped free broken ice cream cones by the Jersey Freeze ice cream guy.

It appears that Springsteen takes pride in asserting this aspect of his identity in his overall language and writing, not just through his lyrics, but in his autobiography as well. Politically very useful.

What some might consider to be the unduly macho tone of the rockstar's remembered "way of the road" (people lending people their girlfriends, all said in utmost good humour, but decidedly darkly medieval), is tinged with what might be cringed at by some as the working-class rebel's benign linguistic crassness (talking to the -albeit intimate- public reading this book, about "the little round tit popping out from the T-shirt" of someone called Margaret). Similarly, the perceived political incorrectness of the context of the use of the word spastic…though it is possible that the fans reading the book would intuit that this is a sardonic allusion to how some sections of society used to converse at given points of time. It still has a raw edge to it.

Born to Run traces Springsteen's music, and that of the surrounding trends and events of contemporary music in a first-hand sort of way. The book, from this point of view, would be instructive, not only for practitioners of governance, administration, activism, and the promoters of the rule of law in general, as this article seeks to draw attention to, but primarily for students (and fans) of the journey of certain kinds of music through several decades. It is an experientially authoritative work on this count, and I'd put it on the syllabus, without going into further detail here.

Structure of the Book; Imagery Used; Influences

The book is intelligently structured. Divided into three broad 'phases', there is a slow, chronologically sequential progression, but with eddies and whirls that flit back and forth in time. The three divisions have chapters, and sub-chapters. Most of these deal with: people in his life, or those who have influenced him (family; people from the music business whom he has interacted with, and, on occasion, formed friendships with; idols from the world of music); his bands, albums, songs, tours, and the stories and thoughts behind them; rites of passage in his life.

There is an interesting three-dream sequence presented entirely in italics. There's also a capsule that verges on a miniature genre-within-a-genre format of writing: his description of his seafaring trip with his father to Mexico. This could be described as an astutely crafted literary tool that has been fitted into the narrative with elan. The writer seems to be aware of having tossed in this ingredient, as he describes the incident itself as having fulfilled a part of his father's seafaring fantasy.

The Church, Magic and Miracles

Springsteen talks of his preoccupation with the interface between the personal and the political. To him, the political was centred around issues of identity in America.

The other great influence in his life is his mother, and, of course, the omnipresent Catholic church.

In the book, there is a repeated use of not just church-inspired phraseology like "let the service begin", but also an eternal dwelling on concepts of magic, miracles, mystery, mysticism.

From drawing attention to the wonders of science (refurbished radios), to guitars, to those of musical talent, it's 'magic' all the way. There even exists a Springsteen album entitled Magic.

The father's bar hangout is thought of as a mystical hangout of men; the mother is a miracle, the sounds of her getting ready for work are sounds of mystery; there's talk of guitar wizardry; of words like voodoo to describe the music of one of his earlier bands, Steel Mill; the mix of black and white influences in the music of the band when it had Boom as a drummer was magic; there was something shamanistic about Clarence's role in the band; even running into an old school friend who used to be a cheerleader at school is described, satirically, as a miracle having occurred; the music of another early band, The Castiles, was "raw, rudimentary, local but effective magic."

California introduces him to the concepts of the musician as a psychic facilitator, and to music being used as an instrument for consciousness-raising, but we're filled in on the fact that his catholic upbringing prevents him from comprehending these phenomena at the time.

He describes the world of the priests and nuns: "…a world where all you have is at risk, a world filled with the unknown bliss of resurrection, eternity and the unending fires of perdition, of exciting sexually tinged torture, immaculate conceptions and miracles. A world where men turn into gods and gods into devils…."

While referring to England as the musical mother country, the cities that had been home to their beat heroes are described as mystical destinations.

One is satisfied that one is not the only myth-maker on the loose!

The Defence Forces

Bruce Springsteen points out that his hit number of the mid-1980s, the protest song, Born in the USA, is one of his most misunderstood numbers, but that later acoustic renditions do serve to demonstrate that there are no inherent contradictions in the things that his music says.

Bruce was inspired to write Born in the USA ten years after the Vietnam war, after meeting two people: Ron Kovic and Bobby Muller.

Ron Kovic, the author of Born on the Fourth of July, was a Vietnam vet whom Springsteen met by sheer coincidence just a few days after he'd bought the memoir at a shop while driving through the Arizona desert. Ron went on to take him to the vet centre at Venice, California, to meet the So Cal vets.

Bobby Muller, who'd been shot in Vietnam, he met backstage at New Jersey. Muller had been in anti-war protests with John Kerry (the Secretary of State of the USA during Obama's time), and had started the Vietnam Veterans of America, and a concert for the Vietnam Veterans of America was held in Los Angeles on 20th August, 1981. Bruce opened the concert with CCR's (Creedence Clearwater Revival's) "Who'll Stop the Rain."

The CCR, I'm told, was in India in the 1960s, touring with the Moral Re-armament Movement (MRA), a sort of cultural group, and visited places such as Ooty, where the third order of the Franciscan Missionaries of Mary (FMM) was founded, and where India's first school run by the FMM, Nazareth Convent, is located, though the groups performed elsewhere, and the event was widely publicised at the time.

Springsteen first came across navy SEAL, Terry Magovern, when he returned from his second great trip to California, having visited his parents who had moved to the Bay Area, and after having accompanied his father on a Mexican holiday. Terry was also the manager of the Captain's Garter in Neptune, New Jersey, where Bruce joined Steve (Van Zandt), Southside and their Sundance Blues Band soon after his return from San Francisco. Terry later became his assistant and close friend for twenty-three years. "Terry's Song" was written for Magovern for the album Magic, after Terry's passing away.

Bruce refers to himself as the Jersey draft dodger number one, and his memoir records the event of him (like quite a few others), successfully managing to dodge being sent off to fight the war. There is mention of "survivor's guilt" at least twice in the book, in the context of the rest of his work and life, but no regret for the dodge.

Friends of Springsteen who went to war include Bart Haynes, who was a drummer for his early band, The Castiles. He was the first soldier from New Jersey to die in Vietnam (Mortar shelling in Quang Tri province).

Walter Cichon of The Motifs also received a head wound in Kontum province of South Vietnam, was left for dead, and was among the list of those missing in action.

When one compares the essences of the greatest democracies of the world, one of the parameters against which my country scores higher, is that we, in India, do not draft people to the armed forces.

The unrelated fact that our Indian Constitution has Emergency provisions- wherein fundamental rights can be temporarily suspended by the government- is arguably the most debatable article of our otherwise exemplary document. This is a provision that has been called into use only once in history. The Emergency. And is seen as one of the darkest phases that the nation has gone through, and the megalith that is the party has done much, since, to demonstrate that it stands for Human Rights, and fights to defend the Fundamental Rights that the Constitution of India guarantees. One is today proud to stand up and be counted as a part of the great global movement that is called the Indian National Congress Party.

While talking of the dodge of the draft, Springsteen has his reasons, and noteworthy, today, is the bit where his perception was: "…bodies were needed to stem the perceived Communist menace in South Asia." Now, decades after the war, it is evident that eventually, it is not wars, but multi-pronged global approaches towards sustainable development and human rights that bridge gaps amongst people and nations.

Bruce describes his present wife (he continues to use this old-fashioned term, as do quite a few people), and band-member, Patti Scialfa, as "…a one-woman, red-haired revolution." The accomplished musician happens to be the daughter of a Coast Guard lieutenant commander.

After Born in the USA, Springsteen says there was an intentional left-turn, which, along with his growing relationship with Patti, was disorienting for the band.

Music and Lyrics for World Peace

The Tunnel of Love album tour, after Born in the USA, merged into the Amnesty International Human Rights Now world tour, and though Springsteen had acquired his largest audience with Born in the USA, the greater significance of the 1988 tour could be thought of as something that's organically evolving and revealing itself in the present day.

It is no coincidence that on the 9th of August, 2017 (the UN-declared International Day of Indigenous People), Springsteen's Twitter account and Facebook page announced that he will make his Broadway debut this year. Through most of October and November, these acoustic shows to smaller audiences are timed to coincide with the annual general assembly of the United Nations at New York.

The grand orchestra that is the development sector has an instinct for leveraging ongoing events to bring about desired results facilitated by impromptu gatherings of an otherwise-difficult-to-bring-together bunch of nationalities or interest groups.

By Springsteen's own admission, when large crowds attend Bruce Springsteen concerts, there are bound to be not just Democrats (whom he campaigns for, and supports), but also Republicans, amongst the audience. Similarly, he draws audiences from countries that might be in conflict, such as countries with various disputes: India and Pakistan.

When Springsteen was recording the number, Worlds Apart, for his post-nine-eleven album, The Rising, a Pakistani Sufi music group happened to be in Los Angeles on exactly the day that he needed a particular kind of sound for the number. They thus recorded the number with Bruce.

The unifying power of music, and its ability to work beyond all geographical and political boundaries remind us that music is an integral part of Nature, and of The Environment.

Cross-planetary forces of destruction caused by the dirtying of rivers, or the melting of glaciers do not recognize borders of countries or states in their destruction. Music, in its reach and appeal, can, and often, does, work beyond such demarcations as well.

It is therefore significant (and useful) that Bruce has not been handed out any very significant UN-centric honours or ambassadorships, as the Boss continues to play Magician in the theatre of the World.

Truth and Authenticity

Springsteen's Foreword to the book describes his town as one where "almost everything is tinged with a bit of fraud", and says of himself, that he was "…a member in good standing amongst those who 'lie' in service of the truth…artists with a small 'a.'"

As one ruminates over the meaning and implications of this admission (or brag?), one finds that truth, authenticity and honesty surface often as recurring themes in the thought processes of the singer-songwriter through the writing of the autobiography.

Some of these ideas are explained to the reader when Bruce writes of his first foreign tour when he was twenty-five, and nervous. He writes, "…

I know I'm good but I'm also a poser. That's artistic balance! In the second half of the twentieth century, 'authenticity' would be what you made of it, a hall of mirrors", and he proceeds to talk of the experience of being aware of his 'performance self', and his 'true self' while on stage, and of the "multiple personalities…fighting to take turns at the microphone."

While Springsteen might have mastered the art of striking the right balance between the demands of communication that go with a given situation, and those of 'authenticity', the articulation here does indicate that he sees these as ongoing challenges that are renewed at each live show. One begins to gain a better understanding of what is at the root of the quest of his continuing live performance saga.

Springsteen says: "In the 1960s the first version of my country that struck me as truthful and unfiltered was the one I heard in songs by artists like Bob Dylan…", and that certain songs "…let me know that someone, somewhere, was speaking in tongues and that absurd ecstasy had been snuck into the Constitution's First Amendment and was an American birthright. I heard it on the radio."

In India, the immediate association with the word 'birthright', are the words of a renowned freedom fighter, Lokmanya Bal Gangadhar Tilak, who declared: "Freedom is my birthright, and I shall have it." As far as we are concerned, it was a term that Tilak coined, that has gained global currency.

If Springsteen was made aware of these events of Indian history as a part of the crash-course on human rights he went through before he played at the Amnesty International's Human Rights Now concert at New Delhi in 1988, then this is an interesting linguistic connection being made in a sentence where he refers to the American Constitution's First Amendment. It is my guess that he was thinking of the rule of law worldwide, of India, and of Mahatma Gandhi. The overall context is, after all, a discussion on Truth.

For those amongst us with the most exacting standards for Truth and Honesty, even Reality Theatre is a nebulous phenomenon, where only a version that unequivocally announces itself, in a timely manner, as being reality theatre, passes the moral test.

Sometimes, however, possibly in the name of using art for social change, one cannot rule out the fact that some versions of reality theatre overstep the limits of truth. In the context of attempts to bring about social transformation, this might just be another form of 'astro-turfing' (not to cherry-pick and dredge facts, but, in this case, to forge reality by bringing it about).

For example, if policewomen in plainclothes, or any group of women, were to occupy public spaces that are not considered safe for women, at times of day that are not safe for women on a regular basis, preferably in empowering, revealing clothing, they would be able to eventually reclaim the space and time as being available equally to all.

Mahatma Gandhi, too, had said something to the effect of 'be the change you want to see in the world.' Gandhi had attended an important international conference in only a loin-cloth, and was disparagingly referred to as a half-naked fakir. The benchmark for women, particularly politicians, to be what they want to be, in public or otherwise, is a task more difficult than this.

Springsteen's interesting and unexpected preoccupation with dress will feature later in this series.

Development-Sector Jargon in the Book

Other than the speaking-in-tongues kind of biblical imagery that runs through the book, there are noteworthy instances of development-sector-UN-inspired imagery:

He describes the Upstage Club as "an incredible clearinghouse for musicians". 'Clearinghouse' is a part of the oft-used jargon of the development sector, and is used to describe a bulk of existing documents, talent, connections or networks that are made available on a platform to be accessed, sorted out, or added value to.

When he was with his father on what he describes as "his seafaring fantasy", he talks of how his "...dad was lowered, like a sack of United Nations grain, into the tender...."

Echoes of this, and other UN-centric imagery lead one to glean an element of the aspirational (or the associative), in how the writer interprets his own role in history so far.

Regarding his work in music, he speaks of having been in a 'transient field', where he was meant for the 'long haul', and says, at one point of the book, that "the above case studies prove, no matter who you are, that's not as easy as it sounds."

Project-cycles in the UN are often looked at as short, medium and long term, where long-term would mean twenty years.

Check-Point Charlie and the Berlin Wall

Further on in the book, Springsteen writes: "I was interested in what it meant to be an American, one small participant in current history at a time when the future seemed as hazy and shape-shifting as that thin line on the horizon. Can a rock 'n' roll artist sculpt that line, shade its direction? How much?"

Springsteen flags a part of his role in world politics in terms of his drives past Checkpoint Charlie, his concerts in the region divided by approximately seven years, and the eventual falling of the wall that divided (the Communist) East Germany from West Germany.

About driving through Checkpoint Charlie, he writes, "you knew the oppression was real…we didn't forget; we'd be back in 1988 to play for a horizonless field of Eastern Bloc faces…a year later the wall fell." Springsteen also mentions that the first trip through Checkpoint Charlie had had a deep impact on his friend and band-mate, Steve Van Zandt.

When bands travel to places to play, there is a cultural interaction and inter-personal exchange of conversations and ideas, perhaps contacts, amongst all those involved at various levels in the immediate logistics of the conducting of a show. But one cannot underestimate the fact that the impact of Springsteen's words, and the band's performance and energy, and the assurance that a better world is possible, played a key role in bringing about seismic socio-political change along this highway (or wall) of history.

This was, ironically, about the same time as when Springsteen says his music had taken an intentional left turn.

Scholars of political science might be able to throw more light on, or confirm the existence of a school of thought that opines that of all the forms of government/state/law (using all these terms in a loosely interchangeable fashion here) that exist, it is prudent to ensure that the best (or most moderate version) of even the worst form of government should also be kept alive in some (albeit rudimentary form), in the crucible of civilization.

Today, as the world is witness to a mixture of disruptive energies, where it appears that the axis has begun to veer, and that nomenclatures of capitalist, socialist, communist and various permutations and combinations of these seem to be caught in a bizarre dance with labels of democracy, monarchy, military dictatorship, all surging towards One World, space, outer space and cyberspace, we need to look at the constructive energy that might exist in All Things Russian mentioned in Born to Run! Or, depending on what propaganda grips you, All Things (fill in the blanks for whatever group, country, organization, person, concept it is that you think plagues the world the most today).

Springsteen describes Bruce at the age of thirty-four as a serial monogamist, and attributes this to the culture of shame and guilt that was imbibed in him by the Catholic church.

Religion, Magic (Again); and at the Super-Bowl With Obama

While discussing the role of religion in his life, Springsteen recalls a few unpleasant incidents of how he (and other children) were treated by the authorities at the grammar school that he attended. Springsteen says that while those violent admonishments "estranged" him forever from the church, the institution was so all-pervasive, that there was no real escape, and that he "came to ruefully and bemusedly understand that once you're a Catholic, you're always a Catholic." He also goes on to admit that "deep inside", he's "still on the team", and says that his mother and her sisters lived and preached the credo of work, faith and family.

In relating events connected to negotiations he tried to make with Mike Appel, his manager, for a new round of contracts, he uses concepts and phrases from the language of Buddhism such as "the middle way" (reminiscent of the Middle Path propounded by The Buddha), and moderation, but in the nick of time, for the culminating sentence of the same paragraph and chapter, he reverts back to Christian imagery, and describes his band and his extended team as his apostles. The manner of the use of language mirrors the reality of his religious grounding that he seems to have come to terms with.

Springsteen's album, Magic, was his "…state-of-nation dissent over the Iraq War and the Bush years." In the course of the Magic tour, in the context of counselling a band member, Danny Federici, who had contracted melanoma (and had earlier been "overstating his expenses and skimming off the top"), Bruce says that "As a leader, even of a rock 'n' roll band, there is always a little of the 'padrone' in your job description, but it's a fine line."

This healing touch, Springsteen has brought to his music, to shape, respond to, and pave the way in synch with a growing collection of world events.

The concert that he did for the Vietnam vets in LA was on the 20th of August, 1981. 20th of Aug. happens to be the birthday of one of the past leaders of the Indian National Congress party, the late Prime Minister of India, Rajiv Gandhi, and is being celebrated in India today as one writes.

Thirty-six years after the LA concert, and nineteen years after the New Delhi concert, Springsteen continues to perform on significant occasions such as for the inauguration ceremony of President Obama, and at the half-time of the American Super Bowl.

When he went back to East Berlin for his second concert, after which the German wall fell, Springsteen seems to have been quite surprised to notice that the tickets said that they were being presented by the Young Communist League, and that they were playing a "concert for the Sandinistas" (question-mark, exclamation mark!)

Russians

Back home in the USA, those who hailed from the Russian steppes in his state of New Jersey were people who included descendants of Genghis Khan, and belonged to the Mongolian race. "Persecuted" by Stalin, and rescued by Tolstoy's daughter from the Soviets, they lived south of Bruce's town of Freehold, on Freewood Acres, as a "planned community." He describes them as being "rabidly anti-Communist", and we are told that they "were sprung from Stalin's cages." Springsteen says many of the children from Freewood Acres were his school-mates.

In the context of describing some of his father's behaviour as "paranoid delusion", Springsteen mentions how his father thought that a teenage Russian friend of Bruce's was a spy.

Springsteen recalls a year when he did "a holiday show for the locals at a Russian social club called Rova Farms on the outskirts of town."

One finds that Richard Blackwell played the congas that evening for Bruce at Rova Farms. The same Richard Blackwell that Springsteen had fortuitously run into far away from home, a familiar face from New Jersey, on his first trip to San Francisco. (More on San Francisco, and Springsteen's tryst with nature and the environment in the next part of this series).

Springsteen was thus, even in his statedly insular early life, familiar with a thing or two that was Russian, as opposed to what the rest of the world might expect of an everyday American's exposure to Russian people or culture of any kind during the days of the cold war.

Anti-Nuclear Protest Music; San Francisco; Environmentalism and Deep Ecology; Nature

We find, in Chapter Forty, The River, that in true Springsteenian form, he draws attention to the Three Mile Island nuclear accident (and environmental disaster) that took place in the USA, through the life of an everyday character. He describes his song, "Roulette", as the "portrait of a family man caught in the shadow of the Three Mile Island nuclear accident."

Thus, a number about an American nuclear disaster (an environmental issue), was his debut, in his words, "into the public political arena." Bruce Springsteen performed Roulette at Madison Square Garden for Musicians United for Safe Energy (MUSE).

Somehow, via the title, Roulette, and the Power of Suggestion of the artist, the reader's mind moves to the Chernobyl disaster, and, indeed, to thoughts on the negative aspects of the role of civil nuclear energy in the emerging energy mix of our planet.

By the time Springsteen got news of his induction to the Rock and Roll Hall of Fame in 1998, his repertoire in the public political arena had expanded to include the Human Rights Now tour that had served not only to extend solidarity, but to also legally empower people who stood in need of strength or liberation, or just music, across the globe.

Springsteen, at twenty-one, made his first foray out west with a bunch of comrades, and one of their dogs. The three-day journey sounds like a rough ride in two vehicles, with no extra money for stop-overs, and one of the human beings not knowing how to drive, but doing so anyway.

In California, Springsteen says, "…we stood speechless before what we saw. Giant old-growth trees, vegetation so lush you'd get lost a few feet in off the walking path…I'd never stood in the midst of nature like this and you could feel its humbling and intoxicating power. I approached a tree the likes of which I'd never seen before…thousands of butterflies exploded off its branches and shot into the hard blue sky. This was another world."

They were at a "human potential spa." Springsteen writes that there were "hot springs tucked into the side of a cliff overlooking the sea. There were the springs, a cold bath, and everybody naked."

Their band played for the locals and the paying guests in the evening, and "it all broke loose West Coast-style…we played the crowd into a frenzy." Springsteen remarks that at this place, "music was a part of a larger tribal 'consciousness raising' event."

From the grandest scale, cut to the microscopic. He describes himself scrutinizing an army of ants as he waits for his parents, by then in the Bay Area, to collect him from the highway. In his book, however, Springsteen dedicates a chapter entitled Eastern Woman to his mother, and describes her as a "raw, rough wonder."

The elasticity in the way Springsteen writes here about nature: grandiose descriptions of sweeping landscapes, distant mountains and the heavens, then the (albeit unleashed) butterflies, right down to the marching armies of ants, is mirrored by his observations of human actions: Unhindered trance-dancers; meditative seekers; "groups of people curled up on a green lawn in white sheets returning to their 'amoeba stage.'"

One would hazard a guess, and go so far as to speculate over whether this might have, retrospectively, been a turning-point of sorts for Bruce. A peep into the fact that everything is possible, that while recognizing and honouring the minutiae of things or circumstances, it was alright, and possible, and do-able, to insist on the pursuit of the largest, the highest, the seemingly impossible goal/s.

The frustration of a person with high aspirations being conditioned to (and resisting) the scaling-down that one's circumstances, religion, socio-political order or upbringing impose on one are hinted at, at the very outset, when, in the opening paragraph of chapter one, he writes: "…my world sprawls on into infinity, or at least to Peter McDermott's house…one block up."

A rudimentary parallel might be drawn, between the approaches of Capitalism and Communism, in the application of the concept of absolutes having been created in terms of the individual versus the collective; the small-scale versus the large-scale; the selfless versus the selfish…and these may then be juxtaposed against other cultural and social constructs that also have a bearing on how people and areas are governed or not governed: the synthesis; the many avatars of the permutations and combinations of the required mix of the required ingredients of the public and the personal, whether in music, in society, or vis-à-vis the world economy.

Springsteen and his raw music enter San Francisco, the land of not only a plethora of environmental activists set in nature's lap, and where "hippies ran free", but of bands that, alas, seemed, at that time, to play more "sophisticated" music than Bruce did.

If Springsteen experienced a glorious desert-ride via Arizona on his first trip to California, he experienced a snow-storm (snow-storms, he writes, can be truly unnerving), on his ride to San Mateo, California, from New Jersey. New Jersey, the place where he was a local star, and people stood next to him, proclaiming: King of New Jersey! (We're also told, in one of the early chapters, that the town of Freehold's first church service and first funeral were held in their family's living room).

Of snow-storms, he writes: "Back east, we usually experience the freedom that comes with a good snowstorm. No work, no school, the world shutting its big mouth for a while… A lot of snow, however…That feeling of freeness turns to confinement. The sheer physical weight of the snow becomes existential and the dread of a dark, covered world sets in. I've felt it twice. Once in Idaho where it snowed circus clowns for seventy-two hours…." Observations such as these that run through the book convince the reader that while Bruce Springsteen does not have any formal academic laurels to tom-tom, his analytical abilities are not restricted to being the product of field-based research such as knowing about the lives of common people from personal experience.

Springsteen's environmentalism is not restricted to him being awestruck by the natural world. His concern for nuclear contamination is repeated in some of the imagery that he uses, such as when he talks of the vessel that he and his father sailed in on their Mexican holiday, as "a bobbing rubber duck in a five-year-old's bathtub." Most netizens would've come across some version or the other of the story of the (i think) Chinese cargo ship that was said to be carrying toy rubber ducks that capsized, and the fact that these rubber ducks are said to show up on far-flung shores, and remind humankind of the far-reaching impacts of any nuclear contamination of the seas.

The World Economy and Trump

The balance that must be struck between the rights of individuals, and the duties of individuals towards the community and the planet are at the heart of much of the environmental jurisprudence of countries such as India. These concepts require a greater amplification in order to meet challenges pertaining to human rights that people face world-wide.

Springsteen writes: "After the crash of 2008, I was furious at what had been done by a handful of trading companies on Wall Street. (The album) Wrecking Ball was a shot of anger at the injustice that continues on and has widened with deregulation, dysfunctional regulatory agencies and capitalism gone wild at the expense of hardworking Americans."

Trump-esque in his concern specifically for the American working class (as perceived by this international observer).

But clearly the very opposite of Trump in terms of there being no conflict of interest in the stands for the working class being taken by Bruce The Boss.

Regarding the making of the album The River in 1979, he writes that he "began to steer the record into a rawer direction…striking the perfect balance between a garage band and the professionalism required to make good records…Along with 'gravitas', our shows were always filled with fun…." This was a progression (or movement, in any case), in the music and style of performance, in comparison to what Springsteen had started out with. There are other indicators that he uses, to trace movements and bolster his descriptions, and these include descriptions of garments, and of spaces.

Music as Theatre: Costumes; Outfits in General

The costumes in which he and his musicians perform, as well as the clothes people wear in general, seem to be of significance to the writer and the performer in him. As are the settings. Music as theatre.

In the days when he was in the band The Castiles (the name of a brand of shampoo), they dressed "more like a British R&B group" and played at places like the IB Club.

Closer to the present day, of when he was about to play at the Super Bowl, he writes: "I'm sitting in my trailer trying to decide which boots to wear. I've got a nice pair of cowboy boots my feet look really good in, but I'm concerned about their stability…I better go with the combat boots I always carry."

Half-way through the book, one finds less of a mention of garb, and this coincides with the overall chronology of the time from where his music takes "an intentional left turn." Uniforms turn to individual choices, and Springsteen discontinues his practice of dictating wardrobe choices to his band-members. People's clothes are suddenly not referred to as much as they were through the first half of the book. (He specifically mentions that he has been writing this autobiography since 2009 in long-hand, and one believes this, so one is convinced that the minor shift in this aspect of the narration is not the inadvertent oversight of ghost writers!)

The pure artistic eye for sartorial style comes across as being one of the passions of the musician, worthy of follow-up commentary further on down this read.

Scavenging and Recycling (also a Part of His Environmentalism)

Just as this ongoing commentary might prove to be a clarion call for direct political support for Springsteen, Bruce's weekly jaunts with his grandfather to literally scavenge from piles of junk: wires, filament tubes and the like, and watch him recycle these into five-dollar radios for sale retrospectively place him at the high table of (and with) pioneering environmental entrepreneurs producing upcycled goods. An additional talking and rallying-point for a political sojourn.

Race Relations

The black migrant population that had immigrated into New Jersey from the 'South' came to think of Springsteen's grandfather as the "radio man", and were his main "patrons". Bruce was "simply the protegee grandson of the 'radio man'."

Touching upon race relations while recounting his role in his grandfather's rags-to-riches venture (Elements of the Bildungsroman have been skilfully woven in, and are reinforced in the narrative via mention of Charles Dickens elsewhere in the book), Springsteen writes: "Race relations, never great in Freehold, will explode ten years later into riotings and shootings, but for now, there is just a steady, uncomfortable quiet."

Bruce writes: "We had black friends, though only rarely did we enter each other's homes. There was détente in the streets. The white and black adults were cordial but distant. The children played together. There was a lot of easy racism amongst the kids…but I never ran into kids who wouldn't play with black kids until I bumped into the middle and upper-middle class." Springsteen understands these nuances of how race relations play out across various strata of society through personal association at all levels. From the radio-buying blacks in their "'Mickey Mouse' camps", to rubbing shoulders with President Obama, Springsteen understands it all. And is able to communicate it to the masses.

He describes the racism of the fifties as being "presumed and casual", to the extent that kids who were excluded from a group-event by a particular person were conditioned to take this in their stride, and to socialize with the same person (who had, in a sense, condoned the social exclusion), at future events as if nothing was the matter. This was considered normal.

Of his black friends when he was young, Springsteen says he was "pals" with the Blackwell brothers, was taken up by the jazz-like demeanour of Richard Blackwell, and reminisces over how he thought of him as "the pope of cool."

He describes two distinct kinds of school gangs, "two socially incompatible teen cliques", in great detail through the overlapping prisms of fashion, style and social status. He identified more with the ones that "copped their whole look from the school's black community." He writes of how the kids return from some of the unifying music on the dance floor "to their UN-designated square of gym floor."

Dance, for Springsteen, was something he'd been initiated into at home by his aunts and his mother, and it was also a carefully honed skill. He does not hesitate to reveal that he went to great extents to practice his moves before he hit the dance floor. He used to attend dance "soirees" at the Catholic Youth Organization (CYO), and at the Young Men's Christian Association (YMCA). Some of Springsteen's music is, unsurprisingly, influenced by the sound of Gospel music.

But Springsteen's two defining connects with the black community are his friendship and musical association with Clarence Clemons, and the flak that he drew from sections of the police ("usually a great part of my audience"), when he "stepped directly into the divide of race" with his number, American Skin, that drew attention to an incident of police brutality on the streets, perpetrated against an African immigrant.

Inclusive Governance

The book also treads a political path when he expresses his views on governmental expenditure in his observations on the aftermath of the LA riots of 1992.

The lyrics of quite a few of Springsteen's songs are, of course, about race and exclusion. The number My Hometown captures "the racial tension of late-sixties small-town New Jersey." In writing about the album, The Ghost of Tom Joad, he says he "traced the lineage of some of his earlier characters to the Mexican immigrant experience in the new West."

The concerns of immigrants, of religious minorities, and those racially discriminated against have been an abiding concern for Springsteen.

He mentions how he once had a girlfriend who was "fabulously Jewish", and how, unfortunately, he wasn't able to conjure up much social bonhomie, in his youth, with another set of Jewish sisters whose family moved into his neighbourhood.

Springsteen talks of "day-dreaming over brown-skinned girls", there are appreciative references to olive-skinned girls, and we're told that on the "Irish Riviera" of the Shore, the "Italians and the Irish meet and mate often…the fair-skinned and freckled can be found tossing down beers…." Race was definitely on peoples' minds, irrespective of how they treated the factor.

Bruce Springsteen points out that his song, "We Are Alive", from the album Wrecking Ball, addresses "new voices of immigration, the civil rights movement and anyone who'd ever stuck their neck out for some righteous justice and was knocked down or killed for their effort." The Boss urges people to "Listen and learn from the souls and spirits who've come before."

Springsteen describes himself as a child of "Vietnam-era America, of the Kennedy, King and Malcolm X assassinations. The country no longer felt like the innocent place it was said to be in the Eisenhower fifties. Political murder, economic injustice and institutionalised racism were all powerfully and brutally present." He views his work as being done in the service of humanity.

While his audience has largely been comprised of white people, he writes that when he sang Promised Land on an Obama campaign at Cleveland, his intended audience were: "young people, old people, black, white, brown, cutting across religious and class lines."

Writer-Reader Interface

On a few occasions spread across the book, Springsteen directly addresses the reader/s. The kind of interface with his audience that Springsteen attempts to craft, and revels in, makes for fascinating reading and conjecture.

Back to Clothes

The book is a-rustle with sartorial detail, ranging from a passing mention of "Nehru suits" that the Beatles sported, to Bruce's mother's exclamations of delight over the picturesque wedding dresses that brides at the church near their house wore. His mother's office, he associated with "perfumes, crisp white blouses, whispering skirts and stockings of the secretaries."

There is an underlying social commentary and semi-political tone, a sociological point that's made in almost every sentence of the writing of Born to Run.

Dress-wise, we find that the principal of his school didn't take kindly to the idea of Bruce attending his graduation meet in his off-beat look. Bruce boycotted the event.

The police treatment towards "longhairs" in nineteen-sixties New Jersey was "intemperate". (Longhairs was not a reference to the long-haired men of the Sikh community at this point of history). Inkwell Coffee House is lauded as a "longhair-friendly local institution."

There was also the infuriating Disneyland experience, when he and Steve were asked to remove their bandanas. Springsteen says he refused to remove his "headscarf" (the Born in the USA "do-rag"), and they chose to avoid the place instead.

The get-up of the Rah-rah and Greaser teenage cliques is gone into in some amount of detail. The Rahs were "the jock, madras-wearing, cheerleading, college-bound slightly upscale teen contingent…who lorded it over most high schools", and the Greasers, Springsteen remarks, "…were in deep pursuit of 'uptown style.' The pristineness of the suits; the high-collared pink, lime green and baby blue shirts; the high-water trousers…." Epic lists that comprised the ensembles of the greaser girls are also released: "teased bouffant hair, white lipstick, white skin, heavy eye shadow, leather boots, tight skirts, dive-bomber bras—think the Shangri-Las or Ronettes crossed with Amy Whitehouse."

The Boss, it appears, enjoys an occasional jam or a ponder over who wore what where, and why, and why not. Here is further potential to expand his fan-base beyond the numbers of those who love his music.

His band was once placed amidst a group of dancers, The Exciters, and he recalls their "slinky gold lamé gowns", of which he declares: "(Teenage heart attacks and rock 'n' roll heaven!)" And at another level, one might interpret these to be outwardly reflected flights of fantasy and human aspiration: gilded sheens of gossamer rising forth from amongst soggy-T-Shirt-wearers and roughers-out of denim.

Springsteen talks of his father's ironed shirts and Brylcreemed hair, and also of how, when Bruce's sister, Pam, was born, and his mother was in hospital, his father got him ready for school, and sent him off in his mother's blouse by mistake.

Springsteen mentions that the book Born to Run is, to a great extent, a product of many rounds of discussions he had on the couch with his good doctor of many years, and that he has done his best, in the narrative, to speak from the vantage point of issues (many connected to his troubled past with his father), having been resolved. Facts such as his father's problem with alcohol, that are necessary for the big picture, of course, have been factored into the text. That said, the incident of his father having sent him to school in a girl's blouse must have been absolute ignominy for a school kid, and mentioning it here definitely verges on the therapeutic.

Years later, another ladies' blouse that finds a mention is when Springsteen says that "the Born in the USA tour was notable for the sartorial horror sweeping E Street nation…I'd grown weary of being a wardrobe Nazi…'fashion' mayhem reigned."

Artistic judgementalism (albeit mild, and said almost in jest) of this kind does not surface in any significant way when he discusses music. It is possible that he is less politically correct while discussing aspects of creativity that do not directly demand the niceties of competitive diplomacy (one does not have specific musical debacles up for discussion yet).

Patti Scialfa (whom he would later marry), and who was a part of the Born in the USA gig, asked him, before a performance, for his opinion on what he describes as "a simple white peasant blouse" that she was in, which he thought looked "kind of…*girly*." He promptly asked her to help herself to one of his own T-shirts that were "stuffed into a suitcase." He goes on to say that he remembers thinking: "Patti looks terrific (in my T-shirt!)"

At the concert in New Delhi in 1988, Springsteen delighted the audience by appearing in costumes that were recognizable from music videos that had been broadcast by Doordarshan. A recent net-search indicates that Amnesty has come out with a set of recordings of the 1988 world tour that are on sale. Apparently, audience tapes also exist, but are not easily accessible, and one will have to check whether the Amnesty pack includes clips of the New Delhi audience. There is, on youtube, the Newstrack video magazine of the 1980s' report of the event.

Apologies for Misogynistic Rock 'N' Roll Attitudes

Springsteen does, in the course of the book, offer retractions from some of his youthful attitudes that he describes as having been misogynistic. As with many cults, so with rock 'n' roll heroes…evolutions need to be declared from the ramparts of grand pianos, and this, Springsteen does with subtle firmness for stragglers, who, it is hoped, will also be readers of books such as Born to Run, and take the cue.

Lifelong Dialogue With Audience

Of the mid-1990s, the days of the Streets of Philadelphia album, and his connection with his audience, Springsteen says: "I don't write strictly for my audience's desires but we are, at this point, engaged in a lifelong dialogue, so I take into consideration their voices."

By that time, Bruce's lifelong dialogue with the likes of me already had a decade of thoughts and endeavours, failures and successes, to show for.

Back to the New Delhi 1988 Concert

Regarding the landmark concert of the 30th of September, 1988, one recollects having gone to great lengths (and, through the lens of some later phase, cringeworthy), attempts to dress up for a rock show (technically, the setlist included most of his pop hits that resonated with a larger audience at the time).

A transparent, pink long crinkled skirt, a loose-fitting white cotton long shirt with an elliptical geometric black print sprawled across the fabric, and full sleeves rolled up and tucked in, puffing out with the hint of a girly country-blouse look (the black-and-white effect, no doubt, indicative of one's intended career-path of joining the legal community), and dangler-earrings, multi-coloured pastel wooden beads in a row. These might have been inspired by the Kondapalli or Etikoppaka woodcraft from the state of Andhra Pradesh. Today, they would be the banners of a rainbow coalition, in all its interpretative diversity.

Added to this, were over-sized bronze high-heeled party shoes borrowed from my friends, the Faleiro sisters, at whose place we congregated and prepared for the event, and probably raided their mum's make-up kit and footwear collection! Shaila was a fan of Springsteen as well, and had managed to swing passes for us for the best seats, though we ran amuck into the audience on the field for a more real experience. Their mother, the late Muriel Faleiro, also happened to catch a glimpse of Springsteen by chance while he was shopping at the jewellery counter of Cottage Industries, and got his autograph for Shaila. These were the days when their dad, a lawyer and a politician from Goa, was a minister of the Union Government, for, among other things, Banking and Finance.

Coincidences

Springsteen comes across as a believer, and a person of faith. Coincidences and chance happenings are specifically mentioned in the autobiography. Add to this, the many coincidences that his fans might be able to throw into the cauldron, and the world of theatre, at least, might be sitting on a golden treasury of chapter, verse and beyond.

Springsteen's daughter, Jessica, was born in the early 1990s on my birthday, and on the date of another year in history, when the USSR was formed. The 30th of December also happens to be my mother's brother's birthday.

However, one is not necessarily clutching at only straws such as these to examine the workings of the mathematical theory of synchronicity, also popularised though a work of fiction and pop-psychology when we were students, that was based on the belief-system of a South American tribe.

The novel, The Celestine Prophecy, captured the imaginations of quite a few readers worldwide when it was released, and some of what it says might be read with some of what Springsteen says, to make sense of the random occurrences of the universe.

To answer, even, questions such as: why me; why now, through the prism of pure Science…and to recognize what it takes to be human, and to continue in that effort…the fight against not only the words and deeds of human beings who oppress human beings, and thus maintain a certain order, but to also combat and course-correct the randomness and hegemony of the unknown, undiscovered, but theoretically existent tyranny of non-judgemental cosmic energy.

This is sometimes beyond the comprehension of currently understood science. Music, and the sensations it causes, the power of individual human will, as well as the force of the collective consciousness are the kinds of things that come in handy when mere mortals strike out to realms beyond the known.

While countries and governments play to the eternal choir of Bend it like Beckham in terms of international geopolitics, at that point of time and space, Bruce Springsteen and the E Street Band and the other great artists at the concert, and the largely fledgling audience (for this kind of live music in India), revelled in the music and the cultural experience. The coincidences were yet to pan out….

The readers are thrown into a layer of suspended animation (or creative energy, or both, or perhaps neither), when Springsteen ends the Foreword with (to me), an intriguing statement: "I am here to provide proof of life to that ever elusive, never completely believable 'us.' This is my magic trick. And like all good magic tricks, it begins with a setup. So…"

This interface that Springsteen shares with his audience, is at once the most tangible component of his life, beginning with the audiences at the bars that he played at regularly, and who put the "cheeseburgers" on the table, to the sell-out successes that turned him into a self-made multi-millionaire, but the interface is also intangible and ephemeral. And it is that intangibility that he seems to wish to decipher, and whose energetic auras he seems to aspire to body-surf.

Here, then, is an autobiography packed with as many coincidences as you might choose to notice, or discover, or just stonewall, as the reader/audience/fan.

He tells us, while talking about his story-telling technique in the writing of The Ghost of Tom Joad, that "The precision of the storytelling in these types of songs is very important…But all the telling detail in the world doesn't matter if the song lacks an emotional centre. That's something you have to pull out of yourself from the commonality you feel with the man or woman you're writing about."

Born to Run is an autobiography, a true story of Bruce's life as observed and narrated by him. In his live shows, Springsteen "wanted the collective identity and living representations of the characters who populated my songs."

Dear character (or potential character, since the aspiration is for the audience to be as all-encompassing as possible), you are also informed, through the narration of the moments when he discovered Elvis Presley, that "You, my TV dinner-sucking, glaze-eyed friends, are living in… THE MATRIX."

Coincidences-and-Audience-Connect (Bringing The World Together)

As characters that populate Bruce Springsteen's writings, those who, for whatever reason, are not in a position to expand the story and scope of their own lives and consciousness in concrete terms, or are in search of a launchpad, or of the experience of dipping their toes into a slipstream -or of drawing The Boss and Others into one of their own, in order to explore the multiverse, may choose to do so by spiralling the boundless energy of this here autobiography into worlds unknown! (I would, however, insist that this be carried out under the overall banner of truth, transparency and non-violence, and for democratically arrived-at and prioritised common agendas of the entire population).

Clearly, we listen to his music; attend his concerts if we're lucky; watch and read his interviews and music-videos; perhaps follow him on Twitter and Facebook, and check his website if social media indicates that there's something new on it. Springsteen's audience-connect at his concerts is epic, legendary. Of course, there's the fact that the fan base is, in some ways, a faceless mass, but as with all celebrities with a fan base, the thing that political planners notice is potential. In this case, political.

I think people are falling short of the right question when they ask him if he hopes to be the Governor of New Jersey. One is thinking more on the lines of World Parliament if and when it happens, or, at least, President, the latter being an any-time possibility in the days of anticipated impeachment. (Pardon the flight of fancy, there is, I believe, a presidential succession act in place).

Bruce has thrown his hat in with the Democrats. So for the next elections, we'll have to also look at who we think are his doppelgangers amongst the Republicans. And personally, I think BS (Bernie Sanders) is still a good idea.

I also think there is tremendous potential to look at how Springsteen could play a bigger and more visible role in facilitating the global inter-faith dialogue through his music.

Springsteen reminds us of how, when he once had a show at Pittsburgh, he "declined" a compliment paid to him by Ronald Reagan. I think some of Trump's speeches have elements of Bruce Springsteen in them by way of tone as well as substance. But maybe that's unintentional, and the influence of Springsteen's language runs deep. Then again, Melania is said to have used almost the exact same speech that Michelle Obama delivered on one occasion, so such things are blatantly possible.

Bruce's amazed tone at the discovery of the existence of Elvis Presley takes one back to that time in his life for a page or three, and calls to mind, some of one's own writings of the 1980s, on having discovered Bruce the Boss!

Bruce-related writings from my diaries contain: pages and pages of just Bruce, Bruce, Bruce, written against the backdrop of evolving ideas on meditation, transcendental meditation and intent-creation; a rave scribbled with a ball-point pen, written in synch with Bruce Springsteen's music (possibly inspired by the fact that the mega barefoot Indian artist, Hussain, had once painted to the sound of music on stage…though I can't quite recall whether I did this jugalbandi first, or Hussain); a letter that I wrote to my uncle soon after the Springsteen concert, and that I requested be returned to me for my records, and that I have saved since the 1980s.

There is something extremely energetic in the author's writing. A particular quality of writing that one might associate with the compressed writing of the lyricist or the poet is sustained with ease through a more-than-five-hundred-page book, making it replete with quotable quotes. Not quite your blueberry hill or shrewsbury cookie, but the entire biodiversity park and bakery, and then some.

On another platform, I'd simply say read the whole book yourself, it's worth the time. Would even recommend that it be translated to other languages. As far as the music goes, Bruce says that he's played to audiences worldwide that have not always been English-speaking audiences, and that this has not been a barrier.

I think it is time for him to play at iconic spots globally, at countries he's never played before, and where he might or might not have a large fan base. Since he seems to be focusing on acoustic sound at the moment, a world tour of a series of gatherings to jam with folk artistes might be what is required.

Unlike the chronology that the book describes, of songs being written, created, and then toured with, one might be looking at trying to explore how Springsteen could create music in collaboration with musicians from all continents as a part of a tour.

Concerts by India's sitar maestro, Ravi Shankar, playing at the Kremlin and several other locations had a tremendous impact when it came to reinforcing the country's diplomatic stances and overtures.

A few years ago, Springsteen toured with his album High Hopes, back to South America for the first time since the Amnesty tour, and to South Africa. These are, hopefully, encouraging indications that there's already more being crafted for an international agenda.

Writing about his first album, Greetings from Asbury Park, Springsteen says that "Most of the songs were twisted autobiographies", that he "wrote impressionistically", and that he "worked to find something that was identifiably mine." At the recording arena for this album, the advantage that Springsteen recognized that he had over many others was the fact that he'd "secretly built up years of rock 'n' roll experience out of view of the known world in front of every conceivable audience." Very like the rare grassroots politician, lawyer or social worker who might not invest in media publicity, but whose hands-on knowledge commands respect, and diversifies the scope of the term 'expertise'.

About Darkness on The Edge of Town, Springsteen writes: "The songs… remain at the core of our live performances today and are perhaps the purest distillation of what I wanted my rock 'n' roll music to be about." Most of his writing in the album was "emotionally autobiographical." Springsteen says that he had begun by insisting that there be no advertising, but Jon "explained" to him, that "no one will know the record exists." Food for thought, indeed, for all those who rely purely on the grapevine. But then again, we're talking about an era that preceded any kind of social media presence, and the Morse code wouldn't exactly count as social media, I suppose.

Springsteen talks of a phase through which he "routinely and roughly failed perfectly fine women over and over again", and that "With the end of each affair, I'd feel a sad relief from the suffocating claustrophobia love had brought me. And I'd be free to be…'nothing'…again." He then talks of the "transient detachment" of being a performer who is always on the road to somewhere else. "You play; the evening culminates in merry psychosexual carnage, laughs, ecstasy and sweaty bliss; then it's on to new faces and new towns. That, my friends, is why they call 'em… ONE NIGHT STANDS!"

Interesting etymological observation noted. And if arrived at without precedent, to be attributed, hereafter, to the author currently under discussion.

English, English! (or What You Will)

Which also reminds me that although there is only a passing mention of India in the book (the 1988 tour), the language, phraseology, and, indeed, subtle linguistic almost-dialects of our urban Indian times have somehow found their way to the world of Bruce Springsteen.

One imagines that this is a part of how India is rapidly expanding in the field of the soft power of language.

There are subtle currents that are required, to incorporate, into the language of power, the twists and turns of myriad cultures. The unique coup of having marked as "Received", unrecognizable brands of English, and of having made the resultant feast a malleable, equalizing mish-mash of words is a spinoff of globalization that the world community can thank India for.

Organically and historically speaking, of course, there was a time when it was newsworthy every time the Oxford English Dictionary announced that the next edition had included words from other languages, including from languages of India.

Springsteen uses the word Melee, which is from the Oriya-language term that means (people's) Uprising. Oriya words being spoken across continents, however, might have nothing to do with the English language, as recorded history confirms. Except for occasional culturally-appropriated and distorted usages, such as Juggernaut: an ancient tribal deity- a row of three half-formed humanoids depicted in different colours and with facial features of the human race, with no religion, held in high esteem in the Avataar-movie-evoking deep and illuminated woods in the eastern ghaat hills of the Indian sub-continent, now appropriated into a version of the Hindu religion that adheres to the discriminatory caste system, with the co-operation of powerful foreign dictionaries to boot. And christened Jaggannath (aka Juggernaut), Balabhadra, and Subhadra by the comparatively new Hindu religion.

Springsteen has served to bring the spoken language of working-class America into the everyday lives of listeners not only in the USA, but worldwide, through his lyrics.

Born to Run, the book, however, bubbles with experimentation and flare that expand the territory of the singer-songwriter into the territory of author par excellence, blending genres with ease within the book, and retaining a continuity in style nonetheless.

A Few Stray Observations about the Format of the Book

There are a few formatic bubbles that drift effortlessly through the book: a peep into an idyllic Thomas Hardy-like rustic setting that Bruce and his friend, Matt Delia (whom he met through Max Weinberg, his drummer), tarry awhile at as observers driving through the country…an oak writing table that's mentioned elsewhere in the book bounces back some of this sound;

a single sentence suspended in the space of a paragraph in the style of a mock mathematical equation (something I have only seen once before, ever in my life, in an essay that I wrote in 2013, what a coincidence!);

narrative elements reminiscent of Hollywood film scripts of the 1970s and 80s that teenagers of the time used to watch, like Footloose, Grease, High School USA, Breakdance and so on, in his descriptions of teen groups of New Jersey;

a do-it-yourself DIY-formatted narration while describing a part of his dodge of the draft (the ability to read and write instruction manuals is definitely a challenging task -or achievement- depending on where the writing originates, and where it's headed, sometimes putting to rest all the demands of political correctness of how all-encompassing a language ought to be…the consumer rights movement might bring about this correction);

a three-dream sequence in italics, where memories of youth mingle with philosophical insight, and hold a seer-like quality that materialise into the written word through the mists of time and consciousness.

These are some of the techniques in the narrative that otherwise remains focused on chronicling and explaining the behind-the-scenes aspects of his life and music.

Lyrics that Echo in the Autobio, A Symbol, and the Writer as a Critic of his Lyrics

Strains of some of the music ring through the writing: "so back into the studio we went", in the book, for instance, has echoes of "down to the river we'd ride" of The River; "one step up, two steps back" harks back to the song with those words while delving into profound concepts of psychology.

The symbol of a radio tower (with button-like ascending lights) serves to act as a silent, sound-emitting presence. (His mother describes it to him as "a tall dark giant invisible against the black night sky"). Like the future of the young Bruce Springsteen's music, it towers over the landscape, "a collective hallucination, a secret amongst millions and a whisper in the whole country's ear. When the music is great, a natural subversion of the controlled message broadcast daily by the powers that be…takes place." Springsteen as the symbolic lighthouse, the radio-tower, that emits glory into the universe in time to come.

Bruce also plays part-literary-critic in that he puts forward his own critiques of his lyrics. This provides the reader with windows to the musical influences, intentions, and surrounding circumstances and socio-political views that moulded the lyrics of each of his albums. A comprehensive analysis of those tracks will call for the writing of an entire tome, and this, perhaps, is already in the works somewhere or the other.

Through this written piece, one has only skimmed the surface of the scope that exists, for the literary interpretation of Born to Run. That task is probably also already being performed by those who have recognized and seized the opportunity of sinking their literary teeth into this platter of ever-reappearing steaks and loaves.

The Private, the Personal, the Political

Springsteen grapples with questions about the extent to which the private and personal merge in his life. He thinks aloud about whether presentation is politics, and he touches upon a key question, the question, to me, which could well be at the heart of the entire work: "Is the most political act an individual one, something that happens in the dark, in the quiet, when someone makes a particular decision that affects his immediate world?"

This is the question, he writes, that he asks via his song "Galveston Bay". The song is about a man who "With great difficulty and against his own grain…transcends his circumstances. He finds the strength and grace to save himself and the part of the world that he touches." To me, the answer is Yes. Individual, tough decisions that go unadvertised and unrecognized, but that have global impacts are a core component of real political activity and productivity.

Springsteen, the singer-songwriter, is already a political personality of sorts. Will he step into the electoral scenario himself? Does he prefer party politics? The answers to these questions, he probably needs to derive from widespread consultations.

He writes that he chooses to play the role of a benevolent dictator in the band. But unlike Trump, who seems to be under the impression that it's worth trying to run the presidency almost single-handedly, Springsteen would hopefully perform differently in purely political heels.

In the meantime, I think it would be worth building and expanding his international presence, primarily through his music, but also through his book.

Synthesizing Coincidences

In conclusion, Springsteen writes: "This, I presented as my long and noisy prayer, my magic trick. Hoping it would rock your very soul and then pass on, its spirit rendered, to be read, heard, sung and altered by you and your blood, that it might strengthen and help make sense of your story. Go tell it."

And this, my friends, is my cue to strum up my epic list of coincidences gleaned from Born to Run…to put observations that have amazed me, into creative perspective…perhaps bring them centre-stage…but in another publication, at another venue…one could keep you posted on this blog….

Well, there ended the edited extracts from the blog-series, but one picks up the baton for *Earth Republic*

While the blog-series was in progress, there was an announcement, by Springsteen, that he would make his Broadway debut (something that I've mentioned on the blog as it happened).

A Broadway debut, no doubt, is something that's planned days and months in advance, so one isn't making any wild claims of the articles having catalysed the show! (One the flip-side of that argument, is the position that even if one writes a little-read blog, it all depends on who's reading it, and that, one isn't exactly the expert on).

A few weeks later, there was the announcement that Springsteen was going to perform in Canada at the Invictus games- the sporting event for injured and 'disabled' war veterans. The one that Prince Harry initiated. Melania Trump was present, Obama was present.

Here's a sequential listing of some of the points in the book that I allowed to distract me away from the leading narrative, and that now land here, to make journeys of their own.

A reader might choose to treat the following paragraphs as a sort of gaming workbook. But any participatory moves need to be made in completely transparent, legal and ethical ways. Reporting back the results to the world would be perfect. With a premium for truth, non-violence, and human rights.

This is still non-fiction, with haystacks-full of one-straw-revolutions to clutch at, unless you're on a roll already, haha.

Disclaimer: The following paragraphs have very little to do with Bruce Springsteen!

The Small "a"

In the Foreword of Born to Run, Springsteen says that he counts himself "amongst those who 'lie' in service of the truth…artists with a small 'a.'"

What does it mean when one goes into the small case while referring to one's self, or that with which one identifies?

In some cultures, this would denote a certain self-effacing humility. A tinge of false humility in order to be approachable, or agreeable, or non-domineering, depending on what your area of art is.

Your profession as art; your hobby as art; your mission as art; just every-day being and creating as art.

But what about the practice of truth as art and existence? Where would you put tactful behaviours, manners, and diplomacy on the scale of truth versus lies?

To that extent, and to the extent of assuming that the mob's reality is reality: is the lie of the artist in the interest of every-day survival more justifiable than other peoples' disregard for ethics? Depends on what the artist is up to, really! Although one is personally meticulous about being truthful and honest.

The contours of artistic licence, if deliberately used as just an excuse to meet the mundane conveniences of the artist, cease to indemnify the artist from perpetrating all manner of falsehoods. Ergo: you can't use your identity as an artist to ride roughshod over other people's rights and truths.

That said, how many people sign off their names beginning with a small case, or defy grammar to write "i" instead of "I?" bruce instead of Bruce? Not an entire tsunami of folks, but quite a few people. And occasionally, perhaps everyone.

Not a very huge coincidence there, then, but enough to grab your attention to read the rest of the page (not that you weren't going to, of course). And this reference to a small 'a' is to be kept in mind for what it adds up to, coincidence-wise.

Shrewsbury

Alright, this is just a straw!

Springsteen mentions a Shrewsbury Club that was somewhere along the Jersey shore.

Shruti, that's my name, and friends sometimes call me shru (pronounced shrew). As a student, when asked how Shruti was pronounced, one used to say: Shru, like in the taming of the Shrew (in the Shakespearean play, The Taming of the Shrew, there's a feminist sort of character called Katherine. One used to play Katherine for auditions).

One's also been Princess Katherine (Kate) in Love's Labour's Lost.

As one tackles the never-ending world of misogyny through one's socio-political work, and writes fanciful paragraphs in solitary splendour (haha splendour, not sugar-free Splenda, ya), one switches on the telly to find that Catalonia of Spain votes for Independence. (I don't need to spelly out what's on the telly, right? Kat-alone-ya.)

And that a senior party colleague of mine closer home confirms that in Kashmir, when people want Azadi, (translated to Independence), all that most of them want is actually Constitutionally-valid autonomy. (I'll betcha they over-heard us at Fletcher, discussing love, actually, over bagels most of the time!)

But that was looong ago. So Catalonia- Kat-alone-ya. Now off to graft the papers on medicinal plants that oughtta include Stevia (there's a plant, I tell ya, it's been there for a long, long time. Along with the all-spice, I think, it was).

And a quick read-up on Shrewsbury cookies (famous in India in Pune, Maharashtra), led one to read more on the town of Shrewsbury.

Notable take-away for this piece: There was a King Stephen of England in the eleven-hundreds who laid siege on Shrewsbury Fort in the town of Shrewsbury. And managed to hold onto it for approx. two decades. Most of the age of the rule of Stephen was referred to as "the Anarchy."

I once had a professor, (RIP 1998), of Environmental Law, who was a Stephanian, and who'd written a book: From Anarchy to Utopia.

I think we're quite done with the anarchy bit for this circle of time. Time to string together the Utopia, to "re-arm Marxism" on our own terms, after figuring out what exactly that means.

Would help to read leading reviews of one hundred years of the October revolution in leading Indian magazines for this. I have a specific, current article in mind. But a workbook's not a workbook if I spell it all out in writing right here. That much about cookies for now.

Dementedly

Had absolutely no idea that other people spoke like this!

In Springsteen's world, there was an Upstage Club that was "all dementedly decorated by Tom himself."

A particular form of usage of the word 'demented' (or 'dementedly'), which meant no disrespect to those who suffered from dimensia or any other mental condition from which the word demented is derived.

But one's laid-back conversations would often talk of things and places and people as being demented. Demented was high appreciation.

In the interest of political correctness, and with age, and with the dispersal of the crowd that adapted to that bit of one's dialect, one doesn't really use such words and phrases much anymore.

But I must say, one can sometimes trace the influence of one's words and views through the way in which people in the world use language. Sometimes, it's unmistakeable.

One played Laura when another friend played Tom. The Glass Menagerie. One crack and it falls through. Kaafi demented. The crack of dawn of civilization as it shall be. As it never was. Or probably as it has always been. Science. Craft.

Formulae

When Bruce talks of The Pandemoneum Club on Route 35, this is the formula that he spells out, and associates with the place:

Woman + booze + man + booze + second man + booze = brawl

Most folks probably won't need to stagger far for the confirmation of this male chauvinistic-sounding theory. (That said, I'm not for prohibition).

But I'm on the point of the coincidence involved in using formulae of this kind in polite book-writing. (The formulae for viticulture and associated tribal livelihoods will have to discussed elsewhere).

Can't think of any precedent other than one's own commentary on Imran Khan's 2013 election campaign as viewed on the internet, that forms a part of this book (*Earth Republic*...specifying this here, despite the repetition from an earlier chapter, for the times when this essay might be used as a stand-alone document). When one fancifully wrote: BO – US + DEO = INK

Who else writes like that?! Four or five years later, (ie., now), I'd alter my formula a bit, bring myself centre-stage.

Cheers.

Timing

It's probably possible for trained mathematicians to brew an entire list of kinds of coincidences that exist in the world and in mathematics.

There's algebra, and something called calculus that plumbs the depths of all such synchronicities of numbers. And values attached to numbers, and their repetition, juggling, and muddling.

In life and art and music and poetry, and theatre, the timing of events and actions play quite a decisive role. (Even without going into an entire monologue on the related influences of astrology, human will, fate, and destiny in this context).

When Springsteen and his friends returned to New Jersey from a stint at the West Coast, he says their return was covered "like it was Odysseus's return to Ithaca", and then goes on to write about how they brought Steve (Van Zandt) back to the band.

"We timed it perfectly to have Steve setting up his equipment just as Little Vinnie came by to pick up his. Nice."

This regard for, and attention to timing is something that not only musicians and lyricists, but also politicians, would do well to emulate. Many do, and that's how you move the narrative forward effectively.

Provocative Criminal Intent...(déjà vu all over again)

In what's come to be a trademark mock-exaggerated style, Springsteen refers to an occasion when the band played longer than usual, and that this was looked upon by the authorities as being of "provocative criminal intent." The electricity was shut down: "Déjà vu", writes Springsteen, of these repetitive events, leading one to wonder whether there are any anecdotes of actual déjà vu that he might wish to relate, that are not only about repetition or nostalgia.

Springsteen or no Springsteen, we are free to discuss the judiciary, the legal system, the ingredients of what counts as provocative, and what doesn't, and who decides or asserts these things. I'd say the gender-parity on this discussion-front is tilted waaaay against single women.

As for Déjà vu, the intersections of psychology, physics and spirituality have been severally mapped. More approachable reading on the space-time conundrum would be most useful.

It's possible that sometimes, people who've read a book talk to themselves in everyday conversation, using words and phrases from books they've just read. It's possible that these are sequentially used. They may have no way of knowing whether or not the people they're talking to, have read the book. But if the listener does happen to read the book someday, then somewhat inexplicable sequences of conversation gather new meaning, and possibly, intent. This, I've observed, in a retrospective review of conversations that took place before I read this book.

Davey

There's a Davey Sancious who Bruce says "had pure musical genius and incredible stage presence." You get the drift.

"From now on, the buck would stop here, if I could make one"

First of all, this reminds me of the title of an unpublished book that was written by a distant relative who's no more. The book of wildlife stories for children was called The Elusive Buck and Other Stories. I didn't ever get to read the manuscript.

Then, there's the name of a famous television discussion show on a leading English news channel based out of India. The show's called The Buck Stops Here.

Springsteen says "the buck would stop here, if I could make one", about how he chose to run the Bruce Springsteen Band. After his band, Steel Mill, he says he "declared democracy dead." He reasons that if he was the one single-handedly doing everything, then he might as well "assume the power" as well.

One can see how such thoughts might cross the minds of business leaders, world leaders and village-heads, and holders of nuclear-button codes alike.

In such scenarios, however, it is in the interest of human survival, to ensure that there is always an even distribution, or balance, of power, be it the economy, or be it the world order.

"…on a car hood in a New York City parking lot. Done deal"

This is how Springsteen signed his set of contracts with Mike Appel.

I'm quite struck by the make-shift replacement for the old oak.

It has an appealing element of fearless urban nomadism.

But what resonates more with me, is the coincidence of the use of a bonnet for an important task: years ago, when a group of friends and acquaintances went to a South Delhi night-club (I can't remember which one), it also turned out to be the birthday of one of the fellow-revellers.

They probably either didn't allow cakes to be cut in the bar, or that probably just wasn't the plan. The cake-cutting was sprung on us at the parking lot. With no knife to be found, I produced an out-dated laminated identity card that I hadn't yet renewed at that time. Good enough, if politely irreverent, and served the purpose!

"… Danny…overstating his expenses and skimming off the top"

At this juncture of party history, I can only think of the need for replacing semi-redundant political leaders with fresh blood (pardon the reference to Dracula).

But truly, quite an energetic synchronicity scattered across the globe when you start counting young world leaders: Macron, Justin, Jacinda….

Lazy-eye

Springsteen mentions a girlfriend whom he once lived with for a while. "She was Italian, funny, a beatific tomboy, with just the hint of a lazy eye, and wore a pair of glasses that made me think of the wonders of the library."

One of my pet theories- well, not exactly theory, it would, at best, find shelf-space in the region of conspiracy theories, or just visualisations of scenarios, is- what if subtle channels of communication were being constantly crafted in the world, to keep entities connected, and all-round pressures even? And in such a way that those concerned would never really know, unless they had to.

And this is not about societies being inter-connected in general, nor about the collective knowledge or responses of groups of people or communities.

I'm talking more about specific links or connections, or trust-building that could be established between specific people prior to them meeting each other (if they do ever meet each other).

Heads of states that are prone to be in conflict, for example, or the chiefs of armies of states that are often in conflict with one another.

What if there were agencies or groups or global good samaritans who made it their business to use scientific methods to build trust between and amongst individuals?

This would involve the use of techniques similar to those that are used to train performing animals. The use of sounds, odours, flavours, language, colours, and the building of associations with each of these.

This tactic could be used, not only for trust-building, but also to manipulate behaviour.

Those who work passionately for the conservation of wild life, and support the rights of animals, even over the rights of human beings, are likely to know of these methods merely because of being interested in animal biology, the social habits and responses of animals, and the animal kingdom in general.

Sometimes, one appears to have a lazy eye in some photographs.

And I was happy to note that there was a television channel that used to have an on-screen reporter who had a lazy eye. It's high time that people with other perceived blemishes and scars and flaws be fielded equally on news reporting.

While some people make their best efforts to ensure that the modelling and film industry's definitions of beauty encompass all kinds of looks and colours of skin, it would be even easier for the news industry to pitch in and make its statements in the arena. Not only men, but also women with all kinds of 'facial flaws' (there's no such thing as a facial flaw), and other diverse portrayals, conditions and genders, ought to be main-streamed on-screen, and appear as presenters, readers, interviewers and reporters on a regular basis.

Whaddya think

The famous review of Springsteen that was written by Jon Landau (and perhaps, later, Jon was made famous because of his review of Springsteen). Jon was twenty-seven when he met Springsteen.

'Whaddya think' has apparently been a large part of their conversation ever since. Which, if you ask me, is not just a good, but a superb thing. Consultations. Opinions of others. The more the merrier, never mind the clichés.

People asking people for their opinions on things, and acting upon these is a coincidence one fervently wishes for the world to replicate before I can say abracadabra.

Talking of the number twenty-seven, in reverse order, the digits read seventy-two (obviously), which was the number of "tracks of rock 'n' roll overkill" that Springsteen and Davey worked with at 914 studios.

I'm sure people talk of overkills all the time, but I'm reminded of a brief verse I scribbled in late 1998, which read "cerebral thrill without the overkill." Brain tumour-kind-of-things, anyone?! And Happy Halloweeeeeeeeeeen! (This bit's being written on Halloween Eve, though the now-it's-now, now-it's-then annual fluctuations of Samhain might be closer to authentic witching powers).

Pizzas and Graduation

Bruce boycotted his school graduation because of a dress-code issue. He wandered around the city doing things like eating pizza instead.
How many pizza connections can you make? And why?

"...oddity...never hassled...."

Artsy coincidence here- might know someone whose name sounds like oddity, and whose delicatessen of stock words and phrases includes 'hassled'; 'never hassled', and on and on and on.

5th of January

Greetings from Asbury Park was released on the 5th of January, 1973. That's the birthday (as in, the exact date, year and all), of a dear friend who was with me at the Springsteen concert in 1988. AND, Springsteen's son, Sam Ryan Springsteen, was born on the 5th of January, 1994.

What a way to begin the year!

Identity Questions Became Prominent

When he was a child, Springsteen's household wasn't particularly political.

But he talks of how identity issues became "prominent" after his success, and that the solutions for these were to be found in the political arena.

Springsteen might have had the working class, race, religion and so on, on his mind when he wrote of identity issues.

But to me, the main connection to be made, today, between Identity and Prominence, is how to reorient humans to their identity in Nature. And how to honour all genders as a result: prominent nipples and all.

People from all strata of society have lost sight, and are unmindful of various natural processes on bodies, and thus possess little or no human sophistication in reacting to these in an informed way. Prominent nipples, for example. (Heard of the Free the Nipple movement?)

A small-town or village-rustic, or urban-clueless male, might get unwarrantedly frisky in the presence of a tribal woman in her traditional gear, or in the presence of an urban woman's semi-revealing party or everyday wardrobe.

I say unwarranted because women dress like this for comfort and maybe aesthetics-in-general.

Over-optimistic men are quick to imagine that the dressing is aimed at them.

Over-hawkish women are quick to imagine that you're dressing to provoke their boyfriends or husbands.

Either way, your right to be bra-free, comfortable, relaxed, strong, and cancer-free are being interfered with.

The right to privacy, and to exercise choices over how to dress is not restricted to spaces, but extends to an individual's rights anywhere.

In places where women being topless is an offence, the law needs to change.

Happy Halloween. Today's the 31st of October. Period.

…the liberating destruction of the Berlin Wall by the people of Germany

Freedom and Liberty. Revolutions happen for these goals, Constitutions get written in support of such aims.

There's all kinds of liberty and liberation.

I suppose these could be looked at in terms of degrees.

From freeing people physically from captivity and bondage, to the liberation of the soul from the human body, and everything in-between. Such as women's lib.

No, it's not a western or modern concept. The lingo and jargon might be. But that's just language. The essences remain the same. No problem is outdated until it's actually solved.

(Where does the interestingly-named Chinese People's Liberation Army stand in this discussion?!). We once sang a hymn: The World Stands in Need of Liberation, My Lord. No, this wasn't a petition before their Lordships of the Supreme Court! And, as far as I remember, Franciscan nuns were persecuted by the invading Chinese army in the previous century.

But that's history, I suppose.

Just like the fact that Vizag used to think of the Japanese as the prime enemy is history, because long, long ago, during the world wars, there was active news that Japan planned to bomb Vizag. That's history. The Japs fund projects all over Andhra, the PLA holds joint events with the Indians, the Americans are everywhere, including at places like a certain spaghetti restaurant, where the home-delivered food sometimes makes it to your dining table with a staple-pin in the grub- no stapled visa, just the stapled spaghetti! This has actually happened to me in 2017. The Italian premier was in the country yesterday, and still gliding about town, one would imagine.

Marquis

Bruce writes of a day when he was lounging at the Marquis hotel, "… an infamous LA crash house for wayward rockers." Quite reminds me of our post-college-year jaunts to the 32nd Milestone, one could summon up enough Halloween-Day grandiose to refer to it as a nocturnal prowling-ground for footloose and fancy-free inter-galactic sojourners (you had to walk in through the face of the Jedi). A-ha!

But talking of Forces of all kinds, Marquis, or Marquee reminds me of an European-style diamond ring that once belonged to my mum's ancestors. Not expensive, diamond-quality wise. Heritage-wise, of course, the sky is the limit. But the point one is making is: It's in the shape of an eye- the Third Eye? Or a part of an infinity loop? That's how Marquis rings are shaped. Everyone wears them now-a-days. Just like everything else. Except ceremonial sacred threads. These were ceremonially sashed across young boys of high castes, granting them permission to study the Hindu scriptures. These days, the caste-barrier is in the process of being demolished on this front, but not the gender-barrier. Who needs a sacred thread, anyway?

BUT a Marquis ring, and I've worn mine sparingly, at first, and quite frequently thereafter. Sometimes, one wore it on one's middle finger on one's right hand, because I think that was meant to be the finger for diamonds, astrologically speaking. Now, it fits on the index finger, so one uses it to point at people with, in an imperious way. Not! Or maybe sometimes. Just for effect. The King of Greece and his entourage were guests at the extended family's island and Palace on Chilika lake in the not-too-distant past. Maybe about a hundred years.

Historically, who exactly was the title of Marquis given to? Sounds gypsy-like to me for some reason. And maybe with some Islamic influence.

Back to Europe, Dracula, and the Dutch connection.

Connect up the islands cross the Bay of Bengal with the Chinese land-route to Europe, and the journey of the tarot. Don't forget where the ancient-ish port-town of Kalinga is located. Think Oriya-speaking empire, think all continents.

Specifically mentions that he hadn't been overseas at twenty-five

What a coincidence! I turned twenty-five and then went overseas for the first time. To the country of Bruce Springsteen. East Coast first.

Common Sense

Springsteen says that the caution with which he needed to approach a new set of contracts "seemed like common sense."

Now, brace yourselves, this is really stretching it! -I mean, common sense is a phrase that everyone uses. Let's not be all delusional here, and imagine that this echoes the stylistics of people we either know or don't know, or whom we share blog-design-themes-from-the-stock-of-themes with (the latter being the modern-day version of how the concept of gotras might have originated. Kidding.) And science help us if the OED attempts to define gotras, or forests, or anything else that the law needs to poke its nose into. To the uninitiated, I say: Just google it, I ought to do so too, just to know what exactly (it is).

Might as well talk about the Commonwealth of Nations. Now THAT bit of prosaic jigsaw-puzzling is bound to resonate with somebody's idea of high poetry. (And let's submit all our artworks for aesthetic trimming, while we're at it).

Ever written a poem and been told: But it doesn't mean anything? No? Good for you. Yes? Was the person watching the sound of music for the most part of their waking lives when they were in high school? Either way, has it made you churn out nice, neatly-tied-up lines of very readable verse? No? Congratulations. Yes? Well, try again.

There's a reason why normal's not normal, and why child rescue centres should and must exist as an option in society. Common sense according to who, exactly? Back to politics.

Gravitas

At one point, Springsteen makes this observation: "…along with 'gravitas,' our shows were always filled with fun." Ha! Gravitas! shows! fun! These days, Gravitas is the name of a news-discussion show on a newish news channel that interviews world leaders and other friends.

Meanwhile, if you happen to be a successful-at-quite-a-young-age politician, or lawyer, and happen to exhibit non-serious behaviour that doesn't quite behove your age, according to loyal perception-managers, you might wish to choose to finish off the grey temples with a good dose of aloofness and immensity. Once you're there, of course, you're free to get back to spraying purple or green or pink hair chalk on what's left of the tresses, but only on Halloween for now. (Gleeful reminder to stand right at the door with H-Day treats, no vinho this time round, please).

J.T.

Whoever names their canine JT? And takes it on a cross-continent tour?! Anyway, they didn't leave him behind. They made it a point to include man and beast on the return journey. Bruce, we're still talking about Bruce and the cross-continent drive.

Inclusive development and governance. Doesn't happen overnight. Calls for rounds and rounds of discussion, outreach, expertise, toning down, toning up, learning, unlearning, reaching for the stars.

If you actually do have a person in one of your circles, whose doggie is of the above nomenclature, you have a v-e-r-y spooky coincidence on your hands…enough to have to say ba to a ghost, and draft it to a Vietnamese restaurant on Harvard Square. Been there, done that. Long, long ago, and back to Halloween!

"…the slow way, sort of…"

The Boss says, of some of his life and music: "Finally, I surrendered to the inevitability of doing it the slow way, sort of."

The slow way - the marathon runner - slow food - the organic life… what meaning will all these terms take on in the century that's ahead of us?

The relativity of it all, and the centeredness of the instant.

"…yacht around the Mediterranean (who doesn't?) and private-plane myself between dental appointments"

Granted. Most don't. (Yacht around the Mediterranean like it's the friendly neighbourhood splash-pond), but more indentures than we know might plan their tours n beats around dental appointments.

I, for one, have found myself engrossed in a faintly memorable transatlantic conversation with a lady who was winging it to her fang-doctor across boundaries.

Creedence Clearwater Revival

Naaah, those are no coincidences, the CCR and their music are quite omnipresent…(But invite me to a book-discussion session via skype if you really wana know). (One isn't doddering yet, and in the very long run, there's always halloweeeeeeen).

"pilgrimage…Memphis Tennessee"

A driving-trip with its first halt at Elvis's birthplace, Memphis Tennessee. Typically referred to as a pilgrimage.

But catches one's attention because one is on the lookout for what to add to one's already existing pattern/s of chance-happenings with a pilgrimage-theme.

Pattern, because it's not just about pilgrimages. It's pilgrimage-plus. You see, over an expanse of decades, a weak signal of an emerging pattern of something plus something. It could even be something, plus something, plus something. If too many such gravitations of chance present themselves to you by way of observed events, then it's probably time to bung something into the test-tube yourself.

But this mention of a pilgrimage (the X factor), doesn't come with an associated Y factor on a first reading, at least.

Pilgrimage-wise, no doubt, there's an entire range of voyages that might count as being a pilgrimage. Including to Mars.

Or the whole set of coincidences could loop back, with half the properties missing from the last set, to draw in an added factor. So you have XY, XY, XY, X. Since there's only X, you could wonder, for an indefinite time, whether the last X will draw a Y and become an XY, or you could bring a Z into the slipstream of the X, and make it XZ, creating new patterns. How do you decide what Z will be? Perhaps there's an existing set of XZ, XZ, XZ floating around somewhere. Binding these would make a sort of linear equation, and a hardy new product. Somewhat like linear low-density poly-ethylene (How, and what little spurious gyan I have about LLDPE, will have to be gleaned from my Facebook archives, or might feature again in future writings. Hint: it's to do with door-to-door sales of swimming pools, a rat-a-tat precursor to door-to-door campaigning in years to come, Halloween trick or treating might make it to a Gen Next CV, who knows!)

Pepper your writing with enough mathematical-looking signs, and you could pass yourself off as a scientist sometime this century. In dead earnest.

My pilgrimage-plus observances could loop back to some Tennessee coincidences, and thus be drawn into the reality of theatrical happenings. (Read my piece on theatre to join these dots).

The Number Thirty-Four

Have you ever noticed any number that suddenly recurs, pops up at you all the time, out of the blue? That's another kind of coincidence (for lack of a better word, and at the cost of sounding repetitive).

Of late, I've found the number thirty-four presenting itself frequently before me in connection with my political work, and in other random contexts, so it struck me as significant (to me, and possibly to the party), that the number thirty-four gets mentioned more than once, and in totally varying contexts, in Born to Run, the autobiography. (Also, the book was published the year I turned forty-three, which is the reverse of thirty-four).

Slipstream

It might sound ridiculous to latch onto a word, and say it's been used before. I mean, isn't that what language is supposed to be about.

But I find slipstream quite an unusual word in regular conversation (unless you're an observatory full of scientists or a sailor or a pilot).

But not unusual enough to be odd if you were to hear it repeated about two or three times a decade. Unless it's a good idea to cram it into an emerging narrative. Which it is.

It was the name of a friend's film company, and fascinated by the concept, one wrote of 'slipstreams' in a short story about a river.

Cleveland, Ohio

Did you know that the inspiration for the title, Born to Run, was from the name of a script about a Cleveland, Ohio band? Not exactly an inspiration, but a lift-off.

The world's a big place, and so chances of people having heard of Cleveland, or having anything at all, to do with Cleveland, that they know of, are not too high. (America is not the centre of the universe, and all that).

When an average reader of English anywhere on the globe is asked what connections they can make, personally, with Cleveland, Ohio, they're not going to exceed one or two, if at all.

And these connections might be as random as me saying we once sang and recorded, on a recycled cassette (you could stick cello-tape on the two gaps along the edge of a pre-recorded cassette, and record live sound over it) and home tape recorder, the song Banks of the Ohio. Funaaaereal, to say the least.

Then there are the correspondences with Father Lawrence Ober (and/ or his team), a Jesuit priest and historian who'd travelled to India long ago, and knew many of our Orissa royals. Was based out of Cleveland, Ohio, when last corresponded with. Kept track of royal family lines and all, and apparently always said it was for a reason. Gathered lineage-related info in a non-scientific way (as far as I could tell), and probably managed an approximation of the real picture most of the time. I now have an entity by the name of Father Lawrence Ober of Cleveland, Ohio, on my Facebook list.

Reinterpreting

With all the revision of history that's flying around these days, one might as well flag the fact that even Springsteen talks about his own reinterpretation of Born in the USA.

There is tonnes being debated, these days, on historic revisionism. Governments and political parties are accused of doing this to suit their ideologies and priorities. Every point of view has its own version of interpreting history. Subjectivity tends to creep in, even in the magnification or ignoring of facts. The most obvious and evident examples of this are usually to do with disputed lands and monuments. Invariably, there is a religious connect. The modern-day row is then all about what to write in the history text books, who will write the history text books, and so on.

As is commonly understood and stated, the news is often described as the first draft of written history. The evident corporatization of News, and of agenda-driven news by a few controllers has now made way for a more democratic aggregator of all news: the internet itself. Whoever has access, and has a view, can put it out there somewhere. Digital divide or no digital divide, this is debatably a much more democratic way to define reality than the world has ever had access to in the known past.

With this realization and tool in peoples' hands, another obvious outcome is what we already see happening before us: the reinterpretation of the past, using the facilities of the present.

In the world of literary academia, interpreting and reinterpreting writings that already exist is the norm. What the writer intended is but a fraction of what is relevant. It would be elitist to assume (even for politeness' sake), that all this is obvious to people, and that nothing new is being said.

Other than writing about the reinterpretation of his song, Bruce goes into flash-back mode, talking about Steve: "Looking back, I think Steve would agree that it didn't have to be that way. We could've done it all, but we weren't the same people then that we are today…What we did have was a lot of passion, transferred emotion and misunderstanding." Clearly, the human race is capable of introspection. And of quoting (deliberately or otherwise), from the soundtracks of television soaps in its autobiographies. No no, not making enemies here, only friends. Ever tried dancing like the lady who was pulled onto the stage in the Springsteen music-video?!

Maureen

When you live in (an albeit secular) Hindu Majority state, then you don't come across as many people with Christian names as the world would otherwise expect. Not even if you've been to Catholic-run schools.

I studied, for a few months (almost a year), at St. Joseph's Convent, Visakhapatnam (nursery and kindergarten), before Mater Dei Convent, run by the FMM at Delhi. At St. Joseph's, Vizag, there was a teacher called Maureen.

My Goan friends in Delhi had a Goan friend back home in Goa, whose name was Maureen (and had a sister named Shampoo?!). (As children of politicians from various parts of the country, we used to talk to each other a lot about our home states. People, places, local issues. Environmental degradation was a major theme of our conversation, to put things into grandiose perspective).

My mother volunteers, annually, for a charity event that's a part of the Delhi Commonwealth Women's Association. One of the main co-ordinators of the stamps and treasure-trove stall that's somewhat like a garage sale, with the proceeds going for free medicines for the underprivileged, is a lady named Maureen. Recycling of products, environmentalism of sorts.

One learns, from Born to Run, that Steve Van Zandt (described elsewhere in the book as 'an early country-rock acolyte, mastering the Byrds' and Youngbloods' repertoire'), is married to a lady named Maureen! This, one realises while reading about the trio's attempted trip to Disneyland. After they boycott it because of dress-code hassles, Steve fumes on about the Constitution, the Bill of Rights, he might as well have made a reference in his rant, to the evolving case-law in Rule of Law countries, on the Right to Privacy aspect of bandana-wearing to wherever-the-heck people want to wear bandanas to.

All just a jumble of unrelated facts, but perfect sculpting-material for a writer, or a poet, or an imaginer and creator of reality! But only for a good and truthful and creative, and, I suppose, charitable cause. (The iffiness in the last bit of what's been said is more to do with the concept of charity interfering occasionally with the concept of rights, than anything else, something that's been dealt with elsewhere in *Earth Republic*).

Benny

Of a time when they were at the IB Club, Bruce writes that they were on their third lead singer. Quite mysteriously (and unlike anywhere else in the book), Springsteen says: I'll call him "Benny." Errrr, why?? Memory-loss? Confidentiality?

Couldn't be because my cousin in the US, when he was a kid, thought people were calling someone Benny (which is what the Oriya word for aunt's husband sounds like). Too much of a melee of disjointed ideas, let's go, let's go!

Twenty Questions

Springsteen married his first wife, Julianne Phillips, in Oregon. Lovely state, Oregon…been there for an international conference on Land, Air, Water Law…about twenty years ago…and even longer ago than that, an aunt's husband studied there. Years later, they had a pet canine named Julie in India.

Twenty questions is the name of a game. The one where you think of a person. And others can ask you up to twenty questions, to which there can only be Yes or No answers, for people to guess who it was, that you'd thought of.

It's a power-cut-time activity if you're in a rural area. Or it could be a zero-in-on-whom-to-make-the-next-PoTUS or PM activity if you want to send out feelers and/or make decisions (as the general delusional public, of course).

But I've had guests come up to me at parties, and ask me if I know to play twenty questions.

Surely, there are better opening lines for conversations. But there might not be better carrots to dangle than prime-ministership!

Denver, Colorado

My penpal was from Colorado. My mom's penpal, Pamela Anderson (not from Baywatch, that was later), was from Denver, Colorado.

I visited and wrote about environmental organizations in the Bay Area, including one supported by John Denver (known, best, in India for his song Country Roads, Take Me Home, but I also liked the number Rocky Mountain High, Colorado). I'm talking about almost twenty years ago.

Springsteen performed at Denver, Colorado's Mile High Stadium. So???

And Bruce Springsteen sang Promised Land when he was on a political campaign with Obama in Cleveland.

Immortality and Walking Alongside Your Own Mortal Self

Some of the most profound paragraphs in Born to Run, to me, are the ones that give us insights to Tunnel of Love.

There is a reflection of views where ideas of immortality and earthly missions and associations fade away in the presence of the inward gaze. A staring into the mirror, and echoes of lines from another song by another singer, "can music save a mortal soul" float into the ambience.

That said, when you surround yourself with the splendour of solitude, it is your mortal self, or its substitute, that is likely to resume its strides alongside your path. Notionally, in any event.

The Tunnel of Love tour morphed, as Bruce puts it, to Amnesty International's 'Human Rights Now' tour.

30th of December

I might've said this before, but I'll say it again: That's my birthday, and Springsteen's daughter, Jessica, the equestrian champion's birthday almost twenty years later, and the date of the formation of the USSR many, many years ago. And my uncle's birthday. So now what?

Are there groups and organizations that talk and think like this? For lack of any other conditionings, probably.

That would be a civilization's cultural impasse of a kind.

Peoples who opt to be apparently listless.

Or it could be the meticulously attained un-grooving of responses via exercises that are geared towards unleashing disruptive influences onto crystalized thought-energies.

1972; 1998; 1999; Not Quite Fish or Fowl

1998 was when Springsteen got news of his induction into the rock 'n' roll hall of fame. That's the year I was in the US for a few months, and, if you google the year for world events, there'll be world events of 1998 to read about.

This was twenty-five years after he signed on for a recording (in 1972, the year of my birth is mentioned), as a solo artist, to create something that "was not quite fish nor quite fowl."

As far as the etymology of the not-fish, not-fowl allusion goes, there's a reference, in Indian mythology, to the ten Avataars (reincarnations) of Lord Vishnu, the Preserver, who, in turn, forms a part of the divine trinity of Brahma, Vishnu, Shiva (Creator, Preserver, Destroyer). The Avataar myths are associated with the concepts of creation and destruction, brought about in order to tackle evil forces. The man-lion avataar was neither fish nor fowl.

These sagas have been variously interpreted over time. It is a tradition of reinvention, and of evolution. The scope of these legends span space, time, the universe, and also the inner-scape of the individual.

The human being in the mythology of the Ramayana, Lord Ram, was said to be an avataar of Vishnu. And the human being, Lord Krishna, in the mythology of the Mahabharata, was said to be a later incarnation of Vishnu.

The victory of good over evil has multiple dimensions, including the environmentalism and power-equations that are the subject-matter of literature across cultures. Contemporary renditions of these themes speak to us through the pages of books like the Trilogy of the Lord of the Rings, and through films like Avatar.

I suppose Avatar (one of the few films I've watched), has universal appeal, and everyone else can also relate to characters, conversations and concerns that 3-D their way to your apple juice and freezing reclining seat if you're the last viewer that the film seems to have waited for in an empty hall.

Springsteen was formally inducted into the R&R Hall of Fame in March, 1999. Around the same time that I started making rare solo appearances before judges of the Supreme Court.

The Supreme Court of India has often led the way for inclusive growth, and for sustainable development. As has the Indian Parliament.

While a balance of all kinds of global forces might have hinged around India in the past, I think it is now evident that India has the opportunity to step centre-stage and call some critical shots.

Aspects of continuity in governance from the UPA to the BJP-led government now have demonstrated, yet again, that democracy is firmly rooted in India.

The trick, however, is to keep it so.

A sharp eye on events in the neighbourhood is advised.

It did not help, for example, for Modi to announce that he wanted to send back the Rohingya Muslims, who had taken refuge in India almost a decade ago, at exactly the same time when Aung San's government was allowing the persecution of Rohingyas in Burma.

This, if you ask me, created an enabling psychological atmosphere in favour of the persecutors. I did mention this on social media, and I think such traces of the subtle impact of the powers-that-be need to be reined in as and when detected or reasonably forseen. Ditto for nuclear.

The Grand Instrument

Bruce reaches a juncture of his career when he feels the need for a "grand instrument and more", to maximise his output. For him, the answer was the E Street Band.

Taking stock of their career moves, and reviewing the trajectory of their output and acting upon it, is an exercise that is today more a part of people's work ethic than there was scope for in the past.

In a vastly populated society, one uses all sorts of markers to aid one's memory to remember or distinguish people by. In a conversation, you'd say, for example: who? the doctor? Or oooh the lawyer, or the person who wins tennis trophies, or the person who broke their leg.

There was a time when people would also say: ohh, that person who changed their job? or oooh, that person who switched companies? See what I mean?

Well, every bout of updating brings with it, its unique solutions. And just like Springsteen needed the E Street Band in clearly orchestrated attendance, I think one could do with a clear-cut set of assigned party colleagues at the national level to add the correct spin to the work one's been punching into the political landscape since the previous century.

I do believe that the party has a global mission that dovetails with its national duties. Time will tell.

The Super Bowl

Bruce played at the Super Bowl, it seems to have been a superb show.

Let's get into just the phonetics now.

In India, you might find folks pronouncing 'bowl' as baaool. This is also how Baul is pronounced. (with reference to the Baul folk singers of Bengal).

In Oriya (or rather, in an Oriya-English mishmash), when people ramble on and on and on in a stream-of-consciousness kinda way, they're said to be bauleeing.

As far as the environmental water-conservation angle goes, in parts of north India, there were, historically, large water-tanks with stepwells known as Baulees. Some of these are considered to be heritage constructions. Central Delhi has one, and it's been the site for adventurous explorers in the past, and the subject-matter of many Sunday writings on the city.

There's more to be read and discovered about the Bauls and the supernatural quality of their music.

… Rambles while it might still be Halloween on some invisible plane in the slipstream of our planet.

CHAPTER V

AND EACH MUST PLAY
A PART OR TWO: THEATRE

When I first heard of Donald Trump, years ago, it was only in the context of the Trump Taj. Some sort of hotel or resort or entertainment centre somewhere in the US. I remember because some folks had visited it, and it stuck in my mind.

Anyway, thereafter, one's caught glimpses of Tump-related news in India, mostly from the glossy pages of newspapers (what Khushwant Singh, in his inimitable style referred to as: Oh, those colourful pages that nobody reads!)…this was when a small team of three of us girls from Mater Dei school went to interview him in the 1980s for an article called Celebrity Vignettes that was a part of a supplement that was prepared by our school for a leading daily newspaper in India. Each school got a turn to bring out this supplement as a part of a Newspaper-in-Education project. The New Delhi celebrities whom we interviewed all said they'd elect Mother Theresa as the Personality of the Year.

Frankly, one might have actually read those Trump-related snippets on main news pages, or business pages…that's how the media has grown over the years here…call it public relations, call it the corporatization of news, call it changing times.

Alarmingly, the case for 'changing times' seems to be more like it. I mean, this IS the news now! We have a US president who was, apparently, on some reality TV show that made him famous in his country. And maybe in other countries. By now, everyone seems to know who he is, almost. They've probably hung out with him more in parts of India than we realize. Because of some business interests. I'm just guessing.

And by the way, one is not, in a blanket-sense, alarmed by changing times in general. That would be Resistance To Change. Of which one is not guilty. (Heh heh, certainly not in those few weeks of demonetization… eeek, pardon the totally faltoo fatta. Regarding change).

Obviously, a balance is struck, with all things, change-wise. There are core values that might evolve gradually over time. This includes non-negotiables (such as values of truth, non-violence and so on).

When I say evolves, it is not code for Oh! Now let's all support corruption with all our might. It's more on the lines of thinking that the phenomenon of corruption has grey areas that need to be tackled in a multi-pronged, phased manner, while continuing to follow and build a brand of politics that shuns corruption (and, of course, violence…defence forces are supposed to be just that: defence forces. They're not there to inflict uncalled-for violence, and they won't).

So, does all this make democracy a charade?

Awards like the Oscars and Filmfare awards are restricted to the worlds of organized entertainment. In politics, there is, of course, Drama with a capital D.

From the kinds of sweeping, arm-waving gestures of NT Rama Rao, to the acoustic wonders of YSR's speeches: when we accorded him the credit on behalf of our government and teams, for having introduced the door-step ambulance service, for which you need to dial 108 (a mystic number, by the way), he used to mimic the siren-sound of the ambulance. So the speech would go: you know the ambulance-service that we have introduced, the 108 service, whenever you've had a health emergency, all you've needed to do was to dial 108, and wooooooooun, wooooounm weeeeeeeein…(claps from crowd). There's been dramatics.

Then there've been props and costumes and theatre-effects. I think even the good, stoic, stolid Prime Minister, Dr. Manmohan Singh, has donned all manner of colourful ceremonial garb of some north-eastern state-or-the-other while visiting those areas. (Disclaimer: It's really uncool and politically incorrect to say some north-east-state-or-the-other…this is how that entire region gets clubbed, as a bunch of people away from Mainland India, with people not being able to differentiate one north-eastern state from the other). But to counter that, we must also realise that it's equally shoddy when people refer to everyone from the diverse South of the Vindhyas as Madrasis. And then the South sometimes thinks of the entire north as Punjabis. That said, people are not really that ignorant. Cuisines are identified, and music, and art and craft, and drama. Not only because of text books, or exhibitions, or cultural festivals. In India, we are free to move about in any part of the country, and we do so. Pilgrimages account for mass tourism within the country.

People know people, people have relatives, people go on pilgrimages, people get transferred from place to place. All this is a part of our unity in diversity. And then, of course, there's The Internet these days.

The forum that dispenses much of this diversity is also the Small Screen. Hindi and English. Regional-language channels tend to showcase more of their own region's culture while talking to their own audiences.

Theatre itself has innumerable moorings in India. From the Marathi *Tamaashaas*, to modern-day *Nukkad Nataks* (or street plays), to dance forms that over-lap with theatre, such as the *Chou* of Orissa, and the martial-art dance-from of *Kalaripattu* of Kerala, the many *Ramlilas* all over the country that enact scenes from Indian mythology from the story of Lord Ram, that includes the burning of the effigy of a ten-headed personality, Ravan, to Telugu *Kalajathras* and *Burrakathas* with socio-political commentaries and satires in Andhra Pradesh and Telangana, to *Dastaan Goi*, the Urdu art of story-telling.

The caravan is endless. Artistes used to perform poetry and narrate stories at the courts of kings, and dancers used to dance at temples.

Folk dances and songs, however, are intrinsically participatory in nature, and do not belong to the realm of performance. This is my view.

Other than the use of theatrical props (sword being brandished and waved around to commemorate the festival of the Goddess), and costumes and performance-techniques on stage and screen, there is, of course, the very substance of what goes on by way of political activity. Ranging from suspense-filled, to tragic, to twists-in-tales, to the ridiculous.

And then there's conjured reality. The repetition of an idea or thought reinforcing peoples' beliefs that this or that must actually be the case; the momentum and matter gathered by rumour-machines; the revisionism; the Mind Games.

Compare this to the world of Reality Theatre, and the penumbras over-shadow all that is or was.

As with the concerns of political issues and processes, so with reality theatre: the cautionary finger points towards questions of ethics.

Where does one draw the line? Aren't the performers bound to reveal the design and scope of their work to their audiences? Sometimes, it's obvious to the viewer. Like when flash mobs break into dance at public places.

But if you're staging a ticketless-traveller-caught-on-a-bus kind of scenario, or a women's effort to reclaim public spaces kind of scenario, do you reveal to the public, the fact that you're just performers? If yes, when?

If it's a pre-announced thing, then it takes away from the meaning of reality theatre. It's a fine art to be able to ascertain exactly when to unveil, to the ambient crowd, the fact that they've been witness to, or even participants, of reality theatre!

In a sense, people from the worlds of news-reporting, history-writing and advertising are the script-writers of reality.

With the advent of the internet, the democratization of these functions has placed magic wands in the hands of every net-nomad, netizen or even occasional user of the band widths.

It wouldn't be delusional at all, for an individual to attempt to mould reality, or to shape and re-shape narratives of bygone, running and future yugas and realms.

Life as theatre…the lyrics of an Elvis Presley number quote from the bard's works, underlining the hypothesis that the world's a stage, where each must play a part.

But if all the world's a stage, what's the point of reality theatre, or even just theatre? Is theatre more authentic than reality?!

Talking of Elvis, Mexico's been making news and catching the world's attention quite a bit, lately. His Fun in Acapulco album, the US had almost extinguished from its memory, until one went from music-shop-to-music-shop, Virgin Records included, from time zone to time zone, asking for the album. It couldn't be located.

The story's quite different today. Perhaps that's why the Reagan look-alike was sitting next to me on one of my journeys, and why one coincidentally found one's self at an urban library-counter around the time Nancy Reagan passed away last year (the Reagan couple are buried at the Reagan library, something everyone might not be well-informed enough to know), which also coincided with some benign rocket-or-the-other being launched off the same eastern Indian coast-line where one was swan-songing the I-couldve-sworn-it-was-bubbly-and-not-sparkling-wine with (did the papers say the rocket was called K4?).

By the way, our party expects us not to drink. And to say we abstain from alcohol. I have views on that, as far as exoticising, regularising and marketing home-made tharra and other harmless victuals are concerned.

Not banning, but appropriate restraint when and where required, are the hallmarks of human achievement, as far as I'm concerned. And tribal communities do have socio-cultural arguments as well. Anyway, one must be very competitive, politically, because of which the degree of abstention has been very high, indeed. One hundred percent, lately. Flavoured chocolates don't really count.

One notices elements of things akin to theatre exercises on certain everyday platforms of community interaction: discussion fora on news channels. With enhanced connectivity and inter-connectedness, even television-discussants seem to be intuitively indulging in multi-layered conversations.

The entire television-screen-space sometimes resembles what's come to be known as a giant echo-chamber. And when it's not an echo-chamber, there are more nuanced ways people have found, of indirectly referring to people, places, things and events.

The use of the catch phrases of specific people, to create presences for them in absentia in an ongoing debate. Not just catch phrases, but also buzz words that are of temporal relevance (for example, a word or phrase that might be prominent on a person's list of tweets or recent posts). The repetition (and relay) of a distinguishable gesture by a person, or a tone of voice.

These, one imagines, inter-mingle with the many-fangled and open-ended toolkit of modern methods of surveillance.

So, for example, if people don't really know each other, but happen to be on the same social or work-related circuit, they might all discuss a topic, and usher into the conversation, the pet phrases of someone they happen to know in common.

More excitingly (or ominously, depending on how close to Armageddon you're prone to think we are), the innuendo/indirect references and covert surveillance connect: If a whole bunch of very well informed people (euphemism), happen to have chanced upon some bits of conversation between people, and if they are not really in a position to admit or reveal that they've come across these conversations, and these people might not even know each other, they've just got whatever they have from some grapevine, then they might still subtly acknowledge, in the course of a conversation (or overheard conversation), (or television panel discussion), the fact that they are all privy to the same nugget of information or rumour (or have common friends, even if that seems absurd).

This, to me, is an exquisite example of reality theatre playing itself out sans script, sans director, but fully loaded with carefully-honed sleight-of-conversation techniques.

If a bystander (or couch potato) manages to cotton on to enough of these references, there are enough floating around to make one believe that one might be snowed into some sort of coup! Just in time, to remind one's self again, that it's a giant echo chamber out there, out there.

But if this is, indeed, the state of the art of reality, then one might choose to muddle it with a dash of historical revisionism of one's own! Even if for fleeting turn-of-the-page conjecture. Alright, not quite, just underplaying the grandest idea of the millennium. And don't confuse grandest with most astounding, or cleverest or worthiest…just grandest, non-opulently so.

Well, since perception dictates much of reality, I must register, here, that I do, in fact, totally have my wits about me. One does realise that if one aligns one's perception to one's own self as being the centre of all things, the thought or idea that appeals to one's self the most at a given point of time is likely to be more magnified in one's domains of existence than in anyone else's. One might also be prone to believing that All Things Are Connected. Well, yes, by one's own cognition, if by nothing else, wouldn't you say?

So that's the game to play now. Not exactly game, not thought-experiment…I think strategists use the term speculative scenarios.

Some speculative scenarios to use the past to steer the future. From my own motley bundle of experiences from the world of theatre. I don't think I just wrote motley to be ingratiatingly self-disparaging (the times for such techniques that once had me have flown their utility in these woods), I think the word motley came to mind at the speed of some undiscovered energy, because one of the first skits (or semblance of a skit) that I ever acted in, was adapted from a short story from a school text-book. (It might have been The Radiant Reader), called The Barmecide's Feast. And the character, Shackaback, carried a motley-looking bundle as a prop. We must have been about ten years old. I was the doorman. This was a skit we enacted at home for a few kids, friends from the neighbourhood. The audience was in splits, and someone even grabbed the bananas from the barmecide's feast before they split, possibly before the great play was over. That's probably why it's useful to have curtains when you stage a play. So that the groundlings know what's not their cue! One might argue that it could be thought of as a rendition of supper theatre, or reality theatre, or audience running onto the cricket-pitch and fielding the props in the days of no flashing third umpire. Let the theatre unfold!

The idea is to scrutinize all one's theatre-related feats (of the kind mentioned above, and ones infused with more formality), and look at the over-laps with reality theatre, if any, and stretch it from there.

Enough to blow a bubble from whatever chewing-gum Obama was chewing at our Republic Day parade a few years ago. WHAT WAS HE THINKING? Is it average ceremonial behaviour to sit chewing gum, when you're the chief guest of a country, and are viewing the march-past and cultural and defence pageantry? Did it have anything to do with the late Mr. Shadow (labrador of labradors), having had the mark of the chewing-gum on his elbow? Or the fact that my vilpine (of the village, a politically incorrect-sounding term I've just coined, because it makes animals out of people, even if just party-animals), (as opposed to vulpine of ouuuuuum-chanting fame) stock of pink centre-fresh chewing gum was freshly opened, and on the table when Obama visited Modi? (During which time I was rehearsing the part of semi-retired world leader). I'm so struck by the coincidence (or maybe I don't actually chew much gum this century), the said candy's still in the fridge-door. So poetically connected, makes me sound like I'm swimming up-river, courting the CIA, KGB, and everyone else that there is to court in my wake! But the world has really shrunk. All these things are close to nothing anymore. And aum is the seed of the Gayatri Mantra, and breath is what aum is made of.

Cut to Curtains. An inter-school dramatics competition that our school participated in. One acted as Laura in Tennessee Williams' The Glass Menagerie. It was staged at the Gandhi Memorial Hall (Pyarelal Bhavan), named after Mahatma Gandhi, at New Delhi.

Lo and behold, just a few years later, Hollywood came out with the movie. By then, we were in college, and I had spent days rehearsing for the same play, but as a different character. As Amanda, the mother of Laura, but we ended up not being able to perform it, because that year, there was the Mandal agitation, and the Rajpal Memorial One Act Play Competition conducted by the Shakespeare Society of St. Stephen's College, directed by students, didn't take place after all.

The next year, when it did take place, another college staged The Glass Menagerie, and my school-mate who'd played Amanda when I played Laura at the Gandhi Auditorium, played Amanda again while representing her college. My college yearbook jogs my memory, and I recall that we had an exchange student, Amanda, which, I'm sure is a very popular name, just like Laura is, and made more famous by a US first lady in the succeeding years.

In our sophomore year, one directed and acted in the play Knightsbridge. I'll have to surf for the script, but I think the character I played there was Muriel. The play had four characters, and not too many frills. However, one effect that I quite liked, and remember to this day, was the introductory music. Pointed out by a helpful senior, the number Knightsbridge, from the music of the Rolling Stones, created just the right ambience to contextualize the otherwise non-committal costumes and sets. We were up against another power-packed, multi-talented performance of the play Passion, Poison and Petrifaction (PPP). There we other plays, but PPP won the Rajpal that year. Knightsbridge came second, and was good to go to other fests, of which the most fun enactment was at IIT Delhi, at their festival, Rendezvous.

More than two decades later, PPP, to me, has almost ceased to denote high-voltage dramas from the yesteryear, and mainly brings to mind, the concept of Public Private Partnership (PPP) that has wound its way into our system of governance and administration. In fact, a few years ago, at a private dinner party in New Delhi hosted by one of my batchmates who'd been a star performer at the PPP play (nothing to do with the name of a political party across the border) in the early 1990s, we found ourselves somewhere between 2012 and 2014, discussing the role of the private sector and the government in the field of accessible health-care, generic medicines, and maybe even intellectual property rights. One would like to believe that such discussions have had a global resonance. The Press Trust of India (PTI) puts out the India-feeds (again, nothing to do with a squeaky-clean political party from across the border).

After PPP came LLL. Love's Labour's Lost. A comedy by Shakespeare, where I played Katherine, one of the four princesses in the play. For the audition, one did a bit from the lines of another Kate, the one from The Taming of the Shrew. Around the time of the LLL auditions, I remember that we had dinner-guests at home (16 North Avenue, New Delhi), among whom was a thespian from the days of when Miranda House used to participate in Shakespearean plays. (From a time when Stephen's had no women students). A few minutes of dinnertime tutoring added to the Oscar-worthiness of the theatre workshops that had been the run-up to the play, and drove the nano or the reva of the Kate-cart a long way! Revealed: a green ride, a green stride, and you may be jogging whilst your boots are green (that just explains the square green boots that were donned in real life in time to come)!

These were important productions, culturally speaking. It was significant to specify to the world, from brick-lined, Macaulay-inspired bastions of brown saahibs, that India and the rest of the world was going to be calling the shots for the English language, as much as anyone else was.

The princesses wore culottes, the princes, bike shorts, and the village belle, a ghagra-choli.

However, those with accents closest to the queen's english were still being cast in the roles of characters who belonged to high society, and those with assorted regional-language or other foreign accents were given the roles of the working class.

The same logic for accents played out the next year for the comedy, The Merry Wives of Windsor. One played Mrs. Page (one of the two merry wives of Windsor). This production had well-researched period costumes. One made so bold as to write a play-review for a leading newspaper, after the production was done! One has come a long way from that kind of self-promotion, to conducting what one strongly believes to be decades of globally impactful work in the areas of policy-making, planning and governance without a squeak of a media campaign.

Talking to a small bunch of people on Facebook, and posting occasionally on one's not-advertised blog doesn't really count as a media campaign, or as a brag.

The promptings for the writing of this book are as much the intention to document history, as to accelerate creative exercises in the world of theatre, and to rattle, or throw open the doors of ethical reality theatre, planet earth, aluminium diet-coke in hand and all, to begin with.

A consumer's a consumer, if you want to solve the Water Justice issue, or the Illegal Bauxite Mining issue, you need to, and must, tackle it at the law-and-policy-making-level, and simultaneously make sure there's proper, well-monitored implementation, with no corruption in the system.

Enter the world of Theatre-in-Education. From the antiseptic and hallowed corridors of Stephen's, where we attended the festivals of all other colleges, but kept our own festival, Harmony, a private affair, one space-trekked to the other end of the spectrum to the post-graduate college further down the road: The Faculty of Law. There, to acquire an altered wardrobe, hours of experience at hanging out and chit-chatting with the inmates of Tihar Jail, the high-security prison, after getting there on crowded Delhi Transport Corporation public busses, attending classes in halls that could pack in an entire booth of voters, playing table-tennis tournaments between classes, sitting on the wall drinking chai, tucking in bread pakoras, and hopping onto pillion seats of bikes to make it to the Centre for Environmental Law, (CEL) WWF-India on time for an evening diploma course on environmental law, often taking the Filmistan route.

Spending hours at Tihar Jail with the city's most dreaded lumpen elements and worse was definitely a rite of political passage. Stamp-marks on one's arm, to enter places, one was more familiar with, as tokens for entering discotheques or night-clubs. So this was high adventure, and if you've done this, you don't require to be personally incarcerated again in order to be in the reckoning for earth president or whatever political post it is, that you aspire for.

One breathed in clouds-full of polluted pre-CNG air back in the mid-1990s. Enough to prompt us to want to participate in the CEL's theatre-in-education project as a grand finale to our dip-in-e-law (at a time when e obviously meant environmental, and not electronic). Haha! Some tot might think I'm an electrical engineer.

So the play that we staged at the Godrej auditorium, WWF India, was called Trinity. We formulated the script for the play that was a musical in parts, through a series of workshops. One played a double role of Lord Shiva, and a Tantrik. Other members of the legal community (I wish they'd all stop saying legal fraternity, that's a bit male-biased), played the roles of Lords Vishnu and Brahma. There were characters from mythology, characters who represented community stake-holders, and trees and beasts and so on. The director's theatre company was called Brechtian Mirror.

That's probably the first time that I've stood on a bench, and boomed out my lines in shudh Hindi (unless you want to count the times when one was four years old, standing on a moodah, shouting vote for congress, egged on by post-emergency election-time loudspeakers at Vizag).

The audience at the Trinity play included a judge of the Supreme Court known for his environment-friendly stances, at least one MP, bureaucrats, and many others.

My friends who'd come to watch it were thoroughly entertained (both by my recital of Hindi lines, and by my Lord Shiva costume that had been hired from Chandini Chowk), and, I'm sure, the rest of the play, and said they'd been rolling all over the floor, laughing.

I do suspect that these are the origins of the internet acronym, ROFL and RAOFL. In the early days of the internet in India, those who had access to the worldwide web did, I imagine, have a brand-new tool with which to chisel the language of the future at their finger-tips.

My friends, batchmates, and lecturers who acted in the play that culminated in the taking of a global oath have all surged ahead on their various career paths, many of them igniting their routes with the glow of justice and equity, from what I gather and observe. This was the third batch.

Unfortunately, the Director of the programme, Dr. Chhatrapati Singh, passed away two years later. I got news of his demise as I was about to sit in on my first class on International Environmental Law in California, taught by Dr. Armin Rosencranz of Stanford University, whom I had first come in contact with when he was invited to deliver a guest lecture at the CEL in New Delhi in 1995. Thereafter, one's attended Armin's family Passover Feast at Palo Alto almost twenty years ago, and returned to India, a young lawyer who sought pass-overs before Supreme Court benches, and legal-eagled some of the conversations on town planning, bridges, fly-overs et al. But that, my friends, was in the previous century. It takes more to regale dinner-guests than Passover tales, so the height of artistic discovery as we converse, and some of the Halloween subtext, is that the ghostly apparitions of the theatre of transparency and justice need to not only make their presence felt, but start making appearances (pow-wow, and a hammer and a hair-cut…also: note to the green room: judges stopped wearing those curly-lock-wigs long ago in India). Plus, make recourse to the law accessible to all.

While in the USA as a visiting environmental law fellow from India, I didn't really act in any formal plays, but did have the opportunity to attend court-room hearings, and watch and kind of participate in a cross-section of types of theatrical performances: Supper theatre at Yale, by the Yale School of Drama (then again, if you're the audience at supper theatre, it's very tempting, twenty years later, to merge the lines between reality and enactment, and intuit an ongoing reality play at a grand scale of space and time into existence!); a high-school production of Shakespeare's King Lear at Marin, northern California; skits during a cultural evening by south-asian students at San Francisco; passed by a street play at the Boston Commons on the east coast, and halted momentarily to watch it; a play on the history of the persecution of women at the Witch Dungeon, a museum at Salem, MA; the broadway musical, Forever Tango at the Marriott theatre at New York City; and an enactment of a bit of history at the Boston Tea Party Ship and Museum – participatory in a touristic sort of way. The audience had prompts for when to shout "dump the tea into the sea!" - and did so, and other clownish stuff, with great gusto.

People playing the guitar and swaying at BART stations, and live bands at bars and restaurants, one doesn't have detailed records of. One has delved into an ancient little pocket book of diary notings to illuminate one's memory for precise details. A few sessions of aum chanting and meditation, and one might be able to recall enough matter to haunt the present with analyses of ghosts of theatres past!

After the Trinity play on environment (for which I'd also suggested the title The State of Nature Vs The Human Race), my work in performance theatre went totally off-stage: conducting free workshops at assorted places, attending, at Delhi, an eclectic collection of theatre workshops conducted by people from overseas as well as Indians over the years, and plunging into street theatre.

All this drama dovetailed into my work as a politico-legal activist: empowering as well as consulting people via the medium of theatre (used occasionally, and not as a primary mode of engagement), and also as one of the methods through which to reach out to various cross-sections of society and gauge people's moods, attitudes and trends towards just about anything you could think of, that had anything to do with law-making and politics.

Invariably, if any grassroots meeting one was invited to attend as a politician or an expert had an element of theatre, I extended my participation to the theatre-component of the meeting as well: for example, while attending a krishi sammelan (farmers' meeting) in the mountains of Uttarakhand to discuss a parliamentary bill (proposed legislation) connected to farmers' rights, it turned out that a naatak (skit or play) connected to the topic organically evolved from the proceedings of the meeting. This was facilitated by the presence of a theatre personality, Jaya Iyer, who, with her vibrant youth groups, had me, thereafter, on speed-dial, so to speak, with a request to holler whenever they thought they needed my presence for occasional expositions of street-theatre performances at Dilli Haat, and at Jantar Mantar. The time that I played Uncle Sam in an anti-MNC-pro-poor-farmer street play, I found that my unadvertised political blog had a recorded visit from a large multi-national seed company. This was about ten years ago, before surveillance was in everyone's face as much as it is today. Street theatre, to me, has been synonymous with acts of bravery, ever since a communist party street theatre activist of Delhi, Safdar Hashmi, was murdered while performing a street play in 1989.

My Delhi street theatre days were during the days of the UPA 1 government, and before it became necessary, in the interest of sending out clear signals pertaining to what one might describe as one's gradual political ascension, (albeit without a formal post), to opt out of grassroots theatre.

This personal decision was taken after a series of discussions with friends and observers at Delhi.

The discussion over why and why not had (and continues to have) a number of variables, and has spiralled, steamed, dispersed and crystallized with many a hot and cold beverage that fuel the oral tradition of story-making and story-telling.

The phase of street theatre remains showcased in one's satchel, with learnings, and the breakthrough of having pranced around the streets of Delhi, spewing lines of Hindi, with not a trace of ye olde worlde Shakespearean accent. This time round, they'd have cast me in the role of Rugby, if it was to be The Merry Wives of Windsor being revisited for a lark. Or perhaps the Rugby-roles are now given to those with posh accents, and those playing the elite roles have more contemporary acoustics to speak for themselves.

In any event, the impromptu Dhimsa tribal dance-steps down a main road of a posh south-Delhi colony for my brother's wedding, on the way to the Gurudwara there, was seamlessly rendered, thanks to years of street theatre! (A more practised and presentable version took place at home at the fort n palace at Kurupam after the local reception).

Activistic theatre also played out after the passage of the historic Forest Rights Act (it has a longer, technical-sounding title that can be googled later by those who wish to).

A musical in Telugu made its way to hamlets scattered along the eastern ghaat hills of Andhra Pradesh, educating scheduled tribe communities and other traditional forest dwellers on the their recently-recognized rights, and how to use this law that had been enacted by Parliament.

Even if one says so one's self, as a key player in the real-life drama, nay, epic, that led to the passage of the bill, one was invited to address some of the audiences for these events, all of which took place in remote hamlets, and often under open skies in the dark, sometimes without electricity. (Folks usually have time for such things after a hard day's labour, post-sunset).

Before the first of these meetings and performances that I was invited to, I had a small session of rehearsals with the youth groups who'd been trained to enact the play. One learnt the steps for some of the dances which were dhimsa-inspired (and one had already snaked and rolled the dhimsa at many a fest and fair, and so one caught on to the moves without much effort).

By this point of time, I think I might say that I had reached a high point of achievement in my ambitions related to theatre on certain counts.

In a sense, I'd say a number of issues about language, and genuine-ness, and the relevance of theatre had somewhat been resolved for the time being.

Certain sets of skills had moved forward more rapidly than others – such as improvisation, engagement of the audience, a control over space, group dynamics, intricacies of inter-personal interaction on stage, and with the audience.

However, more subtle renditions of characters, and long-duration plays had taken a back-seat. I have always maintained that that is something that is best represented on screen.

The theatre workshops that one's organized over time have been in Telugu, English, and with translators, even to a primarily Tamil-speaking group of social workers working to create awareness about the treatment for tuberculosis; for tribal kids and grown-ups in villages and forests during festivals (with themes of: Biodiversity; of honouring tribal dialects and languages; and of the human-animal conflict, with a focus on the havoc that elephants had been playing in those areas at that time); at the Alliance Française in New Delhi on World Environment Day; at a school in Noida, Uttar Pradesh, that was celebrating Environment Week; for the All India Children's Adivasi Science Congress at Visakhapatnam; at a leading school in Delhi as a part of its annual examination requirement for students; at the Waltair Club, and for a friend's training and theatre company in Visakhapatnam, to name most of the formal workshops that come to mind.

Of the myriad cultural events that one has had the opportunity to attend in India, especially Delhi, I've saved a few cards, invites, tickets and ticket-stubs. These have been recently tucked away into albums, and wait in the wings for a round of animated story-telling in a future production. Prominent among these tickets and passes, is the ticket/pass to the 1988 Human Rights Now concert at New Delhi, and technicoloured tales from those tabs, and ticketless draws at Nehru Park, with greats like Abida Parveen holding New Delhi in thrall will be reminisced about in the due course of time.

The rarity of a fluffy-eared rabbit on the bar-seat of a bicycle that rode from 19 Meena Bagh, via the India Gate area, to school (the chevy was deployed occasionally), to make it on time for Alice in Wonderland might have left Lutyen's sparse early-morning traffic startled in the late-1970s. A time when rare rabbits were sighted, and the roads were quiet and unpolluted enough to hear a stage whisper! (How we glorify the past!)

CHAPTER VI

GAMES ARE US AND OTHER COINCIDENCES

People want to make money! Preferably through honest means! Change that to only through honest means, please. They don't want jobs these days, where you sit behind the same desk from when you're born till you die.

There was a Hindi serial on TV in the 1980s called Yeh Jo Hai Zindagi (I think this is the one I'm talking about) - a comedy that's set in an office. To me, it was a depiction of how, day in, and day out, and week after week, people go to the same place and back, right until their retirement party. Unnerving and daunting, to say the least.

Which is not to say that I don't fancy the idea of playing parliament-parliament, one's appetite for such sport having been whetted during an era when visitors were permitted to walk right into the well of the house when the session was not on in the Lok Sabha. Obviously, I went and sat on the Prime Minister's seat.

With parliament being televised like the courts ought to be as well, the privilege of legging it to the well of the house and raising incessant slogans that would send baul singers, old and young alike, into early retirement, seems to be reserved for the members themselves.

The entire IPL of cricket demonstrated to India, and to the world, how sporting activity can acquire the status of serious industry.

Many conversations were held, thereafter, with friends and experts from other sporting fields and games. Not only about general policy-level stuff, but also about how games that have their origins on the subcontinent could be popularised to create various levels of sporting activity. To give an impetus to the teeming number of games that actually exist, and that millions are already familiar with.

The Kabbaddi League came into being, demonstrating that great minds think alike, and I have no doubt that it is a matter of time before viable, crowd-sourced methods of creating and funding sporting leagues emerge from all the experimentation, and make it to the finishing line sometime in the near future. The democratization of the uses of technological devices makes this possible in today's scenario.

Sports and games as vehicles to honour local culture are something that can, in my opinion, never be under-estimated. Hanging out at inter-panchayat volley ball matches in Andhra Pradesh; planning and participating in an appropriate reception for India's gold medal winning Olympic champion (who happened to be a tribal woman from north-east India) at Delhi; visiting archery classes at tribal schools with NGOs; cheering the Indian women's cricket team from the corporate box while they played England at Visakhapatnam; participating in the ceremonial vestiges of outdoor hunting and shooting (brinjals on poles and target-shooting) festivals…even the local folk dances are referred to, locally, as games. Some of these experiences have given me comparatively unusual insights into the world of games and sport.

The Asian Games of 1982 that were hosted at New Delhi brought a wave of knowledge and interest in athletics and a number of other team and individual games to kids in Delhi and India. The national TV channels covered the events in great detail.

I recall discovering the astounding world of gymnastics, and being told that in countries like China, they trained and trained people, and made it the sole purpose of selected groups of youngsters, to be medal-winners for their country. Almost factory-like.

I was in class five those days. Close family from outstation congregated at Delhi, with event-schedules from the newspapers put up on a door, and everyone rushing around, attending the events they'd chosen to buy tickets for.

An elephant, Appu, was the mascot of the games that year, and there were a number of souvenirs, including from ice-cream carts selling ice-cream in Appu-shaped plastic boxes. One went for quite a few events to various stadia: hockey (where Pakistan trounced India at the finals); table tennis (since it was one of my games); equestrian events; cycling (to a velodrome); swimming, and probably many more that I can't remember.

Our school is located quite close to the National Stadium, that's down the road (Rajpath) from India Gate and Rashtrapati Bhavan (the President's house). Although we didn't have sprawling grounds (the space we had was good for basketball, long jumps, soft ball, kho-kho, table tennis, indoor badminton and a bit of hockey), it was easy to make it to the National Stadium after school hours. I did, for a few years, to learn a few strokes of left-handed tennis. And went on to become a lawyer, to attend the Supreme Court that was down another road in the vicinity. My young tennis partner went on to become a Master-Chef!

Marching, and training for the march-past on sports day was pursued with semi-obsessive dedication. Legions of marching-squads with student-instructors occupied the by-lanes of the tree-lined, two-storied government residential colony outside the school's gates, booming and barking out commands of stand-at-ease; attention; about-turn; forward-march; left-turn; right-turn, and squad, halt! At the crack of dawn! Flag-bearers of the school's four houses: Ashoka (of which I was the Captain, thus finding a berth in the School Cabinet), Tagore, Nehru, and Gandhi, and of the school's crest (a ship out on a stormy sea), and of the school's motto: To Love Through Truth, and their armies, hounded the locality for weeks in the run-up to the sports day. Fledgling banners that would be waved in true earnest, when we eventually set out into the world.

Being located on ground zero, you sometimes don't notice that you're probably a very happening part of the world as your squad synchronizes its marching a furlong from where the annual Republic Day parade, and the Beating Retreat marches take place. You're emulating the best. The school diary had a Pledge. (India is my country, all Indians are my brothers and sisters, and so on). I don't know if other schools had such a pledge.

While at Delhi University, one was a part of a three-member women's rifle shooting team that won the Delhi Gold Medal, organized by the Delhi Olympic Association. And the silver and the bronze over the next two years, and competed at the nationals against teams from various states and security forces.

Thereafter, I was seized of all manner of ethical and environmental concerns, and perhaps a touch of Arms and the Man…and in any event, rifle shooting was an expensive hobby, Shaw was the clincher. Years after that, one's probably been quite far-sighted (literally and otherwise), and the only talk of guns these days, is about what gun control laws ought to look like.

It helps, I guess, if you have a vague idea about weapons, and, in fact, have done a mean number of paper-targets yourself. Like when one was at the undergrad college interview, and the principal in 1990 (Dr. John Hala) asked me which guns I'd shot with, and one was able to knowledgeably rattle off the list from the greatly-reduced armoury.

All sorts of knowledge comes in handy. (Coming from a politician, some wheeler-dealers of Delhi are likely to wonder whether one is talking about arms deals here. And would then discover that that, sadly for them, is not the case).

All arms deals ought to be transparent, and online, and probably are, by now. If not, this ought to be made a priority. But more about war games on some other turf.

Back to fun stuff, and bizarre stuff, I don't know what exactly counts as voodoo. But about dolls and toys. I had a sardarji doll, and then we had a sardarji Prime Minister (and relatives!); I had a rubber toy duck, and now there's a person called Donald at the helm of affairs in the world; I had a doll named Rohini, and the country's space satellite got named Rohini (which is also the name of one of my friends); my doll from the USSR wore an icy pista-green dress, just like a party dress I used to wear those days (I'd named her Martina Navratilova, and realised, later, that the tennis star was actually Czech); there was a stuffed lion-face that I called Lion Man (because, those days, people had to book something called trunk calls from land phones, for long-distance conversations, and go via a line man, and to check if you could be heard, you had to yell out to the line man: Line Man?? Line Man?! who was listening in to one-and-two-minute conversations anyway). Today, there's a make-in-India Lion logo.

By the way, I don't agree with this Make in India tag at all. I mean, which century are you living in? What kinds of jobs and businesses are you trying to create? This entire make-in-india thing is just a populist gimmick for the perceived stragglers who deserve better. Ask the correct kinds of economists what I mean. And ask yourself what kind of environment you'd like to eat, breathe, drink, sleep, and generally be in. Those who have the luxury of jet-setting away to make-in-somewhere-else-land for good if the need arises must be aware that their opinions are likely to be coloured by this bias.

Yoga, Jane Fonda workouts, Lodi Garden walks and football sessions, swimming lessons at a populist seaside aqua-centre, trips to various gyms, hikes, bicycling, river-rafting, outdoor adventure, table tennis, and fitness in general. These are my other visiting cards to the world of sport and fitness, and are also being launched into the conversation so that people and governments take the sporting-activity-and-people's livelihoods link forward, and start living the future already. Will there be foot-bridges across the China-Pak Economic Corridor, one wonders. To do the sethu-bandh aasan and the surya namaskaar as a part of my yogic earth pilgrimage before I get to Stonehenge.

P.S. On sprucing up the pouty, former-PM-esque rubber duck today for photographs (the human Donald's on a twelve-day tour of Asia, meeting Xi, and agonizing -and rightly so- over nuclear proliferation in the region), I turned the 1970s Disney rubber-duck over to find an elephant Walt Disney logo, and the flap of its bowler hat says Dewey. (This would've been signed Shrewtree Drewee if we were in the twilight zone of fiction-nonfiction. But we're firmly rooted in non-fiction, schizophonic or not schizophonic). Phonic, not frenic. A skill or talent, not a disease.

The ASEAN Summit's on, and I'm reminded of the congratulatory piece I wrote, when a former pouty-PM from our party spoke at ASEAN in the 1990s. The piece wasn't published, but I did read the entire thing out over an (in every likelihood, tapped) phone, to beau three from our days at 16, North Avenue (also one of the addresses from which I corresponded with a host of ivy-league and other universities, recording my statements regarding my future political plans and the like).

Back to the rest of the discussion:

Gaming these days hardly ever means bowling at a bowling alley like it used to in the 1990s in Delhi.

At Kurupam, during the summer vacations every year, it used to be durbar-durbar (courtroom-courtroom) in the downstairs drawing room when it was empty at mid-day, with my friends from the village; shaking berries out of trees; carrom board; attempting to cook rice and daal outdoor, camp-style; burying dead love-birds from the cage upstairs near the old swimming pool; sometimes having someone catch and milk a goat; rolling down haystacks; playing musical pillars, and a crazy game called parrot, where the floor had ludo-board-like markings…a live session would be preferable to a reading of the minutiae. There was a card game called twenty-nine, that required the application of your mind, and that one played with a resident grand-aunt during the vacations.

The disguises, and detective-games with imaginary clues and suspects that give credence today, to theories of whether life imitates art (some people actually believe it does, or could) of the 1980s, and the classroom-classroom game, where plucked leaves, garden plants and trees were all students being 'minded' by us, class monitors-in-our-dreams-and-games in the late 1970s, until the real-life class-leader badges started being pinned on at real-life investiture ceremonies at school, were all high entertainment.

The new excitement that keeps people glued to their devices and screens (and inner sparks) is all online. It might be a good old game of scrabble, or a complicated, intellectually challenging mystery or puzzle, or something that keeps the kids engaged, emitting futuristic gizmo-sounds, and probably building children's motor skills, and moulding an entire check-list of other skills that the bots have worked out.

Society navigates its way through these advancements, agonizing over what to do when internet predators attack children and the gullible alike with self-destructing games, and hackable toys.

Offline board games, too, have made a big come-back, I'm told, with challenging rules, and created to not bore people out of their wits.

My question, for some time, has been: if so many connected people, in so many places, have the time and inclination to play games online, why don't we up the stakes a bit (if not the ante), in the real world of games-plus-reality. Harness people's leisure activities to serve humankind, and one step further than expecting the treadmill to create, store and disperse mechanical energy for electricity.

The scope for the golden treasury of technology to be able to assist the differently-abled is mind-boggling. Responsible and socially sensitive planning needs to play an intervening role, and help re-prioritize the planet's resources with the aim of regaining paradise for the marginalised. I use the term regaining, because much of what is counted as disability, if deconstructed, can trace its origins to human intervention (good or bad, that's debatable). Such as the Ogouchi's syndrome. If the planet were permanently dark (with only fireflies and the moon and stars), I'd have super vision. Lights on, and it's Advantage, Power Corporations. Deuce, I tell you, it's time to serve a deuce!

CHAPTER VII

A Peer(less) Commentary or In the Name of Tabdeeli: A Soliloquy, 2013

Brief news, views and reviews (not intended to be comprehensive in any way), of the speeches and events of Imran Khan's 2013 election campaign. All viewed and written about through the internet from New Delhi.

Notes for me to use in some future writing project. There's lots to go gaga about when it comes to Imran Khan, and i'm not writing about that. These are well-meaning ponderings on how to bring in the glory (electoral victory), and how to make a speaker like this optimize results. An intellectual exercise of sorts.

I'm viewing these events at random through publicly available youtube clips and clips from the official facebook pages and web-searches. This is not meant to be an analysis of the media coverage or internet or television portrayals of the events, or of the effectiveness of the social media. These are scattered comments on the events themselves, and how they can be improved. From one politician to another, if you will. ☺

On the 10th of March, there was the Peshawar Jalsa (This snippet on the pre-election Peshawar Jalsa, i had emailed to a journalist friend). The live coverage that had been announced and was expected didn't happen on the PTI livestream site (at least, i wasn't able to access it). But the recorded speech was available on youtube later.

Chairs had been lined up for the audience on a maidan. This is an unusual sight for a public meeting of this magnitude on the subcontinent – and i would imagine, anywhere else as well. One wonders why they chose to lay out seating: was it to avoid any sort of stampede and make the atmosphere more 'methodical?' Was it to make the crowd look bigger? Was it to impress Imran Khan? Was it a desire to make the crowd feel comfortable? Was it a tool to assess the number of attendees? (i suppose one could speculate endlessly, and even wonder whether a plastic or a chair company was trying to advertise its products, whether there was any significance to the colour of the chairs -red-, whether the expenditure on chairs for such political meetings should be avoided, and so on). But these are just passing thoughts, and might not deserve an entire paragraph!

From the looks of it, the crowds seemed to have been controlled well, though there was a news report that the steps to the stage had collapsed due to the people's eagerness to reach the star. This might explain one of the photographs that shows him climbing a ladder to get to the stage. This is an image (and the photographer has captured the moment well), that is likely to strike a chord with the audience and win its greater admiration. i say this from experience from one of my own campaign roadshows here in India about a decade ago, where the bravado of clambering onto the top of a vehicle and then ducking electrical wires (due to sheer necessity, of course, and not for the drama of it), apparently sent years of selfless service into oblivion in comparison to such feats!

When Imran Khan spoke, the jostling audience did, at one stage, seem to disturb the dais, actually causing him to interrupt his speech midway at least twice, asking them to move, sit down, and even reaching out to firmly push them out of the way. The people and organizers around him ought to be alert and take over such functions. It does not help to have a political leader addressing almost fifty thousand people and having to worry about fending off enthusiasts mid-speech. Having said this, i must admit that the move lent him a touch of uniqueness: made him real-life and quite literally, connect immediately with the masses as opposed to grandiose idols being whisked on and off stage.

Of late, he has made deliberate efforts to not be projected as a one-man show which might have happened during his earlier elections and political career of the past sixteen years. The emphasis on intra-party elections, the announcing of party policies on various aspects of governance by various experts in the party, the projection of his party functionaries on the PTI's internet television website as well as in the Pakistani electronic media are all evidence of the gathering and growing energies of Team Imran.

The speech at the Peshawar Jalsa was received well. It was a receptive audience whose support he already had. As far as the speech goes, i think that while he's tuned into the issues and concepts that are important to the local people there, and conveyed that well to them, he needs to cut down on references to Tony Blair, Margaret Thatcher, British political parties and so on.

Also, while it is important for him to make the point that people from all walks of life, such as tailors, are and will be position-holders in the party, he needs to bolster these astounding signs or symbols of change with a reiteration that the people in these positions will have the capacity and ability to discharge their duties.

While effectively voicing what might be the disgust of the people against misgovernance, he should be careful to remember that although it is important to do so, and thus establish the fact that he and the people identify with each other, it is equally important to demonstrate to them why he should be their leader. Why he, being as much a part of them, is not as much of a victim as they might be, and will therefore be able to help them. Perhaps that is why he mentions world leaders, and sometimes wears suits and blazers on the campaign trail.

On this occasion, however, he sported a grey fan-like turban. Quite different from the other (i think) Pashtoon cap that one sees him wearing to the FATA areas. In the course of the speech, he divested himself of this gear. From a visual point of view, i noticed that for a few minutes, one of his supporters who was standing behind him was perched on a high foothold, and the overall silhouette to a distant audience was this tall individual behind Imran, towering over him and dwarfing him while he spoke. Such things, however, are sometimes left better unplanned. After all, it is the spontaneity and authenticity that such an audience picks up.

To add to an oft-quoted quip that Imran uses: These people, you cannot fool any of the time. He was a good man, doing a good thing. They knew who he was, they had just had their local party elections. They were optimistic about the forthcoming elections and that is why they were there. Perhaps he could have spoken more about local developmental issues. Perhaps he will, the next time he holds a meeting in a remote area.

For now, one looks forward to watching his evolution at the mega rally that's planned for the 23rd of March.

My Comments on Imran's 25th April, Lodhran Speech

One of the rare occasions on which he mentioned women, and addressed the women present. Good. But he stuck to generalities (as with the rest of the speech). The only specifics were direct challenges to Musharraf (probably works in this context, but i tend to keep political speeches directed at parties, their policies and misdeeds, but not attack individuals).

No local issues dealt with, except for a mention of the local PTI leaders. Overall, the "macro" kind of matter needs to be interspersed with localized issues, specific localized poll promises. A personal rapport with the people of the specific area needs to be created. An on-the-spot assessment of what these issues could be can be done en route depending on whether or not there are local people in proximity to talk to.

At this particular meeting, the people didn't seem too confident on hearing a belligerent tone. An ongoing rapid assessment of the receptivity and mood of the audience while making the speech, and adjusting the speech accordingly on the go would help.

While it is good to emphasize the presence of the "naujawans" by addressing them, it should not be at the near total exclusion of other categories. It's good that he's started talking about farmers and addressing them.

More frequent mentions of the election symbol (a cricket bat, granted recently by the election commission), wouldn't be bad.

In another speech yesterday, i noticed that they wanted him to speak in Pashto, and he said he'd do so afterwards, but i'm not sure if he spoke in Pashto later. At least a few words immediately would have been effective.

Other than the political cause, they are also interested in Imran the person, so depending on the circumstances of each event, if it can be made relevant, brief personal anecdotes (with which they can identify, and not too many tales from abroad which might alienate them), would make the speech memorable for the listeners.

He also needs to focus on the fact that the audience is not a mass of sheep but that each of them is an intelligent human being, capable of opinion, analysis, doubt, originality etc., and his acknowledgement of this should reflect in the tone that is employed and not only in the way that he throws so many statistics at them!

Vehari Jalsa, 25th April 2013

Here, the crowd was a much more upbeat one than the previous Lodhran one. The point on free water for irrigation was appreciated greatly by the crowd. A couple of wisecracks -PJs- to an audience like this proved to be perfect.

26ᵗʰ April Jalalpur Pirwala Jalsa

Content-wise, noticeable improvements from the previous day's speeches. Addressed not only the naujawans, but also the buzurgs and behenons. Spoke of local governance. These were good developments, but there's room for improvement in terms of delivery, content and fine-tuning of tone.

27ᵗʰ April Bahawalpur Jalsa

Great improvement in the chemistry with the audience. The fact that he's observing them as he's speaking and reacting is evident (a distinct change of style as hoped). Excellent. i think there was a local poll promise made, though i'm not sure if that's what it was, but it did get a lot of claps. The brief breaking into the local dialect (here, Punjabi), worked well.

Time now to start working on building more of an emotional rapport with the audience (in a real sense, and not in a theatrical way). The only real way to do this is to think about/meditate on the people and to genuinely acknowledge to himself, the many ways in which he is, indeed, one of them. It was good to hear him introduce this concept in its most nascent form at this speech when he said Hum (us).

i also watched an interview posted today (27 April) on youtube, on a programme called Hum Log. Here, there was a point when he ridiculed the fact that people only want their own gully or street repaired and that they don't think for the whole country. He would have come across to the masses as being a bit clueless about the immediate concerns of poverty (i'm not saying it comes across as that to educated intellectuals etc., but it sounds very different to a person in a village). It would help if he paid a genuine compliment or two to the audience (not repeat the same one at different places, but say something gathering-specific where relevant).

Speeches ought to talk about how/why access to health and education will be better under his government IN ADDITION to improvements that will come about in these sectors as a result of corruption being done away with and other such systemic change that he intends to bring about. ie, Strategy/ies followed by Action Plans ☺ (as this demarcation is sometimes referred to and understood, especially by straight-jacketed-in-their-thinking UN wallahs!).

Examples of the kind of actions he could talk about are: availability of medicines, attendance of doctors, school buildings and infrastructure, mid-day meals at schools for children etc. There ought to be some non-controversial specifics regarding how the situation/condition of women will be made better. Affordable and safe public transport. Specifics related to agriculture: crop insurance, irrigation, infrastructure such as warehouses and storage facilities, loans for farmers, sorting out of land related issues (not just talk of computerizing records), street lighting, communications services etc.

27th April Sadiquabad Jalsa

The cricket reference (about the 'weak' defeating the 'strong' – the Pak team under him in India) was woven in well and got a good response.

Introduction of the local candidate and a bit about her was a positive trend (should, however, keep in mind the fact that there are always supporters of those who didn't get tickets around who should not be rubbed the wrong way).

In addition to talking about manaoing Jashn after the polling (which is being received well everywhere), there should be a line that establishes the intention of a long-term personal engagement with the audience (what i use in some speeches is the Telugu equivalent of Phir Milenge).

28th April at Khan Bella

Watched the footage through the facebook official page, of the clip where it says "a leader loves to be with his people" (when the audience was asked to come closer to the stage). This was a well-chosen (mutually applicable) and truthful "emotional" angle.

Which reminds me that the other connect that could be alluded to/ invoked/displayed is the common "consciousness" without mentioning structured religious contexts. ie., a reference to the essences of the spiritual or philosophical connects that might exist (not within the framework of texts, religions, philosophers, politics etc., but a connect to what he knows or might know to be mutual values, desires, aspirations).

Apart from just mentioning his own spiritual (to use an easy word), beliefs, attitudes etc., he should take it a step forward and establish how that is/could be a common factor between him and the people. And this should not be done as a superior or as an instructor, but as a discussant.

Anyway, the footage shows an admirable and justified optimism among the people. One hopes that there will be a day when one can personally say shabaash to the millions after they bring about peace! i predict victory for the PTI!

28th April Mandi Bahauddin Jalsa

A substantial part of the speech dedicated to/addressed to women. A good effort in terms of time spent on the topic. In addition to education of women and the emotional connect about valuing of mothers and about not letting any harm come to "our women" (this, predictably, got lots of claps), he could also add points on women's health, reproductive health, nutrition, vocational training (in fact, vocational training and training in semi-skilled and skilled labour should be mentioned even in the wider context).

Such discussions could replace some of the excessive time spent on talking about the respect for green passports and visas at airports and internationally. (Even if they all have relatives working in other countries, the larger number who are actually going to go to the polling booths are not going to totally appreciate this slightly egoistic and elitist point: at a much future date, i might write about how this is the very attitude that makes the rich of a country exploit their own poor in the name of "strengthening the economy").

Somehow, the mention of coal reserves received a fascinatingly uproarious positive response! i hope they don't proceed to become a nation of crony capitalists when they come to power.

i think the time has come for him to start announcing, dramatically and matter-of-factly (i think he's a good enough presenter to mix both), that he is there to tell them that he now knows that the PTI is going to form the government on its own. (i know he's been talking about tabdeeli, but there is a slight distinction here).

He should be encouraged to make his own speeches based on a few main points, as this seems to work well. The personal emotional connect with the people needs to be worked on. No suggestions will help, except to tell him to use his own intuition at each gathering, to get a feel of each particular gathering, and say or do something accordingly. This will only work if it is something that is totally spontaneous. Any sort of additional suggestions will ruin the effect. Limited bits of humour seem to be working well, but these digs and jokes should be good humoured, respectful of the poor, respectful of other countries and others, on the whole.

As an aside, i should mention here that just today, (28th April), i viewed an interview on youtube, of Asad Umar dated 16th April "Aaj with Reham Khan." An odd observation of mine here was that the anchor was either consciously or unintentionally, talking like Hina Rabani (and probably even asking questions that she would have asked)! i suppose when people watch interviews, they all have a hawk's eye out for the body language in the responses! Anyway, just to assume for a moment, that there is something to my observation, then one just assumes that it could have been the opposition looking for reactions, especially to the question pertaining to the denial of a party ticket to Faisal Javed, i thought. Were they exploring the idea of attempting to sabotage the work of the PTI by trying to poach him by offering him a seat, one wonders! Also, since the name of Fauziya Kasuri was mentioned, i googled her name (have read about her earlier as well, while reading about the PTI), and noticed that her husband is a seasoned international affairs person (read his brief bio), and the fact that he'd met BJP leaders in India in Calcutta last year as a part of some conference on Peace. i'm making a mental note, here, that i should find out more about this, and whether it's just incidental to that individual's outreach capacity, or whether it reflects some element of their party's foreign policy.

29th April 2013: i've also just looked at a couple of clips on the PTI tigers website. One is a BBC interview where he is en route a meeting, and the other is of him addressing a crowd on the 24th, from a bullet-proof glass cubicle.

Regarding the BBC clip (and in the context of the fact that there are going to be overseas supporters and reporters following him more intensively from now on -going by twitter, or maybe some other facebook page that i'm not actually signed up to, but visited via twitter), i think he should be very clear in his mind, that his chief concern, while on the campaign trail, is/ are the local voters. Everything that is said should be directed to the masses of voters. Let there be no confusion at all about who is important in this scenario (and that should be the masses on the ground and local supporters). This should be palpable (and demonstrated) to the local people, voters and the team present. And as an aside: i wonder who/ who all (if anyone), is/are hacking into my computer?!! My most realistic guess: The Media. ☺

And totally relieved that he did away with the glass cubicle. Respect.

This morning (29th April), i watched a 28th April programme, Agar, on Ary News. This was an interview of Imran followed by some clips of his speeches. i noticed that he maintained a standard, 'controlled authority' kind of stance throughout the interview which was good, especially considering i imagined that his anchor was depicting various 'interviewer voices'. If this is a part of an extremely fine-tuned media strategy, it was executed well.

If it was his instinct kicking in (more likely, really), then his instincts are certainly worth following.

The video clips that followed the interview showed his usual kind of speeches from the past, including a bit of one at Rahim-Yar-Khan (i don't know on which date this speech was made, and i might have watched it earlier as well), where he does, in fact, mention how he doesn't know why, but his heart tells him that they are going to win. If i've heard the speech before, then it struck a chord and was effective. If i haven't heard the speech before, well, here's yet another uncanny way in which he's quite a bit like me! (which, thanks to a good ad strategy, a lot of people might be justifiably thinking –that they are a lot like Imran-?!) The best part is, it's all true! (He's not creating any false impressions). Cheers.

…Another thing that i've just remembered about that interview is that while discussing pre-poll surveys (and this does not at all indicate my personal opinion or bias vis-à-vis the results of those surveys), he dismisses things local (in this case, the surveys), as being inferior (not in these words, but as such). And uses the word 'international' as though that's an indicator of excellence. For the actual tabdeeli that he is in the process of bringing about, he needs to eradicate what's left of the colonial mindset within him (the people don't possess his version/perspective of the colonial/now elitist hangover…this is something that he needs to learn from his people).

Oh, and i've started writing all this as late as the last few days ago on a whim. Instinct. And experience tells me that in this case, this is precisely when one needs to intensify the campaign. One more piece of unsolicited advice from me personally (in case someone in the PTI is actually reading this somehow):

i think all the crowds are in a mood to love India. Let him say something to the effect that the rivalry with India has always been in the context of playing cricket, but that the people of both the countries, including himself, actually love each other. Then observe the crowd's response. (Don't choose a wishy-washy audience for this one, though there don't seem to be too many non wishy washy audiences around!). If the response is good, capitalize on this point.

On the afternoon of 29th April (ie now), i viewed an interview on ATV news of Imran Khan with Farah Hussain. This was published/ posted on 22nd April. i haven't been documenting the names of channels, anchors and programmes (or my comments) of dozens of other Imran Khan programmes i've viewed through youtube over the past few months.

But i need to add my two bits here, about how i (like many others, i presume), am pleasantly surprised to learn that the electronic media has been so active in that country. And am also very taken up by the skill and the "way" of, by and large, all their anchors, and this one in particular. One can tell a Pakistani anchor from an Indian one. It's a matter of style, and here, they have an edge. i'm not denouncing all our Indian anchors in one fell swoop, but overall, by being less shouty, as it were, the Pakistani anchors manage to make the discussions much more weighty. There is less of the anchor's/interviewer's personality being injected into the programme, making room for a more meaningful portrayal of the interviewee. If this is any indication of their overall national character, we have a lot to learn from these anchors (and maybe employ these graces while dealing with other nations including theirs).

Anyway, to get back to the programme i'm talking about right now. It touched on a few India-related aspects, which i want to key in quickly for this fast-increasing collection of notes of mine, because all this will, Inshallah, become even more politically relevant after 11th May which is their polling date, and after the results are out:

He says that it is now in the interest of Pakistan, to have aman, or peace, with all its neighbours (he says this while being questioned on some old statement of his, where he had apparently spoken against India's stand on water-related issues), and to improve conditions within his country.

He says regarding Kashmir, where things are, indeed, very problematic, he thinks there should be a political solution. He even mentions that (he thinks) that it is even in India's interest, to look for political solutions.

He says there will be scope for great progress if trade relations are improved between the countries, and describes Pakistan as a future "energy corridor."

He also mentions at one point, that when he talks about local government, that itself is the much-needed revolution.

When asked about transportation on the polling date in Pakistan, he brought up the example of India, and said that in India, private vehicles are banned on the polling date, but if, in Pakistan, both public and private vehicles are going to be banned on the date, then it would be disastrous. He said he was going to bring this up before their election commission, and ask for at least more polling booths so that people could walk up to them. He gave the example of some areas in his Mianwali constituency which are hilly pahadi ilakas, and said people have to walk way too far to reach a polling booth.

His tone throughout this interview was quiet and soberly analytical.

At one point, he was asked about whether or not he agreed with the view that although he draws crowds and does campaign actively, he does not literally mingle with the people on these occasions. His answer was that he's not one to get into such drama. That he is what he is, and cannot be like the politicians who land up at demonstrations with hand fans to protest loadshedding just for photo opportunities.

The anchor, at the end, said God bless you, and added that they were honoured that he had given them his time. (But this last line, and the fact that the anchor referred to him as Sir, are not why i began this note by praising Pakistani anchors!)

29th April at Attock

Found a clip of today's Attock speech. Nice touch when he said he can see a golden era ahead (would like to hear more about these visions some day!).

Noted the anecdote about the man on the flight with 'nau' children who won't be meeting his children for two years. Have heard it in a few earlier speeches or interviews. The anecdote, for the time it occupies, is just ok. But the main idea in there (of ek din log idhar naukri dhoondney aayengey), has been drawing a good response even minus the anecdote. (For me, it was a line that stuck in my head not because of the line itself when i first heard it in an interview, but because of something in the rest of that interview - which i watched on youtube in January).

Also noticed that the reference to the hand fan protest drew some laughs.

Improvement in the way the women were spoken to at the meeting ("this brother will not let any injustice happen to his sisters" as opposed to "we will not let anything happen to our women").

He's introduced a nice way (that fits his persona, at least), to say that victory is certain (that he's now feeling sorry for his rivals). The clip i watched didn't have the entire speech, so i don't know what else i might have missed out on here.

i wonder how the party is doing by way of election funds, and hope they have things under control on that front.

i also hope they've started making a basic post-election plan of action (by way of an immediate list of things to do with responsibilities assigned) if they win. But before that, of course, are the pre-polling and polling day preparations. Frequent contact with the election authorities, even to clear minor doubts, is always advisable.

On 30th April, watched the 29th April Murree Jalsa speech. The initial point on a localized (irrigation?) issue was received very well. This immediately established, to the people, that he was not just a star that had dropped from heaven, but knew something about their immediate area and was now fit to be a politician. (Despite all the electronic media coverage, remember that chances are that only a small percentage of the rural voters would have watched entire interviews of his to completely realize his metamorphosis from cricketer to politico. Thus, beginning a speech in this fashion is useful, and establishes that point).

About some of the language used: everytime he refers to the 'you can't fool all of the people all the time' quip, he should replace "pagal" with "bewaqoof." Otherwise, the crowds aren't comprehending this point too well.

In this particular speech, at the end, when he said "sun lo…" (everyone listen to me…we shall celebrate on the 11th), the "sun lo" sounded a bit like a threat (to those who were still undecided about voting). Of course, they clapped in relief when they heard the full sentence!

The worst thing to do is to interrupt them when they are cheering you or clapping, saying there are only ten minutes (and that too, to read out endless statistics from that sheet of paper). This is where the cricket-captain (or corporate honcho) persona should be shed.

Go with the flow, it doesn't matter if you are slightly late for some of the meetings as long as you reach all the places you've said you'll touch. Don't let your schedule be unconsciously guided by somewhat-extraneous-to-the-campaign demands on your time. Till the 11th, you belong to your local campaign team/s!!

[i had to revisit this paragraph to say that in future meetings, he did start waiting for the crowds to clap, cheer, and even started sounding semi-apologetic about rushing through some of the later meetings, even saying that he wasn't bothered by the sun as he's played a lot of cricket, he was worried that the people might be feeling hot!]

While speaking, there is no need to intuitively say that some of the people at the back are without "josh." Such details, take silent note of, and tackle through the substantive content of the rest of the speech.

Isn't there some Urdu word or phrase for corruption? At this kind of a gathering, all of them are not too certain of its meaning, though they know it might be crime or violence or something bad on the whole that you're speaking against. (its different when you're addressing a local but urban or slightly affluent set of people in town). Not suggesting huge detailed explanations, but just replace the English word "corruption" with a single Urdu word…in India, we say "Bhrashtaachaar."

Your enthusiasm should ideally remain the same irrespective of whether you're addressing five people or fifty thousand. This happens when you truly value and respect each individual. That is when you become a visible, felt representation of the concept of Democracy.

30th April, watched the 29th April interview by Shahzeb Khanzada on To the Point. Imran's given him some election predictions in writing? Really?!! And very familiar-looking body language here. So many puzzles!

30th April, watched the **29th April Talagang Chakwal Speech** on youtube:

Here, it was not just a question of where the camera was focusing, one could tell that there was actually a slightly different kind of response from a section of the people. Since i know nothing about the area or its background, am not even bothering to google it, let me attempt a purely instinctive analysis of the response. The 'youth' cheered the change of government and sometimes the anti-corruption points. However, what was interesting was the response (or lack of it), of the crowd of middle-aged and elderly people sitting in (many) front rows.

While this was a largeish gathering, there was a shamyana and chairs for some rows. The substantial percentage seated on these were there to either just listen, or with half-made-up minds and brought there for various reasons, mainly convinced, by the youth, to at least attend the event. If this turns out to be the case, feedback must be sent to the youth, congratulating them on their ability to have carried out this task. This will enthuse them to, even now, turn this phenomenon into votes from the seated ones. The seated ones ☺ were not too enthused, in fact, they were rather uncomfortable, with the idea of corruption being tackled and land records being computerized. While these are, certainly, some of the priority items on the agenda, they have to be presented to the listeners through their perspective.

If you stand in a village full of people, telling them that corruption at the village level will finish because there will be good leaders, they are not so foolish as to think that Imran himself is going to do that for them locally (except, perhaps, in his own constituencies). In which case, they will, in their minds, be evaluating whether or not the person who has been given the party ticket will be in a position to do this. During the speech, there was some mention of the local candidate, and he seems to be an affluent person planning to run (or running) an educational institution. i got the feeling that perhaps here, there is support for Imran, but the people are not convinced that the candidate (whoever he is), can solve all their problems.

For the pre-polling and polling dates, you need to make sure that people from the 'other camp/s' are also approached by the party and given some importance (ie their advice on seemingly minor specifics but of importance to them, be sought and acted upon before the election date).

Also, at gatherings like this, when you say land records are going to be computerized, and all problems will be solved by opening your computer etc., please remember that most people don't know how to use computers… i'm not saying that i'm against computerization of land records in an ideal situation, or in a planned way. But when it's thrown as a plan to an electorate that's at this stage of development and of the polls, it's not going to inspire any confidence. In fact, they will feel threatened by the thought of such an eventuality and vote for the other party.

Furthermore, they are also aware of the many issues related to land that need to be sorted out through democratic processes before God-knows-what goes into the computer records. This is how they'll be thinking when you say what you said. Even the youth. The claps related to this topic were more as claps for ending high-level corruption. The silence was because of these doubts on aspects that will impact them more directly.

Clearly, he was able to sense some of what the people there were feeling when he made the Freudian slip of 'vote for the tiger' and in the sentences that led up to it.

i also think the people here were waiting for him so say something that he didn't bring up, or didn't know he ought to bring up. i don't know what.

Is there a possibility that the other side had paid them to sit there and behave grumpy (not a difficult feat to accomplish because everyone wants to see Imran the cricketer in any case)?!

Or is the fact that many in these parts belong to the army (as he mentioned in his speech), have something to do with this?

30th April, Isakhel Mianwali Speech

Watched a clip of this speech. Here, the crowd was silent, almost worshipful. Unconditional support from them. Good that you thanked them.

While campaigning in Mianwali and other areas where you have personally been interacting with them over years, do also assure them that you will not forget or neglect them once you become the Wazir-e-Azam!

Good that you let the cheering continue for a bit (did i see you quickly looking at the camera for appreciation?!) But you couldn't resist mentioning the time constraint again, saying they are the ones that have to keep standing in the sun?! Anyway, that was a minor observation.

Also noticed a slight alteration in the reference to corruption, where you said the patwaris will not be done away with, but will have a small role, but that land records will be computerized.

Another observation i've been meaning to make (just to ask you to ponder over the implications of this concept -since they will be doing so- they are all great philosophers, like you know, though they might not be literate or have formal educations) is this: you keep saying that those who have destroyed institutions can never be the ones to improve them. Politically convenient to say in this context. But the deeper idea attached to this doesn't seem to be too convincing to them. You are basically saying, in a sense, that there is no hope for a wrong-doer to improve. And don't forget, that in these polls, the larger effort is to draw the average person on the road away from arbit activities and into better governance. It goes against the idea of "there is always hope everywhere." Maybe they don't want to buy your brand of pessimism as that's what it essentially comes across as in the larger scheme of things. (Perhaps your own personal subtext here comes from the fact that you've successfully moved on from attempting to salvage the conventional institution/s of marriage?!)

30th April at Kalabagh, Mianwali Speech

Personal familiarity with the area and its issues and people is evident. Wise to have put in a word about "think about the country, vote for the party and not for community" etc. However, the lecturing/preaching regarding communities etc. was a bit too long for an election speech. Save that kind of evangelism for non-election-time hangouts.

30th April Daud Khel, Mianwali (posted about half an hour ago)

A very well received speech. Fantastic speech-to-speech progress.

In Mianwali, this aapka ahsaan kabhi nahin bhoolenge line works perfectly. Repeat it! (even at future meetings).

At this meeting, it was quite funky to have referred to the government that is coming next as aap ki jamaat: tehreek-e-insaaf kee.

Another thing that i've noticed earlier and would like to draw your attention to is that when you say that 'this is your fight, do this for yourself, you are doing this for yourself, vote for the change you want, for your own vision' etc: point appreciated. This has also always been my basic premise in my seventeen years of active (though non-electoral) politics in India.

However, your additional line, where you pointedly tell the people to their faces that they're not doing this for Imran Khan makes the people feel like you're alienating yourself from them. They know you well enough for you to not have to say it yourself to them. In fact, in the tradition of hospitality that our people on the subcontinent hold so precious (and that you've even mentioned in your book), it is just not on to spurn them. To them, it sounds like a spurning. You might be doing it for A Vision. They are doing it, at least fifty percent, for Your Vision. If it makes them feel good to think that they're giving you something, acknowledge it. Don't belittle them by telling them that they can give you nothing. In fact, that is not even true. There is lots you can learn from them, especially about local government and your own culture. This, they have been giving you.

30th April: Oops, had missed viewing a brief clip of the **29th April Taxila Speech and Jalsa**…just watched it now. Amazing crowd. Wow!

And, needless to say, when it's too loud and you can barely be heard, resort to larger movements (like you did while wielding the bat).

30th April, Speech at Mochh (from some other website found on google)

Very receptive audience. Too many statistics being read out from that paper, of which some were not followed up by explanations of why they were being read out. Avoidable. Also because when stats are handed over at the last minute, you don't even know if they have been verified to be the official stats that they claim to be. Don't want to rake up unnecessary controversies by reading out arbit eleventh-hour stats.

Noticed that you ended by saying aap ko kabhee nahin bhoolengey. That was nice.

Today (1st May 2013), i watched a clip of a **30th April Mianwali Jalsa** (don't know where exactly this one was, but i'm guessing it was later on into the evening): The atmosphere was completely charged, it was one of the best speeches from the campaign trail so far (which is not to say all the speeches should have exactly this content, but for the atmosphere there, this was the perfect speech). Well done.

Another thing that's been staring me in the face and that i should have reacted to much earlier is that it is most counter-productive to keep mentioning any other party's election symbol during the speech. This might be hard to believe, but when the voter turns up at the polling booth at the last minute, and is frazzled by everything that's going on around them (and here, one is talking about the people who are not too savvy process or logistics-wise), then you don't want them to associate you with the word 'tiger' just because that's all they've heard and taken away from your speech while gawking at you!

Which brings me back to the point that many people are only listening to the tone/s of your voice. That and gestures convey much more at these events than detailed statistics etc.

Did notice the expansive gestures at this particular noisy meeting. They were natural, fluid and you were relaxed.

Again, your familiarity with the area enabled you to enlist with confidence, the names of the various local leaders who represent you in the area.

This brings me to my next suggestion for the day. But this will have to be done where appropriate and without making it sound like a muquabala: say some things that appease/complement/encourage/endear/entice people who are supporters of other parties. Don't imagine that they aren't listening. Do this well, and start winning over votes that nobody ever thought you'd win!

1ˢᵗ May at Sibi, Balochistan

Viewed not the entire speech, but a clip of it from somewhere midway. The main point that was made here in Balochistan was about how he'd bring back an effective system of local government. He said that before the British came to Hindustan, the system of local government (baldayati nizam?) was successfully in vogue. He said that this is what he intends to bring back to Balochistan. i think he used the term "aseemit baldiyati nizam" which means unrestricted/ boderless local government?

He introduced the local candidates, made each of them raise their hands. i think he could treat the local candidates with a little more reverence and at least know or remember their names in advance. (unless he deliberately did this in order to send the message across here, that irrespective of who the candidate is, vote for the bat…there was cheering for vote for bat and maybe there were strongly contested party tickets involved here).

This was a very low energy speech.

1ˢᵗ May at Loreliee, Balochistan

He said that he'd hold discussions, political dialogue, collect people (unite people), and work towards getting them justice.

Whenever he talks of local government, he talks of how it has worked/used to work in "Maghareb" (north-western Africa?) for years. [later, he stopped using this term].

He addressed his Pashtoon bhais and said there had been a lot of problems, and that the war had to end. Loud cheering for this. It goes without saying, that wherever he's mentioned the war having to end, there's been huge support. Once again, he made the local candidates raise their hands and almost remembered all their names. Could do these introductions a little better, though i've not viewed the entire event, it might have happened outside of the video clip!

The reference to small-scale reservoirs for the area drew a lot of support, as did the mention of the work for a pending local road that he named.

Overall, a low energy event. He didn't seem too involved in the event, for some reason. Wasn't giving it everything like all the previous events. Is something troubling or bugging him? Or is he just exhausted?

1ˢᵗ May at Samanabad, Lahore

A high energy meet and speech. Here, it was all about harnessing the need for self-esteem and bringing about change. The chants from the crowd were of Wazir-e-Azam; "we want change" (in English), and other things that they all found entertaining. They even requested him to repeat parts of his earlier speeches that have become trademarks of his campaign like calling out to "Mia saab!"

1ˢᵗ May, watched the TV programme News Eye: Naya PM Kaun via youtube on i think the Dawn channel.

He described himself as a democrat with leftist economic policies, as being anti-imperial and anti-war. Totally my kind of politics, in case there were doubts! And very importantly, he talked of his proposed energy mix, and one of my nagging doubts was put to rest: he didn't include nuclear power. He's never promoted it, and i don't think the discussions on energy in the manifesto/energy policy ever talked of it, but it was good to hear, once again, from the Chairman himself, about an energy mix that does not talk of nuclear energy.

1ˢᵗ May, Jacobabad, Sindh Jalsa Speech

For the first time, i heard him use the word "Panchayat" while talking about local government.

There was an emphasis on local government in this speech. While talking about health, he also mentioned medicines this time.

Quite uncannily, he also reached out, for the first time quite deliberately, to supporters of other parties, like i was thinking (and had written about earlier today). He told sympathizers of Bhutto that Zardari was not Bhutto, and that Zardari was using the Bhutto name but not doing the kind of good work that Benazir Bhutto was known for.

2ⁿᵈ May: i'm waiting to watch today's speeches. Watched a clip with music with the theme Naya Pakistan where they show Imran and supporters on a roadshow. Quite nostalgic, it felt! (to think about being on a roadshow).

Acha, now before i forget, i watched some of that Sept 2012 Google Hangout yesterday. Haven't heard you saying anything about what you'll do for people with disabilities. Please mention your commitment to the "weakest sections of society," and specifically talk about the disability sector in that context. [later, there was a video clip on the facebook page, of a person on a wheelchair going and voting].

Also, good job yesterday, on wooing voters who might have half-decided to vote for the other side. Now, if you think it's worth the risk, and if you can look everyone in the eye and say something on this front, then now is your golden opportunity to redeem yourself in whatever way your heart tells you to, about Tyrian. (No, no i don't think the "public" is clueless about this, i think they've been giving you the benefit of the doubt for all your choices regarding Tyrian, perhaps you just need to explain your choices to them).

You might not choose to do this through a public speech, but make your comments on the topic public through some other medium to a prioritized audience (maybe while addressing those overseas Pakistanis who have landed up there to help out and whose snaps have been circulating on the social media sites?) Just a thought. This move might win you the votes of a number of undecided urban educated young women, especially from the intelligentia.

Apart from votes, it might also get you better publicity and more Naya Pak donations from moralists. In India, for example, while the public is not at all judgemental about the personal lives of its leaders, it would be impressed by someone who is seen as being brave enough to redeem/ attempt to improve a situation when they don't really need to do so (if that's the case).

So far, the public has only heard from you about Tyrian on the electronic media when you've been "questioned" about it. In your book, of course, you have brought up the subject. But perhaps a little more clarity than what the book says would help to get you that final global push/sympathy/support? It might even open up more doors of clean funding for the elections! (No specific source in mind, just an instinctive thought) ☺ [there was nothing on this later, unless one tried to interpret that urdu couplet that was recited the next day].

While surfing, today, for Imran's campaign schedule, i came across a post that says that today, he's going to some of Nawaz Sharif's strongholds. Again, i don't really know too much about the history of Pak politics n all, but my gut tells me that these are places where, if the other side is seen as being friendly with some other country (eg., India), and if they are projecting this as a plus point for themselves, then Imran, too, should stress on his good relations with countries like India. He can very truthfully say that he has political friends and supporters in India!! (me, who else?!) Don't underestimate me :D

Important to note that this is all instinctive and might sound simplistic, but in the long run, we (peace-loving India), and, indeed, those who want peace everywhere (my theory is, at the end of the day, all human beings do want a good night's sleep, and so, irrespective of what anyone thinks, everyone is a wimpy peacenik), we need Imran to win this election.

He and his party (not just him the individual hero), will improve things after that. They are a part of the formula for world peace. My somewhat debatable implications of world-wants-a-good-night's-sleep theory (actually an unimportant aside) apart: It's as simple as having to tackle the root of the problem. That's what supporting Imran to win is all about. He can do it (electoral Victory). Warm regds, Vsd. Just entertaining myself here, with the V sign, dunno what all it stands for in different parts of the globe and galaxy ☺ Fascinating.

Also, i'm not a mathematician, but I'm beginning to think that BO - US + DEO = INK might be the beginning of a superb formula. But there's lots more to put in before it's a complete equation?! Ok, this bit, i'm so talking to my creative self, i should put it on my poetry blog and forget about it for a few eons…in any case, it's not a part of my commentary on the IK campaign. Must remember to delete this and paste it elsewhere before someone reads it and starts taking this as good as gibberish paragraph seriously! :D (anyway, i owe this paragraph a brief translation: i only meant that all the good guys n gals –individuals – from all over the world need to bring out the best in their own countries and fix everything!)

2nd May, Just Watched the Zafarwal Speech that was made today. He said it was a farmers' gathering, and said his emphasis would be on small farmers. Yay! And he also said he would encourage SMEs (small and medium enterprises). Said this bit in English, i think it's worth looking for a translation for SMEs, as it's a good point.

He made a point that he's been making for a while now, about how farmers in India get a good deal from the government compared to Pakistan, just across the border. At this place, there were quite a few claps for this public praise for India!

He also recited a couplet in the context of difficult times which has also been quoted on the official facebook page. Though i need a detailed translation, understood. Also quite endearing, how he sometimes laughs at his own jokes (though this is not, per se, very attractive behavior: dying of laughter, that is, while cracking one's own jokes).

Just viewed today's **(2nd May) Speech at Shakargarh:** Here, again, while making the same point about how India gives its farmers a better deal than Pakistan does, he specified that the State of Punjab government across the border gives its farmers a better deal than Pakistan does. He then exchanged a look/smile with one of his supports, my guess is that this was because, yesterday or maybe the day before that, in one of his speeches or interviews, while criticizing corruption everywhere (i think including India), he had also made a reference to Punjab, and although he might have meant Punjab, Pakistan, it could have come across to some people as Punjab, India. So the specific reference in this speech, to the Govt of Punjab could just be to rectify that.

It was also interesting, the tone in which he mentioned that India was just across the border, it was almost a tone of reassurance to the people, which they took very well.

Otherwise, there could be a number of political factors for his having said that, ranging from personal equations with Indian politicians (one can only speculate), to indicating his party's disapproval of the current UPA 2 (more likely the latter, since one of his main planks is anti-corruption, cannot see him as being a big fan of the doings of the UPA 2, barring the honourable exceptions, in any case).

Also, if he must read out so many statistics, this time, they were presented better: ask a question, and answer it with the number (i might use that myself sometime, considering i rarely use statistics while making speeches, unless it's while giving a talk as an expert).

i think he ended the speech by praising the women that had showed up at the rally, saying they were there to fight and finish the bad governance.

2nd May, Just Watched Today's Pasroor Jalsa on youtube.

He's got better at articulating the point on local government, and the word Panchayat was mentioned again (second time now, out of the videos i've watched). On local governments, he said the villages will be in charge (have control) of things like education and law and order. Might have also mentioned health like he's been doing in this context. Significantly, he said the role of the Patwari will be reduced, and this will minimize the scope for corruption. This last point is where one can see the idea sort of fine-tuning in his mind. Good.

He's also going on making the point about how Allah has given him everything, and this time, he said Allah has given him more than he knew to imagine. It was overall, a good meeting, but he just short of snapped at guys who kept cheering (kinda interrupting) when he was well into a good point! Theek hai. Also interesting that he specifically addressed the buzurgs here, and told them to bring about the change for a new Pakistan for the sake of the mustaqbil (future) of their children.

2nd May, just watched a 30th April youtube clip from a news programme Kamran Ke Saath. Here, Imran discussed the role of the army, and commented on some of the things that Gen. Kayani was shown saying in a speech that he had made, and that had just been aired on the same programme. He said that dialogue is the work of Politicians, that the politicians so far in Pak, had failed to hold dialogue, and that it was sad that the army was stuck in areas. Overall, quite a balanced and acceptable stand on Kayani, i felt, though i know very little about the subject.

Also, at the beginning, the host asked Imran whether it was ok for him to have said that he was going to eat tiger tikkas, and whether this was halaal. Imran laughed and said that there is a way, a style, of speaking at a public meeting, and he clarified that this was intended in that light-hearted spirit. (The tiger is the election symbol of Nawaz Sharif's party).

3rd May (Today) Mansehra Speech

Initially, the mike wasn't working. He tapped away tantalizingly and waited for it to work. Jokes apart, someone should check sometime, as far as the mike goes, whether this was deliberately done by anybody. Also, it should be standard procedure to have a powerful portable mike handy at all times just in case things like this happen, these things are quite temperamental in the likely event that it wasn't sabotage. Even when the speech started, the mike stopped working, and it was at a point where the continued working of the mike was essential: he had just started explaining that when he says Jehad, he means a fight against corruption and injustice through the democratic process. But obviously, the initial line hadn't given these explanations. Imagine what would have happened if the mike hadn't started working again! Anyway, it did, so, whatever.

He had a new anecdote this time, which he asked people to listen to gaur sey. It was about a man he once met at an airport in Sopore who was waiting for the corpse of his brother. Apparently, people had died in the cold while trying to go, in khoofia ways, to Europe, for employment. He said this man's story had made him sad. Apart from the fact that this might have been an experience that stuck in his head, it makes him sound like one who is a little clueless about the world (for one such event to have been so educative)…if this was long ago and he was very young and still learning about the big bad world, he could have clarified that. My main point being: what was the point? Unless the local crowd gleaned some meaning from it that i can only hazard impressionistically vague guesses about.

He spoke of how something has to die/end for newness/improvement to begin in the context of "naya Pakistan." He also repeated that couplet (i'd better check its detailed/literal meaning, i was hoping he'd translate it in the course of the speech).

3rd May Abbotabad Jalsa Speech

Like the Mansehra crowd, euphoric crowd here as well. An improvement in these two speeches has been the fact that while talking of local government and saying that decisions will be made at local levels, he is personalizing it by mentioning the name of the place where the speech is made, opposed to the name of the (corresponding bigger) place where decisions are currently made.

He also asked people specifically not to vote for independent candidates, and he said this was because independent candidates have no vision. As we all know, this is not necessarily true. It was fine to ask people not to vote for independents, but this was a bit of a lame reason to give, it sort of ridiculed the people's intellects.

The good part (he's been saying this often), is: don't look at community, who's related, blah blah, just look at the "nazriya" (vision). Vote for this party because of its vision.

Finally he said, Mat bhoolna, Kay… Kay: PTI… Naya Pakistan!

3rd May (Today) Battagram Speech

While he made excellent points on the need to bring about a new government that brings justice to the people, he specifically spoke against the need for roads. To deliver things like education, health etc., roads are definitely required. He could criticize corruption and corrupt contractors and politicians who make money from roads, but opposing roads in this blanket fashion is quite elitist. One thing all these people want, which many of us have, is a road to their house, or at least near it.

For the first time, he made a mention of how there are different laws applicable to men and women, and said that was a bad thing. Excellent.

4th May, i'm off to a party after having watched a play, will view today's speeches late tonight or tomorrow morning.…

4th May (past midnight here in Delhi), Watched the Speech at Swabi

When he said that the villages will settle disputes, especially land disputes, and that there will be free justice, he also mentioned (for the first time during the election campaign, at least from what i've heard so far though he's mentioned this before elsewhere), the word Jirgas. (The tribal and other traditional local institutions of government). i think this concept has a lot in common with our Forest Rights Act that we introduced here in India (and, i reckon, traditional systems of land governance by various tribal and indigenous communities across the globe).

He made a special mention of a PTI person who had been allegedly murdered by a PML(N) person.

He also said, at the beginning, that mashallah, the Pakistani quam was very samajhdar and understood everything (i think he said this in response to various slogans the crowd kept raising that were points from his speeches).

4th May, Charsada Speech

He began by saying that Muslims who spoil the name of the religion are worse than kafirs. I think he said his specific reference was to Maulana Fazl Ur Rehman who had been the 'friendly opposition' for five years when Parvez Musharraf was in power and had killed Pashtoons. i think he said Fazlur Rehmn had again killed Pashtoons by being in league with Zardari for another five years. He had made this point in a speech yesterday or the day before that also.

4th May at Naushera

Related a legend/story from the religion, where the religious leader had said to a seeker, in reply to a question, that he himself was too old to change his religion, but that for anyone to be a true Mussalman, the main thing that the person had to do was to be a truthful person. To tell the truth was the priority in Islam.

5th May, just viewed today's **Minar-e-Pakistan** election speech at **Lahore** from a facebook page:

Superb expansive gestures signifying benevolence, confidence, peace, well-being, omnipresence etc. To be emulated by all!

He praised the unity in diversity of Switzerland, saying although people spoke different languages there, they were united by one nazariya or vision. i wish he'd cite India as an example of unity in diversity.

While promising to make a lawful, progressive and strong country, i wish he'd add on that bit that he's mentioned at least once long ago on some television programme (if i'm not mistaken), about how he dreams of a strong Federation comprising his country and all the neighbouring countries.

In this speech, while discussing the historical aspects of Islamic rule, instead of just saying Maghreb like in the earlier speeches, he clarified by mentioning the past glory of Morocco to wherever. If there's a speech-writing/suggesting assistant/s, they have refreshed their reading in the course of the campaign. Good. But someone please tell him that any self-respecting person from the subcontinent will not say Middle East, but will say West Asia (i heard him say middle east, and i think it was in this speech).

The other country that he mentions now and then is Australia. This time (as once earlier), he mentioned, in the context of coal reserves and top soil, that compared to Australia's excellent six inches of top soil, his country has six feet of it. Frankly, i'm quite ok with their party's energy mix for their country for now.

By the way, that Patti Scialfa lookalike (kidding, have researched her and heard her on insaaf tv, excellent work), shouldn't quell the enthusiasm of the young women supporters!

5ᵗʰ May, Speech at Khushab Jalsa, just viewed on a facebook page:

He started by saying he can forsee a khushalee ka daura ahead.

He mentioned (local?) names of PTI leaders, including doctors, engineers etc. (for this, he was looking down and referring to a paper, better than waving it around like in some earlier speeches).

The point about roads that i had earlier thought problematic was clarified when he told the people that he is not promising them just roads or metro services or bridges, but promises to build them an entire nation. Good way of having got out of that bind! And congratulations to whoever for the statesmanship in rectifying this. (haha this is beginning to feel quite realistic!).

5ᵗʰ May, Chiniot Jalsa Speech

He's stepped up his interpretation of Islam, an excellent move. At this rate, deserves to be annointed an Imam some day…it's a fair and good interpretation, i feel.

He was chewing gum. Or paan. Or something. He made his point about the effectiveness of social media again (he's been making this point now and then), saying you can't fool people these days, there are cell phones, and word about everything goes around in no time…in effect, that there are no secrets.

5ᵗʰ May, Just Watched Today's Faisalabad Speech

Noticed that this time, he began by addressing the farmers, labourers and the working class. He specified slum dwellers, rickshaw wallahs, taxi drivers, factory workers and other people who are usually the subject matter of Springsteen's songs! He also addressed the town "Faisalabad," called out to them in a rockstarish way. And lifted the hand of the party candidate (i presume), who was standing next to him, again in a Springsteen-lifting-Clarence-Clemons'-handesque way.

Which reminds me of a clip of an English news item i watched on Imran's elections. They described him as Pakistan's own Obama. i'd be happy if, a few years down the line, some anchor, in the context of the US elections, described Springsteen as the US's own Imran. ☺

He spoke of building a strong Pakistan, one where the people from Balochistan, and the FATA areas, and Punjab and Sindh, and people of all religions are treated equally. He said he's for equality before the law, and went on to explain how Islam views all human beings as equal, irrespective of whether they are Hindu or Sikh or Christian or from the Kailash area (he didn't specify Buddhist, but definitely meant them as well). He got a lot of applause for this. This is how the majority of the citizens feel (very positive towards India), is what i gather from this and other similar crowd responses.

His eyes had a wild, Bruceish look and he kept asking for people to move from the path of the spotlights.

I somehow feel that it will have a good impact if small children are seen (being carried) at some of these venues. But i realize that's a bit of a bizarre suggestion…unless there are some around anyway, and they are made visible. (Have come back to add this: looks like great minds think alike, just watched another clip from yesterday's Lahore Jalsa, and i find a kid with a flag did come on to the stage!!).

He clarified that when he says he'll collect taxes, it doesn't mean he'll increase taxes, just that he'll make sure people pay their taxes. He said that in fact, he would try to reduce taxes if he could.

Depending on how the speech is going, he could tell the crowd what they mean to him in emotional terms. This speech was very good.

6th May, looks like there are a lot of Jalsas to watch (and catch up on) today…i'm just back from the dentist's and taken a quick look at one Lahore jalsa.

The insaf tv facebook page says that he's been doing big meetings till sunset, and then smaller ones everyday at Lahore. i think if he's so certain of winning his Lahore seat, he shouldn't waste more time on Jalsas there. He should start the day very early, there's good attendance at early morning meetings. And then maybe rest a bit mid-day (or keep smaller en route kind of meetings for mid-day). Since these are the last few days, i think he needs to campaign from sunset and into the night, there'll be crowds. And i hope he hasn't left any campaigning for beyond the 8th. Will have to monitor the poll date preparations round-the-clock, almost!

The Indian papers (including the Hindi ones), have a piece on how Imran is known for opposing American drone strikes, but is also getting legitimate financial support from American donors. Of course, depending on each paper's politics, they show this news in different lights, but i don't think it's a problem.

6th May, no videos of today's campaigns out yet…but here's a point worth noting: while speaking of foreign policy, he said he was in favour of his country not interfering in Afghanistan.

6th May, Just Viewed Today's Speech at Kasur

Good emphasis on local government, justice, education and health. Quite a bit was said on education. He specifically addressed children and told them that although they can't vote, they should tell their parents to vote for the bat! That was quite cutely done ☺ And for the first time, there was genuine affection (towards the children), in his voice.

There were some lengthy stories related to corruption by the other parties. Not so sure if it's worth narrating very long stories to such huge gatherings.

And now this would be my word of advice to all parties and to those conducting the elections: While ensuring that the elections go smoothly, also make arrangements for law and order post-results. The euphoria should not lead to squabbles and stampedes on the streets.

6th May, Just Viewed Yesterday's 5th May Speech at Jhang

He dedicated a large section of the speech to addressing children, and narrated how children in Pakistan had helped him to fund-raise for the Shaukat Khanum hospital.

He also made the point (that he's made earlier), about how his party plans to spend five times more on Taleem (education). Quite poetic as I'd had a breakfast discussion on education here the same morning!

And while one logs off for the moment, there is a dancing peacock and a peahen outside my office window here in New Delhi ☺ Really!

And here's a note (to myself) within a note (to myself): Looks like assorted people have been harmlessly hacking into my computer, making minor changes to this document, like punctuation marks, formatting and so on, which I keep correcting (though i could be mistaken, and i might've made careless mistakes while typing. Most likely, a mix of both phenomena). The most obvious being the lines at the bottom of the last two pages. i wonder if these lines are for footnotes, and whether the hacker/s are suggesting that i start making footnotes?!! Or did i hit some footnote button by mistake? Whateva.

How interesting: Just read an update on the official facebook page, that tomorrow, his first meeting is at 11 am at Karachi. This sounds like a different kind of routine from what had been described of the routine so far on the Insaf TV facebook page, and about which i had written something in this commentary of mine earlier today. Anyway, good to know that there's such a meeting planned. i feel it'll stir a few more constituencies.

Another thought: i read that Musharraf's party is boycotting the polls. What have you done, strategically, to woo those voters? It's never too late. The other parties must be acting swiftly on this.

And before the campaign period ends, are you planning one comprehensive television address to the entire nation? (Not an interview, or the telecasting of a speech, but an address on a channel or channels that are widely telecast). i think there should be one, and it will ensure that sweep.

If yes, such an address should also include the following ingredients: a brief, modestly narrated account of your own political journey; a section that addresses the party workers (ranging from congratulating them for their efforts so far, to instructions, and suggestions for the polling day); main points on what's wrong with the nation; basic poll promises (your vision, but make it sound practical) to the nation from local to state-level to national to foreign policy; your broad idea of Islam and finally, some personal/emotive content.

I wonder who is hacking into this?!! It's not impossible that the PTI is…and that some of these suggestions are being taken on board (and that that's not just my imagination), in which case, i have been wondering who's getting all the credit for all this?!!

6th May, Just Watched Today's Allahabad Speech

He made a more detailed mention of tribal areas, FATA, and said that the PTI is the favourite party in those areas.

He said that Kashmir will be solved through political dialogue, and he will bring peace (aman) and that this will lead to khushali.

Delivered this speech very well. The camera, for this one, was focused on him, and he combined being at ease with making an effective speech very well. Sleeves rolled up, nice muscles!! And when he concluded saying zindabad, he raised his hand in a fist, looking very commie indeed. He also said that he would not let any injustice be done towards women, and would go to court if any injustices were ever done to women. (like you can see, he's gathering the support of various players!)

He also said that if any of his candidates turn out to be "do numberee" people (corrupt), then he has a dry cleaning machine, he'll put them into it and make then ek numberee!!

6th May, Today's Speech at Gujranwala

Spoke against corruption. Said that the PTI has the support of the minorities and named Hindus, Sikhs and other religions, and said PTI will not let injustice happen to the minorities.

6th May, Today's Speech at Sialkot

Huge, euphoric crowd. He said Naya Pakistan will be the kind of Pakistan that Iqbal wanted. Justice, Equality, Peace, an emphasis on education. Only watched a brief clip from a news show, so don't know what the rest of the speech contained, will look out for a longer version of this event.

7th May, Just Watched the 6th May Multan Speech

Massive turnout. Anti-incumbency and anti-Nawaz sentiment, anti-corruption at its height. And support for Imran. He will get an unprecedented majority from here. Speech was good.

7th May: Haven't yet viewed any of today's meetings, but just heard a little while ago, about Imran's injury at Lahore (what was the need to have another Lahore meeting?) because of the stage collapsing. Watched the NDTV report, and tracking the twitter accounts of Awab Alvi and others… they say he's probably been taken to Shaukat Khanum hospital, has head injuries and was bleeding (NDTV reporter who was an eye witness). News reports on the net also say he was semi-conscious but that it was not serious. Just peeped into Jemima Khan's twitter account, she says he's conscious. Phew.

Praying for him and the others who've been injured.

7ᵗʰ May 10:42 pm: Ok, Faisal Javed has tweeted, saying Imran's in high spirits, and the doc from Shaukat was supposed to make a statement… anyway, all ok with his health overall, looks like. …he's got stitches….

8ᵗʰ May: Just watched Imran's "address to the Nation" on the official facebook page. Spooky or what! (The fact that a national address was made like i'd thought they should, except that it was under most unexpected circumstances). Anyway, he spoke a few lines and the points were from the earlier speeches, to which he added that now he's done everything he could, it's for everyone else to vote on the 11ᵗʰ of May, "apney liye." Lying there in the hospi and speaking like that, he reminds one of images of Kasab that we saw on our Indian TV channels. Perhaps it is a way for a politician in Pakistan to appeal to those indulging in violent politics, to give democracy a chance.

Also watched Faisal Javed's announcement with updates on Imran's health and saying that the 9ᵗʰ May Jalsa at Islamabad will take place, and that Imran might address it.

8ᵗʰ May, just watched, on youtube, a special interview that he gave yesterday before the fall happened. The programme was called Kharra Sach.

This interviewer (who, oddly, reminded me of a Churchill fan), said he'd ask the questions as if Imran's victory was certain. (In fact, he said he was about to vote for some other party, but his children had convinced him that Imran would win). Imran laughed.

In the course of the interview, he brought up some post-election scenarios and asked Imran what he/his party would do on various issues.

Among his many replies, Imran again made references to Nitish Kumar's good governance. At a later stage, when Imran was talking about strengthening local government, the interviewer prompted him, saying you mean Panchayati Raj. Imran said, yes, that's exactly what Nitish has done! (i need to check whether Nitish has, indeed, been doing a better job than other states when it comes to Panchayati Raj! Believable).

Every time Imran was told that people had a lot of hope, he folded his hands in jestful (but well-meant) prayer and laughed.

One point that he made with greater clarity was about the delegation of work. He said setting up of corporations did not mean private sector. That politicians could oversee and decide policy etc., but (public sector sort of) corporations controlled by the government should take over functions of the railways etc.

Another point that they discussed was post-election mischief makers: Imran was asked what he'd do if rival parties pretended to be his guys (wielding his flags etc.), indulged in violence, and then tried blaming his party for it. This was a very well-researched question. i had earlier written in this document, about the need for post-poll law and order, but this exact version of disorder hadn't crossed my mind. A good lesson/tutorial point!

8th May: Ok, i just read on PTI twitter that he'll address the 9th May Jalsa via video. Better. Too over the top to expect Imran to go for a Jalsa so soon after the injuries.

I also read somewhere else that the PTI might ask for elections to be postponed. i think this is an awful idea. No point at all in doing that. It's not going to help anyone or make any difference, going by all the known trends and circumstances.

8th May: Just noticed that the official facebook page, about half an hour ago, has uploaded a clip from a 6th May recorded clip from Imran, where he's telling the people about the upcoming meeting (9th May Islamabad at "D" Chowk). He says that at this meeting, he's going to make non-political points, that everyone must listen, and he's going to talk to his quam/people about his Dil kee Baatein. (He had also said, at a recent speech, that he doesn't know why, but his Dil is telling him that he's going to win the elections). Interesting: will look out for this speech! (Of course, i will semi-delusionally continue to look for whether or not the points that i'd suggested for a last address to the nation before the elections are "incorporated" into the speech!). Semi delusional because either someone's hacking into my comp and reading all this, or the file has a funky virus, in addition to totally arbit coincidences such as the word Churchill being mentioned in today's newspaper!! (Almost as though it was a pointer towards the Churchill-like character that was the anchor in the interview i described).

8th May: By the way, it turns out that most of the Jalsas (that had to be cancelled) today, were Lahore Jalsas.

9th May: Noticed only today, that it looks like someone from the PTI visited my blog. (A PTI environment specialist who is now a candidate). So someone from the party has seen my blog, though i don't know in what detail. Though i can keep dredging out bits from speeches and documents of theirs that i look at in an unorganized way: like a broad line or two on Natural Resource Governance that, mashallah, seemed to resonate with my old note on my blog, with the same topic.

Now looking forward to watching on the internet at about 7 pm, the Islamabad speech, or what's being described as his "address to his nation." Should i say Break A Leg?! (Serious grunt: even the language of theatre should do away with all this imagery of violence. Inshallah.) ☺

CHAPTER VIII

Bought Online: E-Shopping Rants and Civil Drones

I introduced myself to the world of online shopping in 2014. This was soon after our UPA government lost power. As a part of the team that ushered in and advised the ten-year UPA 1 and 2 INC-led government (as a humble, but even if I say so myself, impactful grassroots party-worker and not-so-grassroots pro-bono party advisor), I found myself suddenly free to go back home to rural Andhra Pradesh, and to make forays into the NCR primarily in connection with my law-related work.

Three years have passed since, and a tryst and sojourn with e-commerce (primarily as Consumer), has been the hitherto uncharted territory that one has hiked through.

The best part of shopping online is that you don't need to commute-obviously! No pollution, no traffic jams, no having to run around from market-to-market and shop-to-shop hunting for the saree that will be the find of the season, jostling people on the road, at the shop-entrance and even in the queue. Instead, you have at your fingertips, detailed information and an exponentially larger array of options. Scouring the market takes on a whole new meaning with the net-search.

True, a few things unique, and a few things exclusive might never make it to the net, but such things, one is likely to hear of, anyway. And true, you can't really feel the texture of fabrics and things. But that's what easy and free returns are for! Buy, try, rave, save. Or reject, return, get the stuff reimbursed or replaced. Simple!

Unless, of course, you happen to be in rural India.

Webstores are eager to sell their wares. Type in your pin-code, and voila! It delivers to the back of whichever beyond you've boxed yourself into. There's always an estimated time-frame mentioned. Sometimes, this works. Otherwise, you could be waiting for weeks on end, and hey, all that was said was that that was the estimated time for the website to be so kind as to deliver the product that you have paid for, all the way to where they're supposed to deliver it to.

And then it's not quite the website, or the company that's selling the things to you that has much to do with where the item's to be delivered. Your rural address. It's on the records. It's been said the thing's going to be delivered to you. You've paid good money, and made your plans according to the understanding that said product will be delivered to said doorstep.

The site or company conveniently hands this responsibility over to courier people, who then sometimes sub-contract the last-mile delivery to lone-wolf freelancers. End result, your products are sent into your neck of the woods once a week if you're lucky. You're more likely to receive a phone-call from the delivery agent asking you to go to some bus-stop or some office at some nearby town to collect your parcel.

This is the private sector I'm talking about, mind you! Things reach more efficiently via the government's postal system of speed post, to be sure. But that's not the point. Private versus public is not the point here.

Here is a huge opportunity to create good competition for local couriers. Basic training or requirements that are relevant to the job, such as a familiarity with the areas to which the products are to be delivered would go a long way in making the service more efficient. Rather than keeping these last-mile courier people off the tax and efficiency radar, it would reflect quite well on the rural economy, if this were viewed as an emerging formidable group of self-employed people. Rural areas also have a similar requirement for trained electricians and plumbers, not only from a present-day perspective, but from the point of view of putting in place, safe and quality infrastructure for twenty-second century green villages.

If things take aeons to reach you, they also take centuries to return. I suppose it is increased connectivity, and modern systems for the movement of goods that will facilitate speedy deliveries and returns.

Which brings us to the topic of the use of drones (unmanned aerial craft) for the transport of goods. I think I recall reading that although this is a topic for Civil Aviation, the Prime Minister's Office had retained the function of making policies for the use of such drones as well.

It might appeal to our imaginations, to imagine drones delivering free medicines to remote areas, or to have micro-drones conducting drip-irrigation like in Israel. There have been advertisements, in the past, in Indian newspapers, that indicate that in China, pizzas are delivered by drone.

Other than all the usual (and very valid) concerns that pertain to security, are the concerns regarding sound and air pollution, and air traffic in general. One needs to approach with great caution, the entire issue of the use of drones, and to not be in a hurry to meet short-term goals such as those of catering to the demands of e-retail package-delivery. Especially if we happen to be the recently-described harried consumers with rights.

The national conversation, which is wringing its hands over the polluted skies of smoggy Delhi has not cottoned on to the civilizational enormity of the upcoming drone policy, and needs to do so post-haste.

If you're a cautionary voice against the emerging drone policy of the NDA government, and your voice is being kept at bay by those defending the emerging quasi-policy by being told that the whole drone thing is totally unregulated, and at least some regulation is being brought in, you must be a green horn, or a complete egoistical nincompoop at the law-and-policy-making table (or you or your friends must be into some murky drone-deals). Not too many apologies for this deliberate outburst, that, I assure you, does not warrant a trip to the loony bin (or I would've deleted it by now).

Who do you think ought to be the next President of the Indian National Congress Party?

There are a number of other miscellaneous aspects of the web-based sales of goods that need to be monitored and streamlined. I hope the consumer rights practitioners are holding refresher courses, or doing whatever it is, that needs to be done (one could go into near-academic detail here, but will refrain from doing so on this chatty occasion), to empower the e-shopper. The e-shopper's concerns, like any other consumer's concerns, are not to be brushed aside lightly. For obvious reasons.

The way websites are designed are sometimes misleading to the customer as far as the process of the return of goods is concerned. You might not be able to activate a Return button for days after receiving the product, and be told that returns are possible only after delivery. (There is, of course, a deadline for returns). Once you miss the deadline because the prominent button still informs you that you're waiting for the product (that's arrived long ago), and you decide to phone the wretches, the voice tells you that there is, in fact, some other page with tiny lettering somewhere, which leads you to a return process. They might have been able to justify this in the absence of the prominent return button. Such fiascos are more often than not, on individual sites that directly sell to you, and rarely on the searchable sites that serve as a selling agent.

The other great thing about shopping online is that one doesn't have to trek half-way cross the world to catch a good or sudden deal or discount. But the flip-side of this is that one's got to be wary of misleading discount-announcements. You read something that says XYZ huge discount, and you click on the link, the next message mentions the fine-print that the front-message neglected mentioning. The thing with the internet is- you would've not clicked on the first link if you'd known about the next thing. Each unnecessary click is a waste of time and money. Some of the understood norms of traditional print-world advertising need to align themselves with emerging technologies. If regulators don't, consumers will need to ensure that such corrections are made.

Either way, a strong consumer rights movement in the area of e-commerce is the need of the hour. This would also serve to streamline and further 'legitimize' the goods and services of web entrepreneurs, who ought to recognize the fact that they stand to improve their standards with user-feedback and competition.

While India grapples with its nascent world of internet-shopping, it is probably still way ahead of many other countries when it comes to the outreach and efficiency of e-commerce.

It would thus be quite acceptable for India to take the lead in areas of reviewing and recommending actions to other countries, especially those in the neighbourhood. It might be an area where countries like China would prefer countries like India to address countries like Taiwan directly, in terms of room for improvement in the online market-place.

CHAPTER IX

LORDY, LORDY, WE'RE SO BAWDY: GENDER ISSUES: ONE-POINT PROGRAMME

I think much of polite company in India (we decide who that is), is quite at ease with discussing the next wave of women's issues. Is capable of recognizing some almost-given-up-on rants and objections as being not merely frivolous or elitist complaints, but often the roots of very serious problems.

The blind-spot seems to be that many fall short of tackling, or accepting the existence of these issues in their own, immediate, every-day lives. I think we owe it to ourselves to spare nobody. If a supposed 'perfect gentleman' is out of line with his words or ways, the rap on the knuckle ought not to abscond its duty.

But it might be argued that everyone picks their battles, and does so in a dynamic way, guided by ever-altering variables. In which case, make this particular point-of-review a frequent one, please.

If someone's suddenly started putting their foot down, more than forty years down the torture-chamber of a misogynistic society, against the boorish behaviour or body-language of colleagues, employees, relatives, friends, voters or the general public, it could well be because the person's current priorities and opportunities give them the leeway for such resistance. Or that the person's altered what their personal trade-offs could be. Like they might not be too keen to stand for elections and pander to people's egos anymore.

Chances are, that those taking the most strident personal stands, and standing up to the onslaught of male chauvinism and misogyny are the ones who are not likely to have read or consciously participated in organized activities of mainstream movements for women's rights, or trans-gender rights.

With formally un-showcased struggles on assorted turfs, the battles of such women and girls are likely to gain them, not awards, applause, credits in glossy paid-for publications and super-successful working-woman status, but wondrous trophies of hostility, oppression, and a plethora of signboards to the loony-bin.

Shake the foundations of the social norms in polite society that expects women to wear bras, and a brand of feminists will inform you that bra-burning was done with and dusted in the nineteen-hundred-and sixties-and-seventies.

Intellectually clichéd, not worth bringing up today. Pardon the malapropish anti-compulsory-bra struggle, but a cause is a cause. No reference to the Balochistan Republican Army or whatever it might be called, if it indeed exists. (Puns are supposed to be base humour, injected into plays by the bard and others in order to keep the groundlings entertained…so the peals-in-response-to-puns are adequately smothered, but just enough to let the joke know you got the joke, who, in turn, cringes artistically, and even apologises while stirring the alphabet-soup tureen).

That'll be one's first and last self-conscious attempt at signing off (with a negative) on the roll-call for humour. Funny is as funny was. Otherwise, don't laugh. Eeeesh! What a self-consciously-written paragraph (but there's probably technology to read not just thoughts, but minute aural inflections, so same difference, either way- documented or not. One reckons.).

No doubt, the zeal for consumer choices and the priorities of the bra-industry over-rode the interests of various strapped-up victims at various points of time, and the whole thing fizzled out.

Or, to be fair, it didn't quite fizzle out. Those who could find themselves in, or create environs where such shackles were made redundant, did so. Certain countries, certain beaches, many parties and homes, and remote tribal hamlets. France.

Keeping consumer options and choices open is, of course, important. Some women might need to wear bras for physical comfort, or while exercising, for support. Or for whimsical reasons, which, if you analyse them, might not be all that whimsical, and would therefore be utilitarian in some way, and thus permitted by stern and grouchy societies.

But most of the time, bras are worn so that a person's nipples are masked, particularly after the invention of the t-shirt bra, and for the robust, so that breasts are not seen to swing. The natural contours of women's breasts being discernible through fabric is pounced on, and termed as provocative dressing. Officialdom is unlikely to touch such garments with the other end of a pointer-pole. This is the point of origin of much of the raw power-struggle between (or, to be more precise and politically correct: amongst) genders. I think it's time to turn the definition of power dressing on its head.

The origins and eddies, whirls, and current social microcosms that dictate these norms are often set by insecure and thus hawkish women (insecure not being said here in a value-judgemental way, but literally and justifiably insecure- financially, within a relationship, or just in terms of establishing their own control over space in domestic and public spheres), AND by men who seek to use whatever trick they may have in the book, to assert their own influence over spaces, even if it means displaying elements of aggressive and domineering paternalistic behaviour.

And then, of course (and mostly), there are the creatures of habit (pardon the pun, no reference to Julie Andrews and the sound of music or other veils). Those who only know how to view what has been dinned into their minds since they were born, as being the normal and proper thing to do or wear or accept. Anything strange or different or unaccustomed-to is held up to ridicule and creates panic.

Dress-wise, much of english liesure-book reading society might feel it's traversed way ahead of these observations and realizations to even suspect that this is how things still are, even in their immediate neighbourhoods.

So all this needs to be said again. In these very basic terms.

In order to keep the discussion going, to accelerate it, to garner support.

To point out to the emancipated, how they could facilitate change even without going too much out of their way (though, ideally, if they did, there'd be exponentially quicker and better results for all of humanity, and definitely for martians).

Much of wardrobe-judgementalism comes from people being predatory or territorial about space. It then becomes about control over space.

However, this is often inter-twined with other aspects of attempted control, and attempts to establish various kinds of dominance over others. This applies within households, as well as in public spaces.

In remote tribal areas in India, for example, women do not wear blouses or petticoats with their sarees. This way of dressing, with no concept of shame attached to displaying the upper body, is still accepted as normal in many tribal habitats. But the change in attitude brought about by specimens of the 'outside world' on this front is rapid and regressive.

There's an impression amongst some feminists, that women being bare-breasted, historically, or in certain tribal areas, is always a sign of their subjugation.

While this could well be the case in some places, it is very important not to confuse these pieces of (no doubt rare and valuable) knowledge, with my observations that are drawn from observing and interacting with people from various tribes since I was born.

Denying the fact that there are, indeed, still some places on this planet, where women's bodies are far less objectified than in the modern world does a great dis-service to the cause of women's empowerment.

The fast-diminishing right to be bare-breasted (of which an appropriate facilitating atmosphere is an important part), needs to be the focus of any discourse on development, girls' empowerment, overall social trends, and even of national (and international) conversations and actions.

On the state highways and in the smaller towns and villages that surround tribal India, middle-aged and elderly women still walk proud and free and respected in their blouseless, petticoatless cloth-pieces.

But passing trucks often do honk in a manic, eve-teasing sort of way when they pass by these ladies.

Younger women and girls do not find it possible or appropriate to dress with the kind of abandon that their mothers and grandmothers still manage to pull off in these remote areas.

The new generations of children and young boys are gradually learning to disrespect this aspect of the power of women in our own societies, and are sometimes the first ones to tease or misunderstand nudity. This is primarily a move away from understanding Nature and its influences on the human body.

There are then examples from the west coast, from areas that are a part of Kerala, where it is said that women from lower castes were forced to remain topless, and had to pay a tax if they dared to wear blouses. A most objectionable practice, but this fuel for quiz-wizardry should not be repeatedly used to disempower the genuine and rightful cause of tribal women elsewhere, which is to be able to continue to remain bare-breasted and powerful in society.

Where society intrinsically knew and recognized the various workings of the forces of nature on the human body, today, men are quick to misinterpret prominent nipples or goose-bumps on the female body as lustful sexual arousal, or more ridiculously, as being a statement of invitation to intercourse.

Added to this are often societally rigid and patriarchal views that if a youth's body displays such signs, then it is time for the person to get married. Single people are seen as people with problems.

A taut penis visible through a trouser, and society thinks it has a frustrated, unemployed youth who needs to earn enough money to get married and have sex on its hands.

Predictably, the 'problems' are usually in the form of challenges to those who wish to continue to perpetrate existing systems of family, property, dominance and unilaterally-dictated conditional protectionism. This is the kind of malaise that needs to be smoked out of the DNA of all world religions, and other minds. This is the heaven of freedom that Tagore's lyrics sought for our country to awake to. I have the same aspiration for our entire planet, which might resemble a flickering blue butterfly from space afar.

Meanwhile, these same areas also have towns full of people who have hopped onto the bandwagon of middle-class morality long ago- inspired by the British, French, Dutch, and even the Mughals, feministically unpopular interpretations of Hindu mythology, and occasionally, by largely benign elements at the top of some feudal pyramids, who are, luckily, likely to be open to dialogue, book-reading, discussion and social transformation, and to participate, whole-heartedly, in democratic processes.

However, the trick is to swing the debate within these feudal opinion-makers, in favour of those amongst them who stand for gender justice. The single women. That would be one's most infallible bet for catalysing change in feudal-minded societies. The rights of single women and girls. I've noticed, in the policy-debate in India, that when you mention single women, the concern, sympathy, and priority is immediately directed towards widows and those divorced. My fight, to get to the root of the matter, is to place the rights of the single girl and woman first. And the word to use is single, as opposed to unmarried. Because labelling humans as being unmarried, to me, is as irrelevant to a person's status as saying that the salt is without pepper. We're talking about salt, what's pepper got to do with the conversation?

There's such a thing, in polite conversation, as being too anal with your metaphors. But outer-space help you if you're surrounded by muscular and docile achievers who know everything, in which case, what's pepper got to do with sexuality, go board a comet until we ask you to pin-point the exact meaning of each and every syllable of this paragraph of clearly not macho republic, but *Earth Republic*. All the people who used to be like this might not be like this anymore, and thank goodness for that.

As we know, no community or family is totally homogenous in its views. Each individual's self-interest varies. All these factors need to be learnt and understood on a case-to-case basis in order to help tilt the balance in favour of the girl child, the single woman, and the LGBT community.

The highest degree of difficulty lies in tackling the instances of misogyny, harassment, abuse, discrimination, oppression, bullying at the level of one's immediate environment.

Even if a girl or woman thinks (or has been brought up to believe) that she has not been a victim of some sort of discrimination or the other -because making such an assumption would nebulously indict her entire family and circles of people she comes in contact with- it must be realised that this is highly unlikely. And one says highly unlikely and not impossible, only keeping a mathematical possibility in mind.

The recent Hashtag-MeToo online campaign to confirm instances of sexual abuse from any time of one's life, in any form, has had such an overwhelming response (and, as per my observations, mostly from courageous and articulate women, first), that I think it is a timely reminder for all concerned about gender equity to take note, and to act.

Regarding Hashtag-MeToo

Here's what I wrote on my Facebook wall (and cut and pasted on my political blog) a few days ago (A large percentage of the people who read my Facebook posts do not use English as their first language, and some of them might be my political supporters or followers, and the tonality of the note primarily addresses such groups). On my blog, however, the purpose was to communicate the points being made to a wider audience, regardless of whom the initial note sounds like it was addressed to:

Regarding the #MeToo online movement in the English language against sexual abuse on the internet:

1. *I agree with the Avaaz post, that this can be termed as Epic in the (very large and significant) english-reading circuit.*

2. *There have also been other articles that indicate that there has been a snap analysis of the kinds of places and occasions and settings from which such incidents have been reported worldwide. (This is called an anecdotal, non-scientific survey, but still has much value).*

3. *It is now time to co-relate the work already being done by those in the area of law-making as well as law-enforcement, and strengthen their efforts with these findings.*

4. *A word of caution, as derived from reading the anti-thesis opinions, so to speak, to this entire effort: refrain from furthering or creating any kangaroo-court or mob-mentality kind of situations while moving forward with efforts to clear-headedly continue moving forward for solutions.*

5. *Regarding solutions, another view that has become quite clear, is that people could enlist the things that all men need to do, to work towards solutions. There are a few good points in a Guardian post, I have another point to add to that immediate set of points:*

6. *Would men who have already done any of the objectionable things that we are talking about (even if on a supposedly smaller or what they earlier considered insignificant scale or manner, even if not really under the ambit of any kind of criminal culpability by any stretch of imagination), be so brave as to own up to their mistakes; unequivocally apologize, and do what they can to make amends.*

7. *I would also advise the MeToo posts to add one more line about what or where, so that they do not make suspects of the entire male population that they do and do not know!*

. . . .

(BTW: Even I posted a MeToo update, in connection with Delhi Transport Corporation buses of the 1990s.)

My #MeToo post was with reference was to an unverifiable, but, in hindsight, definitely a targeted pushing-and-breathing incident on a DTC bus from Shah Jahan Road to Delhi University in the early 1990s. I was in three-quarter denims and a bush shirt.

Another post from my Facebook wall in 2016 would be my most topical #MeToo complaint, though it's not the incident that I chose to hash-tag. Here's the FB post:

FACEBOOK, 1ˢᵗ Oct., 2016

DASARA DAY #1 MESSAGE (and specific complaint)

Greetings on the first day of the ten-day run-up to the Dasara pooja.

(i am in Gurgaon, Haryana, for a few weeks, and not at The Fort in Kurupam, as a part of my boycott of the toleration of unacceptable behaviours by an old

domestic staff -cook- against women -ie myself- at The Fort in Kurupam). (Keeping in mind all factors, i have been calling for the sacking of the said old recruit since 2014, and not gone to the police, but have only achieved the limited goal of the culprit not reporting in to work when the other family members are out-of-station).

In Kurupam, the Dasara festival has nothing, or very little to do with Raavan.

I think it is more of an annual exercise to do with focusing on invoking/ propitiating/meditating on divine energies (scientifically speaking: contemplating on and tapping into hidden, unknown, forgotten, undiscovered forms of matter).

Priests trained at the Maharishi Mahesh Yogi ashram (which does not make caste distinctions), have been brought by our family to Kurupam to perform these poojas in recent decades, and the process has always involved tribal communities, and still does, starting with us. (Elements of the caste system that had crept into the pooja-aspect over the past century are gradually being weeded out…we have been around for quite a few centuries).

Animal sacrifices are made within the framework of the existing law which takes customary laws into account when i last checked on counts of hygiene, prevention of cruelty against animals and wild life protection. It is a time of feasting.

The private premises in the Fort wherein the swords (the main symbols of divinity) are placed for worship are also thrown open to the entire public, irrespective of caste, creed, race, gender or religion during these ten days.

I see these as occasions to keep the society of earth networked, and the pooja aspect, if nothing else, is a psychological tool that extends individuals and groups opportunities for self-analysis; the developing of will-power and intent-creation; the making of affirmations and resolutions; the recounting of succcesses, achievements; of sharing and being thankful for what there is to be thankful for. (i have done my bit in this connection since the turn of the century, not only at the fort, but in near and far-flung hamlets of the eastern ghaats, and amplified these voices for the world via united nations processes and beyond).

I will post daily messages for the next ten days on this topic.

With blessings to all.

The final chapter of this book features a compilation based on the rest of the Dasara 2016 posts.

The right to dress as one pleases, and the duty to educate society on how to react respectfully towards cultures of nudity lies with every human being who believes in the spirit of the constitution of India- of the values of human equality, freedom and dignity.

The very concept of Dignity, and the fact that different people have different ideas of what constitutes dignity, needs to be examined under the magnifying-glass of power-struggles amongst classes, castes, and religions that seek to define dignity itself.

Often, one might not be personally bothered about what others think about the way one dresses. However, the moment the perceptions of others begin to influence their actions, and thus impact one's every-day life, then it becomes necessary to alter that perception. Not by succumbing to the ill-conceived, dogmatic perceptions and prescriptions of the critics and abusers, but by taking steps to alter their perceptions on how things ought to be. This calls for a long-drawn, multi-pronged approach. But, as with all deadlocks, the possibility of bringing about instant, non-violent transformations should never be discounted.

How to dress is a personal choice, and forms a part of the right to privacy. As a recent Supreme Court judgement has recognized, yet again, such a right is not restricted only to space, and the control over space, but is, in fact, an individual's right that can be exercised anywhere. This point has been flagged in the piece on the right to privacy here in *Earth Republic.*

Mahatma Gandhi might have been described as the half-naked fakir at an international forum, and one might, as of today, fervently hope that the Democrats come back to power in the USA, but to me, Donald Trump is also the president with a First Lady who was once a topless model.

To me, he has that end of the ambit. Whatever his forces defend, if it means that women without blouses will be honoured in the ultimate analysis, I might bet my horses on such a person, or at least such a country for now.

However, this is not to wish away or overlook the many stories of the abuse of women that Trump himself is said to have indulged in. There are reports of highly condemnable attitudes that reek of patriarchy, and need to be defeated without hesitation.

From My Facebook Wall-Post, 17th Oct., 2016

This, too, is being said.

I just want to know from trump now: does he think it is ok to say (and do) the things that he is alleged to have said in connection with it being ok to grope women without their permission, and that he now dismisses as mere locker-room talk?

Locker-room talk or not, it betrays a state of mind that is unacceptable for an aspiring world leader (or anyone), to begin with.

Unless he wants to clarify that he has evolved beyond such utterances?

(i'm more for a bernie sanders kind of figure, and was for wynona la duke in the past, and i know that campaigning for such people would tilt the balance against hilary. to do or not to do?).

By the way – as far as india's opinion goes, we shall be well-advised by the chairperson and members of our external affairs committee.

Meanwhile, one hopes that all Gen-next politicians, especially women, manage to turn the rheostats just so, so that they can assert the kinds of dressing they wish to assert, without being elbowed out by competitive males and females within and beyond the arena.

Deep necks, transparent formal clothes, office-goers unbound, dress to re-dress at conservative family dos, and show them the central path to the digital age, if and when required, if you know what I mean – push the boundaries, you'll take them far!

CHAPTER X

EARTH REPUBLIC NOW: THE INTER-FAITH CONVERSATION, SCIENCE, THE HIGH SCIENCES, GOOD GOVERNANCE, AND WORLD PEACE

World Peace, or the minimization of conflict at a given point of time, with the potential for generating lasting peace, is something that most of the world aims for.

Except, probably:

the arms lobby;

those who might be intrinsically inclined to covet and grab the means of survival of others, even when not warranted by need;

and those who bear grudges, or have been wronged, in some way, and seek retributive justice.

One could go into the causes, effects, and the assumptions that have been made, vis-à-vis each of these factors (there could well be more, and it would be useful to enlist those as well), and extract solutions from such an exercise.

The entire expanse of the world's resources, ranging from the intangible and the nano-scopic, to the mega-scape of the planet, the solar system, passing meteors and beyond, including the electromagnetic spectrum, is tapped into, exploited, and regulated by those who are able to do so.

The workings of pure natural energies, with little human intervention, are a bit like the working of market forces.

Being human (or being any kind of non-robotic self-driven thinking entity, perhaps), has the potential of bringing into play, the workings of value-based energies (negative as well as positive).

A rough categorization of people's propensity to behave in a particular way can be gleaned from the religions they profess to belong to, or the broad belief or non-belief systems that they associate themselves with.

Such views are ultimately reflected in people's actions that relate to governance, and the distribution of natural resources.

There is an ongoing inter-faith dialogue, at a global level, that has been bridging the gap amongst world religions. The scientific interpretations of these views, and, conversely, the scientific theories behind various belief systems need to form a part of the global conversation, in order to bring about a parity in the human rights situation in the world.

This is not to say that one wishes to impose an inescapable new world order on all of humanity.

Achieving fine-grained democracy is of paramount importance, and is achievable, given all the technology that is present these days, and is available to enough people to realise its potential.

An eventual world order where all humans have equal human rights could, technically speaking, be on the horizon.

Ethical issues connected to semi-humans, androids, and other creatures will continue to be debated. These, we need to view through the prism of the rights of the transient energies that we, with our present-day human bodies, might well morph into sometime this century – clumsily, at first, via organ transplants, artificial limbs, and other technological facilitators.

A greater accessibility to technological ways, means and devices could well be the point at which degrees of scientific sophistication dovetail with the knowledge of aural energies as understood by yoga, Buddhist traditions, and the world views of indigenous communities world-wide.

While keeping such horizons on the radar, it is essential to not lose sight of immediate and proximate challenges and emergencies in present-day governance.

These need to be tackled firmly. Disregard for contemporary human rights in the name of the future advancement of the civilization as a whole cannot be entertained.

I now share with you, select prior writings of mine, from my Facebook wall.

FACEBOOK 3ʳᵈ Oct., 2016

DASARA DAY #2 MESSAGE

It's nearing midnight as i write the Day 2 message.

But in ancient perception, days don't range from hour-to-hour, but from sunrise to sunrise.

As the world witnesses the accelerated uses of scientific discoveries applied to emerging technologies, one wishes to draw attention to the role and importance of ethics (human rights and prevention of cruelty to animals) in modern-day science, as well as the high sciences.

What is or isn't ethical, or what does or does not violate human rights, and what the law should ban, restrict, regulate or encourage in the field of modern science is often the subject of public debate. (for example, the creation of genetically modified organisms; human surrogacy; surveillance; kinds of warfare etc. etc. etc.).

When it comes to the High Science/s (activities the world over that are often labelled as ritualistic practices or as being based on blind faith such as elements of shamanism, wicca, voodoo, mantra, tantra etc.), it is my opinion that many such activities, when viewed through the scientific prism, would actually qualify as being scientific experiments based on theories, and possibly some tried-and-tested procedures/formulae being replicated.

So while i agree that many such practices might have a scientific basis, i am of the firm opinion that the corollary to that is that they should then be subject to regulation similar to the kinds of regulation that exist for modern scientific activities. (Temple as laboratory!)

It is also not disputed that all such practices, just like any other activity, need to stand the scrutiny of Constitutional rights and guarantees. However, i find that this is not adhered to when it comes to caste discrimination in connection with the performance of rituals.

To me, this discrimination has absolutely no scientific basis, and if there are communities or individuals who believe that there is any scientific basis for promoting such discrimination, then such scientific experimentation or belief-based practice should be banned as being unconstitutional and unethical.

This has been my message on a day when one has surfed for, and accessed new decks of tarot cards (i've been reading tarot for sixteen years now, and have used the Rider Waite and Universal Packs so far…will write about the new packs once they arrive).

FACEBOOK 4th Oct., 2016

DASARA DAYS #3 and #4 MESSAGE

Various people observe various festivals in India in various ways, depending on what the immediate community around them does, and, as individuals, i suppose, depending on what each individual's temporal mind-frame prompts them to do.

At any given point of time, there is enough of a mixture of individuals in society to make each aspect of a festival relevant.

For example, some may associate the Dasara pooja with food-related enjoyment, some, who might look forward to guests and visitors, some to games and merriment. Some look forward to the reassuring visit to the deity, and some, to the prayer-and-meditation aspect of the event. Some might associate it with a lot of work, and the opportunity to earn extra money. It may not be the same people who enjoy the same festival for the same reasons each year.

One might have temporarily 'graduated' from organizing local meetings, and games, and exhibitions and recycling events and cultural events. However, this spirit continues to be taken forward by new generations in evolved ways. (Including social media posts of dances, pandals, and festivities in general. If you would like to post any of these on my wall during the Dasara period, please do so. I will review, select and post these on my timeline for some days, or perhaps permanently).

Meanwhile, here in Gurgaon, i am reading a book on Chakra Clearing, and the Sacred Indian Tarot deck is scheduled to arrive today via e-commerce. (The other decks that are scheduled to reach me during this holy season are the Green Witch Tarot, and the Buddha Tarot…the decks i've used so far are:

Rider Waite -since the turn of the millennium-, and the Universal Tarot since approximately 2009. One is looking for a good Kabbalah-based tarot pack). i am also dispatching to various publishing houses, my new-age fiction novella: Deep Wood Trance.

Needless to say, these things do not take up all of my time, which continues to be dedicated to political activity.

FACEBOOK 5th Oct.,2016

DASARA DAY #5 MESSAGE

The book on Chakra Clearing, one has just concluded (reading). It was written in 1998, and the lady happens to speak often in the voice of my late maternal grandfather! He loved buying books on spirituality, and read or skimmed through most of them. Also, he couldn't abide communists, but otherwise stood for freedom. Followed the path of faith.

*The Sacred Indian Tarot hasn't yet showed up. Uncharacteristic for the otherwise prompt internet-commerce services. But i have received a notification saying the delay is probably due to inclement weather (a phrase often used in the Harry Potter novels that are about a school of witchcraft and wizardry, esp when Quidditch matches are held with teams from cold places with players with names like *fleur*...fleur also being a word that i dreamt of in print...'the river fleurs....' and talking of flour, in Hindi, that's ata, which, in Telugu and Oriya means aunt -father's sister-).*

It is not impossible that one has acquired some clairvoyant and clairaudient skills. (Or has recently started noticing that one has these abilities). But very intermittent, unpredictable 'readings'.

This could either be because of my Gayatri Mantra and Aum chanting exercises and general elevatedness (! -via truth, not substances), or it could be the active use of known technologies by unknown entities/countries/parties/persons/creatures/machines, for the purpose of communication, or could be both.

Such communications could be helpful or hostile or both or neither.

Anyway, in the context of the electro-magnetic spectrum and nuclear energy and biodiversity: the human and other bodies are all inter-connected. This is what the chanting-people also say. A bit like the movie Avataar (i've watched the first part).

FACEBOOK 6ᵗʰ Oct., 2016

DASARA (DOUBLE-COUNTED DAY THIS YEAR, ASTRONOMICALLY-DAY #6 TO BE OBSERVED TOMORROW)

The Sacred Indian Tarot card deck arrived last evening.

The first card that one drew in a reading was The Empress card, which depicts the Goddess in the Shashti form (the version of the deity that is observed on the sixth day of Dasara, and on which children are honoured).

Today, to me, this symbolizes, of course, all children, and especially my lovely nieces. (Interesting trivia at The Fort is that my father and his four sisters were all born in a room that was then called the Shashti room. It is the room that i currently use as a bedroom, and which my paternal grandmother used to use for many years. For many years, there used to be a row of faces painted on the wall in red paint – one to depict each child. And there were larger wall-paintings of a variety of animals in a yellowish brown colour on the other walls.)

Since this is like a sort of rest-day this year, for the pooja, i shall tell you all the gist of the story of the dagger that i bought more than a decade ago, and that stands on an old wooden god-pedestal in an alcove of the same room today. (The large knife is now a part of the morning pooja on the tenth/dashami day, with all the guns).

On one of our epic road journeys to dense forest-villages where tens of thousands of people were rallying to fight against bauxite mining, we set out to express solidarity and extend help, both political and legal, to our troubled brothers and sisters in the hills.

I began the day, having done the surya namaskar yoga at dawn, and, accompanied by a group of individuals from our village, drove to the Aruku area from Kurupam. It was a hectic and successful meeting, that set off a chain of wonderful events and improvements for the good Peoples of the Earth. We stopped, as ususal, at a dhaba or two en route, when we passed towns or their fringes, and even gave a ride to an official for a short stretch on the way back.

On the return journey, there was a group of boys trying to sell hand-made sword-like agricultural and kitchen implements. i was impressed by their enterprise. They were standing by the roadside, in the midst of the wilderness, holding up these swords, dancing like warriors, to attract the attention of passing cars to sell these handicraft!

I bought one, and this was quite close to another hamlet that sells some of the best mango cheese (aam pappad) in the world. So some blocs of aam pappad were bought.

When we returned to the Fort (by the way – fort means fort plus palace) at Sivannapeta, Kurupam, these items were taken out of the car in almost ceremonial fashion, as though a deity with accompanying prashadam was being brought back from somewhere.

From the next Dasara pooja onwards, i sent this sword in to be made a part of the pooja.

For some years, i debated as to whether or not i should send it into the locked pooja room with the deity-swords and new images where poojas are performed everyday all year round. This would mean that the sword, too, would be treated as a deity.

To me, all these are symbolic depictions and psychological tools.

Finally, i decided that it would not be placed with the deities, but with the weapons during the weapons pooja on the main day.

That is the story of that sword.

I sit in a central room at a round table every day at the Fort when i'm there, and track world and local events from the round table using technology. (And interact with a wide spectrum of people via social media and the internet in general).

Locally speaking, we have, over the years, in the context of the need for a Ground Water Policy, discussed the many lakes and water-bodies of Andhra, and how they need recharging. (That was made a part of the National Rural Employment Guarantee Programme). But of course, much to be still done on the water and sanitation front.

You are seeing the results.

Have you heard of the legends of King Arthur and the Knights of the Round Table?

Some of my friends and i have studied about them while studying English Literature. It is very interesting. There are many books about King Arthur in the Kurupam library that my ancestors used to read when they were not reading Shakespeare.

Today, i am using the dialect of English that some people use locally in Kurupam.

The Mandala Buddha Tarot pack is scheduled to arrive early.

I have spoken to people in the village over the phone today, and discussed, among other things, nomadic tribes with one of them.

More later.

FACEBOOK 7ᵗʰ Oct., 2016

DASARA DAY #6 MESSAGE

First, to continue from my earlier messages on the tarot activity here – yesterday, A Mandala of Cards, The Buddha Tarot did reach.

It is a very interesting pack, with an even more interesting book on the subject.

Unfortunately, the cover of some of the cards were defaced by a melted rubber-band that had bound the deck.

Furthermore, the box containing the book and cards did not contain the pouch that the cover of the box said it would (However, everything was properly sealed in manufacturing-style plastic wrap).

The e-commerce process does have a "return" process that i initiated, but then again cancelled, because of various logistical considerations.

I hope this does not mean that i am allowing such companies to continue to send out defective products. (the earlier sacred indian tarot had a minor fault that i overlooked).

Essentially, all points related to more efficient e-commerce, and even consumer rights pertaining to e-commerce need to be compiled well from the point of view of consumers, especially rural consumers. (though what i've just described was in an urban area), and be acted upon.

At the level of other discourse: human beings often mistake leniency or goodness for weakness. What is the best way to deal with this irony, and not compromise on one's leniency, disarmament, etc. while continuing to demonstrate actual strength. Answer: Insist on clear and unequivocal (ie straightforward) but peaceful communication by all, rather than implied messages and gestures.

The first card that one drew from the Buddha Tarot was a card depicting the Chakras. And the chakras, to me, would be at the crux of the significance of having opted for the Buddha Tarot deck!

FACEBOOK 8th Oct., 2016

DASARA DAY #7 MESSAGE

This morning, i have done one round of surya namaskar yoga on a broad ray of sunlight that enters an eastern room of a multi-storied tower in the millennium city. The green rubber yoga mat here is aptly called Obsessions.

Electrical energies get grounded when you're on rubber, which is why footwear made of such materials is recommended, especially when there is lightning outside.

Rubbeh also means God in Punjabi? So, to crack a part of a code that i probably dreamt up some years ago: 'without rubber' also translates to without god (people such as scientists, atheists, non-religious nature worshippers such as indigenous communities across the globe, as well as, i suppose, to some — the devil?!).

Anyway, today, i drew a card from the sacred indian tarot with the intent of attempting to divine what today's message here should be. i drew the final card in the pack-The World card (pictorally depicted in this deck as 'brahman', or the deity that depicts brahma, vishnu and shiva, all in one).

So, i suppose the message should be an all-encompassing message for all of creation (and non-creation). Of all that is known, and unknown.

The seventh day of Dasara also focuses on the "fearless" embodiment (or aspect) of the goddess.

These are my words to you:

This is how to be fearless, and to free yourself from all fears: Resolve all your issues by following the path of truth. The path of truth requires one to recognize all subjectivities in thought and practice, and to resolve these.

The ways to do this are many. A mix of all ways may be used. (Ranging from organized meditation, to conversing with others, to seeking the advice of various kinds of specialists and professionals on various subjects of your concerns, to the path of faith, surrender and even alteration, desertion, abandonment of outdated truths and realities for emerging new ones).

Essentially, this involves two steps for each aspect of existence:

1) Identify the point of conflict

2) Strategize on how to overcome it

Using the Gayatri Mantra as a simple tool for guiding such a meditation and contemplation is one of the most organized ways to conduct this exercise. It enables one to look beyond conditionings and recognize solutions in areas that might have been clouded by conditioning. One shall talk at length, on the forty-day meditation of the gayatri mantra one hundred and eight times on another occasion.

For now, let us turn to creative solutions for The World, and the role of each individual in the search for World Peace.

There exist many dimensions of existence, as propounded by scientists, spiritualists, knowers and believers.

However, the current dimension that we are all tuned into, is one of concrete/material/physical reality in terms of our own bodies and the tangible matter that surrounds us.

Correct? Well, partially. What is so tangible about radio waves and micro waves and the use of the television remote control? But they form a part of our very material existence.

And these are only some very basic examples. I think there are many more, in the areas of nano-technology, micro waves, use of the spectrum, displacement of matter, and much more.

And here is the main point: As these energies and facts of science and existence gradually unravel into everyday life and markets, human values will change.

The realisations from these discoveries of science will change day-to-day human living in such a manner that many things held valuable and precious will be viewed through a very different hi-tech prism.

Furthermore, the very nature of human existence (of the human body) will alter, though gradually. It is already happening. People started with gold teeth, they now transplant organs, alter genes.

Alongside this, it is possible to map each individual's mind very accurately, and store a life-time's sensory and intellectual experiences.

As it is, we know that all the cells in a human body regenerate at intervals. (So technically, when you meet a person after many years, you are meeting a new set of cells that is bound by a comparatively more durable energy-network).

Given these observations, it is time to transit the planet into futuristic methods of all the activities that it concerns itself with.

However, the weak, the poor and the less privileged cannot be made subjects of experimentation for this (For example – even if one thinks that spirulina capsules are the answer to solve the world food crisis, one cannot impose this as the only food option on the masses while simultaneously allowing the production of planet-destroying foods).

These are some things to contemplate on, for those who wish to, until tomorrow. Literally speaking.

FACEBOOK 9ᵗʰ Oct., 2016

DASARA DAY #8 MESSAGE

Today, the eighth, or ashtami day, is considered very important. The sandhi pooja (which usually falls close to midnight on the cusp of the ninth day), is a high-point of the pooja at Kurupam. While there are animal sacrifices made through the ten days, our main bali/sacrificial animal – these centuries, a goat, is carried out in keeping with the law. (hygiene, prevention of cruelty to animals in terms of method of killing, and within the ambit of the wild life protection act and other international treaties and conventions).

The sacrificial animals are bred livestock, while the olden-days' traditional hunt or shikar (not to be confused with the bali), used to be on the tenth or vijaya dashami day.

Interestingly, my facebook feed tells me that today is the ninth day of the ninth month of the Chinese astronomical calendar, and is the Chongyang or Chrysanthemum festival in China, Japan, Vietnam etc. (known by various names in various places).

On surfing the net to learn more, i noticed that a traditional sweet that is made on this occasion in China and other places off the east coast of India, is the Chongyang Cake. On reading the recipe, i find that it will taste exactly (or quite a bit like) one of the sweets that is made in our village and in other parts of Andhra, known as Boorulu and Garulu. (rice flour, pulse flour and sugar or sweetener all steamed…in our areas, to make it more tasty, they have started deep frying it and adding cardamom and sometimes, coconut. i would recommend vanilla essence also. by the way, vennela means Light in Telugu!).

So this was the reach of our old decentralized oriya-and-other-languages-speaking empire at one time. (The famous ancient port town of Kalinga is not far from Kurupam, and there are many elements of Buddhism, and, who knows, even Jainism, in these areas). Of course, since those times, and even after joining India, the goodwill of our empire has grown and extended much further, in fact, worldwide.

Today, i have meditated on the mystery of the truth behind the clairaudience that i seem to encounter. For this, i used the Buddha Tarot by Robert M. Place. (Also of note, as far as today goes, is that it is a landmark day for one of India's political parties that is known to stand for the rights of the Scheduled Caste community. Many from this community have opted to follow the path of the Buddha, often to escape the evils of the caste system that had crept into Hinduism. Others might have followed it having been inspired by Gautam Buddha, who wandered the surrounding regions. Apparently, Nepal plans to open a consular service in Vizag).

The card that i have drawn from the deck today is the Padmakini -The Dakini of Lotuses ("Dakinis are goddesses dancing in the vast empty space that is consciousness…they connect us with the divine").

Perhaps i have a piece of the jigsaw-puzzle of my answer….

In mundane-activity news, one ought to consider making an Empire Chongyang Boorulu Cake for Dasara Day once i'm done cooking the raw nonveg from the Green Chick chain of shops here in north India. Or maybe next year!

In Hindu mythology, the Goddess kills major demons on this day (though the picture that one always associates with demon-killing is the Maheshasura Mardhani, i don't know for sure, if it was the same event).

These days, some of the evils in society are corruption, exploitation, race, gender and caste discrimination, and crimes against women. These need to be tackled in an enlightened fashion. The pen (or keyboard, or Mind) can be, and is, mightier than the sword.

As far as other world events go, the ballot is also a good weapon, topically speaking. The words of Donald Trump, demeaning women, need to be defeated by the american electorate.

To be continued on Navami day

FACEBOOK 12ᵗʰ Oct., 2016

VIJAYA DASHAMI MESSAGE

Happy Dasara, world.

The sun has risen on the day that succeeds dashami in India. The tithi (or astronomical hours comprising, in this case, Dashami day) is still going on.

And it is still the dashami day on western parts of the planet.

I did not post a navami, or ninth day message as i had inadvertently set the computer on flight mode, and thereafter, as the internet speed was very low.

I hope the festive season was one of introspection, fulfilment, thanksgiving and intent-creation for all.

After many years, I have spent Dasara away from Kurupam (though I will be back soon). Here in Gurgaon, my brother and his family visited me, and in the evening, i opened and started reading the Green Witch Tarot written by Ann Moura, and illustrated by Kiri Ostergaard Leonard, which was first published in 2015.

I expect to find a resonance from it, with the novella, Deep Wood Trance, that i had written long ago, and which i am in the process of having published.

The first card that i drew from this pack yesterday was the three of wands (of getting better results than expected), in ventures such as book-writing (and, i suppose, all things!)

The next card that i drew in connection with similar matters was the eight of chalices, which signifies a shift to a higher level and method of working.

I hope the ripple-effect of all successes (past, present and future, and timeless) continue to be experienced by all, and are acknowledged by the electorate, to begin with!

FACEBOOK 18th Nov., 2016

As a cultural narrative/construct, it would be worthwhile to imagine that there exists a republic of earth including all earthlings, with an unwritten constitution, with one human constitutional monarch (not the queen of england)

FACEBOOK 31st Oct., 2016

Religion (or lack of it) and Governance, with spl ref to the public sphere, esp work ethic while honouring nature (and associated Holidays):

For the efficient management of all natural resources via good governance, other than the required inter-faith parity on human rights in terms of Personal Laws (ie those pertaining to birth, death, marriage, adoption, inheritance etc.), we also need systemic parity on a set of points as far as the inter-faith-parity-for-good-governance for world peace bit goes.

Let me start the listing of such points:

1. Official Holidays, Public Holidays, Work Holidays in all sectors including the unorganized sector:

In all areas of work (organized and unorganized), it would be useful to discuss the scientific as well as socio-scientific need or preference/s pertaining to the observation, celebration, and various other ways of practice of so-called festivals, significant astronomical days etc. in-as-much-as these infringe on professional commitments.

In India, this would have a bearing on national holidays, state or other local holidays, other forms of leave…in the government, as well as public and private sector, including the unorganized sectors of employment.

Let the discussion begin. (To find a via media between honouring the ways of nature and the needs of the modern world in this field)

FACEBOOK 21ˢᵗ Oct., 2016

Personal Law/s in India (Upgrade all, but no uniform civil code)

I am FOR the constant monitoring and upgradation of all personal laws in India, from the point of view of ensuring that each set of personal laws adheres to the Constitution of India, especially the fundamental rights guaranteed to individual citizens.

The system already provides for this. It must be made to work efficiently. Efficient in the broadest sense of the word (non-biased, non-corrupt, high degrees of excellence and so on.).

As with all law, constant upgradation based on evolving times, including the role of science, must be factored in.

I am FOR the strengthening of all democratic mechanisms that would serve to monitor and ensure this.

I am NOT FOR a monolithic uniform civil code.

HOWEVER, when individual freedoms with the accompanying "reasonable restrictions" (and associated collective rights) kick in, some of the personal law/s become/s redundant.

This has already been happening over time, but it is currently important for the political wing of state to own and accelerate the Human Rights (and associated Fundamental Rights)-scrutiny of all personal laws from the point of view of bringing about socio-economic justice for children, especially girls, homosexuals, trans-gender people, single people, people with various belief-systems, those not aligned to any formal religion, those with disabilities, those who are still impacted by the caste system, and those whose livelihoods, economic bearings and civilizational standing are rooted outside of mainstream economic activities and/or processes, such as, primarily, tribals.

Please note that while doing so (and ideally, this should go without saying)-while assessing the need for societal and governmental intervention, do not judge these categories of situations/people by either the best or the worst that the given situation is capable of bringing unto the person.

For example, please do not overdo the case against child protection services, as that would not do justice to children who genuinely require societal intervention of some sort.

Similarly, do not fall into the trap of assuming that all scheduled caste people are in a permanent state of wretchedness, or that all tribal men will help all tribal women all the time.

Basically, do not oversimplify the discussion. Ironically, much of the larger discussion takes place over the electronic media, and that too, the english media, and this is a medium that quite often needs to be brief.

This powerful medium should be used with as much skill as possible, to ensure that the priorities just mentioned are met, and all the purportedly niche areas of concerns in personal law (such as the rights of erstwhile princesses to their ancestral homes -palaces and forts-) are adequately addressed and met.

FACEBOOK 27th Sept., 2016

WATER FOR PEACE, NOT FOR WAR:

To repeat some basic points on water (similar points recently made on my wall in the Cauvery context, now following up on Indus, or for that matter, all rivers including Amazon!)
equity amongst human beings in terms of access to quality and quantity is important;
macro-policy on prioritization of water-use is important;
do not equate large farmers or agricultural multinationals with small farmers;
do not confuse farm labour with farm owners;
gender-justice within farming communities (and other water-consuming human communities) is important;
double-check to ensure, while discussing policy, that the technical definition for drinking water does not include irrigation water;
blacklist nuclear energy-generation as water-guzzling and water-polluting;
cropping patterns would need to be altered via macro-policy in a calibrated way, keeping water-efficiency, environmental health and equity amongst farming communities in mind.
WORLD PEACE will be because of water, not world war!

To be discussed in these contexts

I hope you had fun reading my random talking-points for drawing-rooms (or chatrooms) everywhere. Chatrooms are so early-twenty-first-century by now. These days, it's all out there, tiara and all! (Tiara was my occasional handle on Chatropolis once).

One has now subjected those who have dared to come this far, to a sitar-recital-full of tonal attitudes and concerns (unless you've flipped across to the last few pages first, which is also fine).

Net-net: The Supreme Courts of Rule of Law countries, and other international adjudicating bodies have a great responsibility on their shoulders, to ensure the continuing evolution and diligent expansion of self-correcting systems of justice across the globe.

So does the world's largest bureaucracy, the United Nations. India is one of the highest contributors to the peace-keeping forces of the United Nations.

Culturally, Modi might run helter-skelter across the globe, caricature-worthy enough to knock on the doors of Walt Disney creations.

However, there is, indeed, much to be said for the demonstrated continuity in governance of this great democracy.

Including jogging the world's memory on the agreed-upon aspects of Indian history, such as the extent of pre-Indian empires that still have their capitals, parts of their geographical areas, and most of their people as citizens of India.

But hands of friendship and goodwill extend far and deep: into history, onto continents, and aspirationally, to realms beyond this planet. (In the absence of credible takers, there's always a joker in the pack)-The oblique scenario for which one has pulled up, in as politically correct and socially non-offensive a way as possible, one's blue-veined leotards. The use of online facilities to unleash versions of artistry for one's personal gifts, not-for-sale, that's involved the making of personalized souvenirs, heritage-themed jewellery that ranges from recycled trash to the real (haha) stuff. (Frankly, I'd much rather plot, conceptually, to be the Earth President, than the constitutional monarch of the unwritten constitution of the planet! I think.)

Politically, we continue to tend the garden (or wander in the woods, which is a good thing), of the world's largest and oldest political party: The Indian National Congress Party, that, since its inception, has had a global and universal identity, approach and appeal. Who wouldn't like to be its elected president?

Many of our founding members and ideologues have historically been from nations outside of India (and, in fact, used to read books of all kinds, ranging from the esoteric work, Isis – which calls to mind terrorism these days, when, sadly, Isis was the name of a mythical creature from Africa-, to modern-day political and scientific thought).

Apart from hard-core political campaigning and strategizing, I have written and spoken about my party's views, and my individual views (especially on forests, tribal rights, the environment, women's issues, and an entire plethora of legislation) on social media and elsewhere often, and talked about the party's history.

The current vice president of my party has coincidentally reflected some of my views at Berkeley, California, recently. A place I happened to have visited and expressed specialized socio-legal opinions at, a few decades ago, the same year that our current party president was elected president. Discussion ranged across the gamut of the developmental and environmental needs and concerns of the weak and the downtrodden worldwide, with a view to having the inputs heard, and, I supposed at that time, incorporated into world economic planning. Something that one believes has happened in great measure.

The relevant links of the macro trajectories of the world's economic planning, and the sustainable development agenda thus fall into place, with my party playing a central role for the planet, and complete the jigsaw puzzle of the party of Truth, Non-violence and of the Word Community for now.

The Congress Party apart, Indian Democracy, its ability to successfully juggle coalition governments in many states, as well as at the centre, is a reflection of the multi-tasking genius that multi-culturally-united societies are capable of jamming and banding together with.

Jazz yatras, jugalbandis, chants, operas, folk tunes, classical music, hymns, quawwalis, ghazals, the sounds of nature, Bollywood beats, the sounds of beasts and of the devil – we synthesize these for humanity.

If Isis is today a bad thing, bring it to the Great Indian Refinery, where evil turns enchantedly good, where lotuses grow from filth, where, if Isis is a terror organization, I will tell you that it is a mythical bird, a book, the label on the G-strings of an obscure underwear company with the said wardrobe essential having made a mysterious disappearance, the lines from a poem I wrote and put on a poetry blog years ago (the cosmos is this osmosis), the fact that the word Islam translates to Peace.

If we're looking for a defusing narrative or a palliative for the defeated, the dying, the frustrated, whom we did not create (as the song goes: we didn't start the fire, no we didn't light it, but we'll try to fight it), then India might want to play trade messiah, cultural messiah, or just plain Friend. Dost. Nestam. Sango. Mitra. You want it, we got it before the Chinese do.

Not what you're looking for? Ok, we've got selfies as well. And roles. Looking for a constitutional monarch of an unwritten earth constitution? Pull one out of the bag! Props for a post-colonial federation that might unite a region? Out with the Kohinoor diamond, and all the other spoils of empire from the orb to the spectre and objects galore! A systems-machinery and technology to run a truly representative world parliament? Once the entire population of the planet has a UN-recognized refugee card, that might be possible. Either that, or bring in governments and leaders who will work for just causes, pronto! Almost done for 2017, and still counting....

www.ingramcontent.com/pod-product-compliance
Lightning Source LLC
Chambersburg PA
CBHW051047250726
48656CB00001B/185